Short Selling for the Long Term

Short Selling for the Long Term

HOW A COMBINATION OF SHORT AND LONG POSITIONS LEADS TO INVESTING SUCCESS

Joseph Parnes

WILEY

Published by John Wiley & Sons, Inc., Hoboken, New Jersey.
Published simultaneously in Canada.

For general information on our other products and services or for technical support, please contact our Customer Care Department within the United States at (800) 762-2974, outside the United States at (317) 572-3993, or fax (317) 572-4002.

Wiley publishes in a variety of print and electronic formats and by print-on-demand. Some material included with standard print versions of this book may not be included in e-books or in print-on-demand. If this book refers to media such as a CD or DVD that is not included in the version you purchased, you may download this material at http://booksupport.wiley .com. For more information about Wiley products, visit www.wiley.com.

Library of Congress Cataloging-in-Publication Data

Names: Parnes, Joseph, author.
Title: Short selling for the long term : how a combination of short and long positions leads to investing success / Joseph Parnes.
Description: First Edition. | Hoboken : Wiley, 2020. | Includes index.
Identifiers: LCCN 2019051847 (print) | LCCN 2019051848 (ebook) | ISBN 9781119527763 (hardback) | ISBN 9781119527787 (adobe pdf) | ISBN 9781119527824 (epub)
Subjects: LCSH: Short selling (Securities) | Stocks—Prices.
Classification: LCC HG6041 .P296 2020 (print) | LCC HG6041 (ebook) | DDC 332.64—dc23
LC record available at https://lccn.loc.gov/2019051847
LC ebook record available at https://lccn.loc.gov/2019051848

Cover design: Wiley

Printed in the United States of America.

10 9 8 7 6 5 4 3 2 1

This book is the culmination of decades of hard work and could not have been completed without the support of my wife and son, close friends, and the team at Wiley.

Contents

Preface

There is a reason some of you may have not heard of me before. I am neither a billionaire nor a talking head; rather, I consider myself to be a contrarian. I have been personally successful regarding the stock market in terms of developing a short and long strategy. I have taken a long time—almost 30 years—to write this book, as I have taken some issue with those who are so dramatically successful and purport to offer a path to becoming a similarly situated billionaire. There is a reason there are so few of them around, and I believe that this book instead illustrates my personal strategy, not premised on the claim that one will become handsomely rich for all time, rather on my ability to become financially independent. I believe this goal is truly attainable and reflective of the seemingly vanishing American dream.

So who am I? I emigrated to the United States from Tehran, Iran after graduating from high school prior to the Iranian revolution of 1979. The United States seemed to hold the most promise for me, so I obtained a student visa and enrolled in college to study engineering. I financed my way through college by working as an X-ray technician at a local hospital over nights and weekends. These were very difficult times for me. My parents in Iran had both passed away, I had no relatives in the United States, and I had arrived with no money. I was able to complete my studies in engineering in three and a half years, due to my advanced placement in mathematics (obtained by taking a qualifying examination). After years of studying engineering and economics, I landed my first job in New York City, at Western Electric, which was the manufacturing division of AT&T.

Starting in the 1970s, amidst the Watergate and oil crisis, contrary to most investors I started investing in the stock market. I soon recognized that short positions, when used in conjunction with long positions as a hedge, enhanced my returns. I began making money, started publishing a market letter called Shortex, and founded Technomart R.G.A. Inc. (also known as Technomart Investment Advisors) to manage other peoples' money. I began to get media attention, and eventually, I appeared on CNN-FN, Bloomberg, CNBC, and radio and TV stations all over the globe. I am grateful to have been featured in *Forbes*, *Barron's*, and *Investor's Business Daily*, to name a few of the publications. In 2011 I was invited by the Bank of England and the Financial Market Committee to appear before the Financial Market Law Committee (FMLC) of the United Kingdom to serve as a keynote speaker on short selling before an audience of members of the Appellate Committee of the House of Lords, which is most analogous to the US Supreme Court. I am currently the editor and publisher of the Shortex Market Letter and president of Technomart Investment Advisors.

This book illustrates the art of short selling, which is quite difficult to master for most because of the scarcity of float and/or liquidity. On the one hand, shorting can generate impressive gains. On the other hand, it exposes its traders and investors, at least in theory, to a loss, and the expenses for carrying charges. In the past decade I feel that both high-frequency traders (HFTs) and institutional traders have had the ability to influence the market through programmed trades and subquotes done in nanoseconds, putting the individual short seller at an inherent disadvantage.

I have developed a relatively reliable selection method, which I call short selling for the long term, that I describe further in this book. The short positions in portfolios of $1 million and up are based on the initial premise of the 130/30 investment model. This means I invest 100% of the portfolio into long positions, and then select stocks to short, representing approximately 30% of the total value of the portfolio. I then take the proceeds from the shorts and reinvest that money into long positions. This gives me 130% of the portfolio in a long position and 30% of the portfolio in a short position. Depending on individual objectives of investors, and market variables, a single portfolio may have a 120/20 to 200/100 ratio of long to short holdings. Using the typical 130/30 model, I select long positions that equals 130% of the nominal capital invested and select short positions that equals up to 30% of the nominal capital, giving a net market exposure of 100%. The book explains this concept in detail and it is my sincere belief and hope that you will find it of tremendous value.

CHAPTER 1

Investment Philosophy

This book discusses my methods for evaluating the market, which differ significantly from those of many money managers. Succinctly stated, I invest—I do not trade. This book is an explanation of my method of investment.

Individual investors have individual needs. This book describes a methodology that allows an investor to determine if this investment philosophy is compatible with their own needs. Some people are risk averse while others want income. Only you will know what works best for you. This book may provide you with the information that you need to help you with your decisions. Please see Figure 1.1.

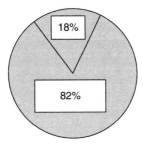

Figure 1.1   The short and long positions in composite portfolios for 2016.

1

The pie chart in Figure 1.1 represents the short (18%) and long (82%) positions in composite portfolios for 2016. The long-to-short ratio is 4.8. This ratio changes year to year, depending on market conditions. In a bear market, there are more short positions than 18%, and in a bull market, there are more than 82% long positions.

The role of any investment advisor is to supply private and institutional clients with practical investment advice. This advice may encompass experience across a broad array of industries, with a special focus on growth companies and short-selling strategies. Many of my investment recommendations have appeared in *Barron's, Forbes, Investor's Business Daily,* and *Modern Trader.* I have been featured in and contributed to a broad array of media, including Bloomberg TV, CNBC, and First Business News. I have been recognized as one of the top wealth managers in 2004–2012 by *Bloomberg Wealth Manager* and featured in *Barron's* (Figure 1.2) and *Forbes.* These media outlets all seem to be interested in my investment approach. I was also invited by the Bank of England to be the keynote speaker at the Financial Markets Law Committee (FMLC) meeting in London. This committee was created by the Bank of England and was chaired by Lord Hoffmann, a former member of the Appellate Committee of the House of Lords, which is now called the Supreme Court, and is most analogous to the US Supreme Court.[1]

I employ a proprietary bottom-up approach to investing that focuses on company research, fundamentals, technical analysis, and cash flow to evaluate superior opportunities for long and short investment opportunities. Strategies may include sector balancing, growth, cash flow, bonds, income, short selling, risk aversion, and other investment strategies. These terms will be explained later, in appropriate sections of the book. I focus on in-house company research to evaluate the fundamentals, technical analysis, and cash flow on the various issues selected. In-house company research often carries none of the biases of research from institutional investors, which often have significant holdings in the companies that they recommend for purchase, which is out of date by the time it is published.

I discourage investors from becoming clients if they depend on the money they want us to manage for living expenses. If you have certain minimum living expenses that require a return on

---

[1]Joseph Parnes has not given or received any consideration for any such media recommendations. Travel and accommodations were provided by the FMLC.

investment, these must be secured first. If you need funds for living expenses, this creates a situation where the investment philosophy of the client is counter to my own investment philosophy. *This day-to-day need for funds clouds the judgment of an investor.* If you are going to invest for the future, and invest to grow your assets, do not use money you need to live. Simply stated, do not invest money if you cannot afford to lose it. Only put surplus capital into an investment fund. Ideally, you should invest, and check in routinely to see how you have done, but do not worry about short-term changes. The current market conditions that are impacted by global traders creates a new environment and produces a more volatile market than in the past. The natural market fluctuations, retractions, hiccups, sell-offs, and so on are to be expected. Do not let the volatility impact your investment judgment. You will want to sell off when there is a short-term profit, rather than hold for the long term. When an issue drops 15–20%, it takes a truly sophisticated investor to see the long-term picture by seeing the drop as an opportunity.

Trading is not the hallmark of my strategy. It is my belief, developed through years of experience, that maximum returns will be lost in a short-term trading strategy. Very often, once a position is traded with the thought of repurchasing the position later, some other factors have intervened and the repurchase opportunity is lost. Many times, once a position is sold out, not only will there be a tax burden to the investor but discipline is needed to reacquire the position. The advantages of having held the position at a lower price are often lost with a repurchase strategy. The inconsistency of traders in repeating their previous gains would subject the investors to a new element of the risk. Therefore, my trading strategy is best described as "not trading." A company with solid fundamentals, good management, a strong cash position, little or no debt, a reasonable price-to-earnings ratio compared to its peer group, and a strong market position compared to its peer group has all the elements of a solid investment. This type of company will be able to ride out various market bumps, corrections, and sell-offs, and should be held for the long term. The shortsighted approach of "take my profit and run" probably reduces the overall return on investment when calculated over a six- or eight-quarter period.

Being a wealth manager, my intent is to maximize performance and its value in the time frame of one to three years, or even five years, by a double- to triple-digit increase in asset value invested. I select long positions based on a strategy of following the technical analysis over time, and fundamentals. My clients' accounts are customized commensurate with the objectives of the investors. I personally and actively evaluate 40 to 60 issues. Then, based on the requirements of the individual client, I usually narrow down investments in a single portfolio of 18 to 24 positions, dividing the assets in large accounts into $30,000–$60,000 or higher tranches. Basically, the more positions in the account, the less the volatility. This degree of diversity helps weather the normal market fluctuations while capitalizing on and maximizing the profit potential of individual issues.

The aggregate portfolio of a client varies subject to risk tolerance and objectives of the investors and the size of the portfolio. I review the movements, corrections, and retractions of each issue. Near-term objectives, intermediate objectives, and stop losses are set and reassessed on each issue to avoid being "stopped out." For individual issues, I look at 10-day, 50-day, and 200-day moving averages, which are viewed as a tool to evaluate the momentum of the various issues, knowing full well that the deviations, plunges, and down-gaps may involve institutional, hedge fund, or mutual fund investors taking positions or eliminating positions (these terms and their significance will be explained in the appropriate sections of this book). When the momentum of a stock overextends its respective movements above the set barriers or resistance lines, I know it is time to reevaluate that stock. On long positions, I look for relative strength as well as flow movements: short positions of institutional investors play a strong part in that evaluation.

Shorts are difficult to master, primarily because of the scarcity of float/liquidity, that is, the number of shares available. Ideally, I maintain 10% to 15% of the initial stock value as a stop loss in short trades, depending on the volatility of the issue. In volatile long positions, I evaluate the stop loss, depending on the retraction, to see if there is a change in the fundamentals of the company, or if the retraction is in response to some external event, such as commentaries made by short sellers, to drive the price of the stock down. Eventually, due to the strength of the fundamentals of the company, the short sales will dry up and the price will rise due to covering of the shorts. By being aware of certain market investors or traders, such as high-frequency traders (HFTs), computerized high-frequency trading (HFC), institutional traders, and algorithm traders, who capitalize on volatility to enhance their performance, I look for them to cover their short position, which typically drives a stock to even higher prices. Contrary to the herd mentality, I take note when the level of bullishness on the subject issue becomes overextended. I focus on technical elements on an issue when the following elements become transparent: overheating, primary/secondary support level, breakdown, topping (on individual issues in the general market/sectors), and trading charts that show ridging/head and shoulder, plunging gaps, reverse cup with handles, volume, deterioration of accumulation/distribution mode, length of the distribution, downward penetration on the 50-day and 200-day moving averages, and formation of the "death cross" pattern. All these terms and their applications and implications will be described in the pages that follow. Other data of importance in short selling are short interest in the New York Stock Exchange/NASDAQ composites, put/call ratio, major indices trends, and volatility index.

While a home-run investment in the stock market is usually spectacular, I am not looking for the "big kill." Those astounding investments with 500% or 1,000% returns in three months do happen, but they happen far less frequently than people taking losses. I always remind people that for many years, Babe Ruth held the Major League Baseball record for the most home runs in a single season, hitting 60 homers in 1927, while playing for the New York Yankees. But in his effort to send the ball out of the park, he also had a huge number of strikeouts, with 89 in the same year. In 1961, Roger Maris hit 61 home runs with 67 strikeouts. Compare that to Reggie Jackson, who hit 47 home runs in 1969 with 142 strikeouts, or Will Stargell, who in 1971 hit 48 home runs but had an astounding 154 strikeouts. You often hear about the great number of home runs of these players, but rarely do people mention the strikeouts, or, even more importantly, the ratio of strikeouts to home runs. When reexamined in those terms, Ruth had a strikeout-to-home-run ratio of 1.48, while Maris had a 1.09 ratio, Jackson had a 3.02 ratio, and Stargell had a 3.20 ratio. This means that Stargell was more than three times as likely to strike out as he was to hit a home run while Maris had a little less than even shot at it. Now we are getting down to useful numbers and into the realm of predictive analytics. If you invest with a money manager, is he going to have the Roger Maris result or the Will Stargell result?

I want to make money for my clients slowly and methodically, by pursuing logical investment goals. I am perfectly content with a single or an occasional double. In the long term, I will accumulate more runs with these "single-base" advancements than by trying to be a home-run hitter.

The short positions in the portfolios of $1 million and up are based on the premise of the 130/30 investment model. This means I invest 100% of the portfolio into long positions and then select stocks to short, representing approximately 30% of the total value of the portfolio. I then take the proceeds from the shorts and reinvest that money into long positions. This gives me 130% of the portfolio in a long position, and 30% of the portfolio in a short position. Depending on individual objectives of the investors, and market variables, a single portfolio may have a 120/20 to 200/100 ratio of long to short holdings. Using the typical 130/30 model, I select long positions that equal 130% of the nominal capital invested and select short positions that equal up to 30% of the nominal capital, giving a net market exposure of 100%.

I have shared these investment philosophies, especially on the use of shorts, in the course of dealing with various media contacts I have had. I have found that magazines are results oriented, so I was pleased when they kept returning to me for material. They were particularly interested in my use of shorts to enhance long positions, and my philosophy of using shorts in lieu of puts, calls, and margin accounts. Using the 130/30 model technique, no more than 30% of a portfolio is in shorts, and then the proceeds from shorts are diverted/applied to other selected issues for their long-term growth rate. Apparent long-term appreciation in the value of these growth stocks makes up for the cost/fees/interest charges being levied by the lenders for the short position selected.

Caution—Limitations and Difficulties: On the advice of counsel, any securities mentioned in this book, with the exception of those mentioned in previously published articles, should not be considered a recommendation to purchase or short this security. These securities mentioned are used for illustration purposes only. The reader must not construe a mention of any stock as a recommendation to purchase or short a stock, or as a recommendation to trade options on any security. This book is designed to present concepts, not recommendations. Please consult your FINRA-registered financial advisor if any questions arise regarding the content of this book. Furthermore, the author does not claim that any device or system can be used to make decisions on which securities to buy or sell, or the timing of such decisions, irrespective of what limitations or difficulties are discussed.

Any graph, chart, formula, or other device mentioned in this book is not to be used in making any determination as to when to buy or sell any security, or which security to buy or sell.

Reprinted from BARRON'S

September 12, 2005   © 2005 Dow Jones & Company, Inc. All Rights Reserved.

And, Now, a Word From the Dark Side

By Richard Karp

Katherine Lambert for Barron's

Parnes argues that the so-called smart money isn't always so smart: "When one institution sells off, the rest follow suit, like a herd of sheep."

ON FEB. 23, JOSEPH PARNES, A PROUDLY "consistent contrarian," advised his readers to short **Ceradyne**, a manufacturer of body armor, whose stock was then flying high. On that frigid winter day, the stock was hot, trading at $29.09. Three and a half months later, on a balmy June 6, Ceradyne (ticker: CRDN) was cold; it had fallen to 23, and Parnes told his readers to cover their positions. Those that did reaped a profit of 35%. Not bad, in a rather listless stock market.

It was a sweet triumph for Parnes, 59, who's seen his share of hits and misses over the years and who often swims in perilous waters.

Parnes is the editor and publisher of the Baltimore-based Shortex Market Letter, produced once every three weeks. (A one-year subscription of 20 issues costs $299.) Hundreds of investor-oriented publications exist, but most focus heavily

on what to buy or hold. Only occasionally do any of them suggest selling anything short. But Shortex, as its name implies, is one of the few newsletters that's sometimes tilted more toward short recommendations than longs.

Going short is dangerous. While shorting can generate nice gains, it also exposes its practitioners, at least in theory, to an infinite loss. After all, if someone buys a $20 stock and it goes to zero, he's lost $20. But if he borrows shares at $20 and sells them short, hoping to replace them at a cheaper price, they could rise to $50, $60 or who knows where, making the potential loss much greater Just ask anyone who shorted Google after its initial offering last year and was slow to cover his position.

For a newsletter editor offering suggestions on what stocks to short, there's another danger. Most investors are longs. Thus, they aren't too happy when their shares go down. Generally speaking, this can produce a blizzard of angry e-mails, nasty phone calls or worse, aimed at the short sellers—who are often perceived as having manipulated a stock, rather than having merely pointed out existing problems. Yet, amazingly, Parnes swears that he has "never gotten an angry message from any investor." His theory on why he hasn't had to face down any unhappy investors: "All our recommendations are fundamental and technical, and we don't hedge our short recommendations with our own long positions."

What initially drew Parnes to Ceradyne was a newspaper story noting that the army was considering refashioning the body armor used by soldiers in the Iraq war. This strongly suggested that Ceradyne's then-heavy production schedule would soon slow. Moreover, the stock's 50- and 200-day moving averages had fallen below the market's over the same periods. "This gave us the feeling that

the shares would fall even lower," says Parnes.

"Most important of all," Parnes says—and this points to a key element of his overall strategy, regardless of whether he's considering shorting a stock or going long—"when institutional investors see this kind of news, they sell off just to prove to their clients that they can react quickly to changes. When one institution sells off, the rest follow like a herd of sheep. They exit heavily to impress clients—and this sends the stock sliding even more quickly." Quite a different take on institutional investors than the widespread perception that they're always part of the so-called smart money.

Parnes emigrated to the U.S. from Iran as a teenager—his parents had already died by then—around 40 years ago. After a few years of studying engineering and economics, he ended up in New York City, where he landed his first job at Western Electric, the research and development operation of AT&T. "These were very difficult times for me, when I first came to America," he recalls. "My parents in Iran were dead; I had no relatives in the U.S.; and I came over with very little money." Nevertheless, there was plenty of part-time work at Western Electric in the early 'Seventies, although he also had to take a job as a hospital X-ray technician to make ends meet.

In the early 'Seventies, during the era of Watergate and Oil Crisis No. 1, when shorts were doing better than longs, "I started playing the stock market, and found that I liked shorting positions, rather than going long," he recalls. He also liked making money, and says he did quite nicely during this period.

In 1979, he began managing other people's money. He started **Technomart Investment Advisors**, which oversees private accounts for investors. He put about 10% to 20% of his clients' money in short positions—"especially if they were

(over please)

Figure 1.2   Feature in *Barron's*.

Reproduced with permission of *Barron's*.

aggressive traders." At the same time, he started the Shortex Market Letter, which listed his recommendations. "I added the 'ex' to 'short' because that was the sexy thing to do at the time," he remarks, frankly.

"Shorts were difficult to master," Parnes reminisces, "but once I learned from experience why some stocks flourished, while others withered, I developed a reliable selection method." He adds: "I always created a 'stop-loss' to protect the positions and the clients"—meaning that, if a stock moved against him, he'd absorb only so much pain before covering a short position or selling a long one.

Today, Technomart manages close to $75 million, of which an average of about 20% is in short positions. But some of Parnes' more aggressive clients prefer holding up to 40% in shorts. "The ratio of short to long positions runs with the stock market," Parnes says. Thus, in the bull years of the 1990s, only 10% of the fund's money was short. In the bearish atmosphere of the post-9/11 Wall Street, an average of 40% was in shorts—roughly twice what it is now.

His followers—including some 500 Shortex subscribers—can put their money in Parnes' fund or play a lone hand by using his newsletter as a guide. And generally they appear to have done well. Parnes asserts that his private accounts have beaten the Standard & Poor's 500 in each of the past five years. Their best reported showing came in 2004, when they were up 22.43%, versus 8.99% for the benchmark index. Their worst performance came in 2002 when, despite Parnes' penchant for shorting, they were down 15.09%. Still, that beat the S&P's 23.37% decline in that bear-market annum.

Some examples of his approach:

Last winter, AK Steel Holding (AKS), a maker of flat-rolled carbon stainless steel, was turning out metal feverishly, in anticipation of a surge in orders fueled by a raging global appetite for steel products. But the company made a miscalculation: The surcharge that it tacked onto its lines ultimately wouldn't cover the rising cost of the energy or raw materials needed to make stainless.

On March 16, Shortex advised its readers to short AK Steel at $12.22. On June 24, Shortex recommended covering it at $6.34—a move that would have produced a 48% windfall in three months. Again, Parnes says, selling by institutions cascaded, battering the shares.

As Parnes told Barron's: "Since October 2004, these institutions had been accumulating AK Steel shares, in effect

bulling the stock from around $7 all the way to $17.50 through March 2005, in order to make money for their clients' eyes." Then, they panicked and pulled out. The upward slope in AK Steel's price trend shattered, on heavy volume.

To be sure, not all of Shortex's recommendations lead to bonanzas. In what he defines as a "very aggressive bear play," Shortex advised shorting **Cal-Maine Foods** (CALM) at $7.88 on April 6. On June 24, the stock was down to $5.95—about 24%—and he recommended dumping it, in the belief that it was unlikely to decline much more.

Cal-Maine, which produces and distributes eggs, started having obvious problems when net sales dropped to $101 million in the quarter ended February 26, versus $165 million in the correspondng 2004 stretch.

Says Parnes: "There may have been traders smarter than I who shorted eggs earlier, when the stock was at $12 or $14 a share, but we believed that, in April 2005, $7.88 was still [too high] for the stock."

Not every call has worked out, of course. Case in point: **Holly Corp.** (HOC), a U.S. oil refiner. On Feb. 23, Shortex advised its readers to short the stock, then trading at $34.35, in the expectation of being able to cover the position profitably in four months. By then, Parnes figured, energy issues would have fizzled out and the shares would be changing hands in the $25 to $27 range. As usual, Shortex specified a "stop-loss" number—$39. But energy-industry trends—and the company's stock price—went the other way. Those who followed his advice took a 15% hit after covering. Those who held on took a bigger one; the stock recently was around 58.

Another play that fell short of Parnes' hopes involved a company he was bullish on: **Quality Systems** (QSII), a maker of information- management software, mainly for medical and dental companies.

On March 16, Shortex recommended buying Quality Systems. The stock closed at 46.38 that day, after a 2-for-1 split. He advised holding the position until August 15, when he predicted that it would be in the high 60s. By early June, the call looked great; the stock was around 60. But by the end of the month, after Quality Systems delivered an earnings report that disappointed Wall Street, the shares had plummeted to 45.

Parnes considered the reaction overdone. Undaunted, he recommended that those who had bought hold on, and that those who hadn't should get in, to take advantage of the "analyst-driven" selloff.

On August 15, the stock closed at 69.50. Recently, it's been trading around 71.

"In fact," says Parnes, "except in the minds of the analysts, there was nothing wrong with the company's growth. But that [single earnings-consensus miss] scared off the institutions. As usual. Too much of what happens in the markets is a result of emotional reaction to the ordinary volatility of stocks as interpreted by analysts. Too many investors," he continues, "including professional money managers, do what analysts tell them to do—without rhyme or reason."

And what does Parnes see ahead?

Ironically, for someone who's made a career out of shorting stocks, he's rather bullish on the stock market's prospects. He's impressed by the profits that companies around the world have been able to churn out, and he thinks that the trend won't stop. "Moreover," Parnes adds. "oil prices are soaring dramatically, yet the stock market is not buckling—a promising sign."

So, what is Parnes recommending?

On the long side, his picks include **Intuitive Surgical** (ISRG), which designs and produces robotic surgical systems; **Joy Global** (JOYG), a maker of mining gear; **Marvell Technology Group** (MRVL), an integrated- circuit manufacturer; and **Sportman's Guide** (SGDE), a direct marketer of discount outdoor clothing and sporting equipment. He expects all of them to have good earnings.

Among his shorts are pet-supplies provider **PETsMART** (PETM); Parnes believes that animal owners' spending growth may taper off from its torrid pace of the past few years. Another, **Toll Brothers** (TOL), a builder of high-end homes, recently reported earnings growth of 20% for the third quarter—but that was below analysts' expectations. And **Winnebago** (WGO), the recreational-vehicle maker, may not be able to match last year's record sales, he says. All of these could be victims of higher fuel costs and rising interest rates.

Parnes is shorting **Boyd Gaming** (BYD), a gambling outfit whose growth rate, he thinks, is set to fall. (He made his call before Hurricane Katrina damaged a Boyd casino in Louisiana; it's uncertain when it will reopen). In addition, he's short **Abercrombie & Fitch** (ANF), which had exceptional same-store sales in August, but which Parnes thinks won't soon see such results again. Also, he says, the resignation of its president and chief operating officer, Robert Singer, "after only 15 months in office is not a good sign." ∎

Figure 1.2   (*Continued*)

CHAPTER 2

The Bank of England Lecture

On January 14, 2011, I unexpectedly received a letter from Joanna Perkins, the director of the Financial Markets Law Committee (FMLC) in the United Kingdom. This letter can be seen in Figure 2.1. I believe I had come to the attention of the FMLC as the result of various comments I had made in the press about the use of shorts as part of an investment program. The Bank of England had created the Financial Markets Law Committee and had asked Lord Hoffmann to chair it. Lord Hoffmann was a former member of the Appellate Committee of the House of Lords, which had functioned as the final court of appeals. The committee was concerned with identifying areas of legal uncertainty that affected financial markets and wanted to properly inform members of the judiciary about market practices. Based on my expertise, I was invited to be the keynote speaker on the subject of short selling at the annual judicial seminar, which is considered the apex of the NLMC's yearly conference program. Other speakers were William Hautekiet from The Bank of New York Mellon, and Andrew Bagley from Goldman Sachs International. This private seminar was open only to members of the senior judiciary, such as Supreme Court judges, other judges with an interest in financial markets practices, and a few select financial experts. The committee had become concerned because new rules on short selling were being introduced into the European Union.

c/o Bank of England
Threadneedle Street
London
EC2R 8AH

Telephone: (+44) (0)20 7601 3918
Fax: (+44) (0)20 7601 5226

Email: fmlc@bankofengland.co.uk
Website: www.fmlc.org

14 January 2011

Mr Joseph Parnes
President
Technomart Investment Advisors
401 Washington Ave Suite 1101
Baltimore MD 21204
USA

Dear Mr Parnes

**FINANCIAL MARKETS LAW COMMITTEE
JUDICIAL SEMINAR**

I am the Director of a Committee established by the Bank of England called the Financial Markets Law Committee (FMLC), which is concerned with identifying areas of legal uncertainty affecting financial markets and making members of the judiciary properly informed about market practice. The Committee is chaired by Lord Hoffmann, a former member of the Appellate Committee of the House of Lords, now called the Supreme Court, which is the UK equivalent of the US Supreme Court.

The FMLC's annual judicial seminar is the apex of its yearly conference programme. It is a private seminar, open only to the senior judiciary, members of the FMLC (see enclosed brochure p. 16) and a very few, carefully selected financial experts, not open to the Press, and well attended by judges and the Supreme Court justices with an interest in financial markets practice.

It is at this event that I extend this invitation to speak on the subject of short selling. I believe your expertise in this area makes you an ideal candidate to present to the judiciary on the practice, which is becoming particularly pertinent at present, given the new rules on short selling to be introduced in the European Union. Members of the FMLC and I would be honoured if you would join us for this private, convivial but important opportunity to educate the judiciary and share experiences about new financial markets practices.

I would be grateful if you could let me know whether you would be available to speak at this seminar, which we have provisionally scheduled for May 2011. Please do not hesitate to contact me should you require any further information.

Yours sincerely

Joanna Perkins

**Joanna Perkins
FMLC Director**

Enc: FMLC Brochure

Services 9610089v1

Figure 2.1   Letter from the Financial Markets Law Committee (FMLC).

Since I was addressing legal rather than financial experts, I made an effort to simplify the financial terminology, provide a background of the history of short selling, and then trace its evolution into the current status. Therefore, financial analysts may find this chapter too

MAY 23 2011 London, United Kingdom
Financial Markets Law Committee
c/o Bank of England
(HO-6) Threadneedle Street
LONDON, EC2R 8AH

5.00 pm	Welcome from the Chairman	FMLC
5.05 pm	A Short History of Short Selling	Technomart Investment Advisors
5.25 pm	An Introduction to Stock Lending	Wim Hautekiet The Bank of New York Mellon
5.35 pm	The Mechanics of Short Selling	Andrew Bagley Goldman Sachs International
5.45 pm	The European and National Regimes Governing Short Selling	David Rouch Freshfields Bruckhaus Deringer LLP
5.55 pm	Thematic Summary - Q&A	Carlos Conceicao Clifford Chance LLP
6.00 pm	Chairman's Closing	FMLC

The FMLC Judicial Seminar forms a part of a programme for the British judiciary aimed at briefing members of the judiciary on aspects of wholesale financial markets practice . It is intended to provide a link between commercial judges and the City.

Figure 2.1   (*Continued*)

pedestrian while others without a financial background may find this chapter helpful. However, what is presented next is a verbatim duplication of what I told the Bank of England during my presentation.

The Presentation

NOTE: The following is a transcript of my presentation before the Bank of England. My rationale for certain aspects of my presentation is shown in parentheses.

There is a long history of concerns about short selling in the UK. After the Tulip Crash in Holland of 1600s and the Cook Island collapse in the early eighteenth century, England banned short selling outright. The London banking house of Neal, James, Fordyce and Down collapsed in June 1772, precipitating a major banking crisis which included the collapse of almost every private bank in Scotland. The bank had been speculating by shorting East India Company stock on a massive scale. Short sellers were blamed for the Wall Street Crash of 1929. Political fallout from the 1929 crash led Congress to enact a US law banning short sellers from shorting shares on a downtick. This was known as the "uptick rule," and this was in effect until July 3, 2007 when it was removed by the SEC (SEC Release No. 34-55970), which, in part, led to the 2008 market collapse. More importantly for UK citizens, George Soros became notorious for "breaking the Bank of England" on Black Wednesday of 1992, when he sold short more than $10 billion worth of pounds sterling. [This event triggered the start of great concern from the British banking community and judiciary about short selling. However, many did not fully understand the entire process, so I had to review what a short sale was.]

In a short sale, the investor thinks the value of a stock will go down, so he wants to sell it, even though he doesn't own it. This is the first of many risk factors that should raise a red flag. If you do not own something, how can you sell it? [So I had to explain this process to the audience.] A brokerage house "lends" the investor a stock, which allows him to sell stock short. The investor "borrows" the stock at a price in order to receive money for this sale. The investor pays a "stock borrowing fee." The short contract remains open as long as the investor wants, for years if he wishes, with two possible options. The short sale can remain open until "covered" or called by owner of the stock. The investor hopes to "cover his short" by purchasing the stock at a lower price. The difference between the "short price" and "purchase price" is profit (or loss, if the price rises above the sale price). It is in this latter situation that the investor can lose money, unless he really wishes to maintain the short in the stock. In this case, the investor may have to post more collateral or cash to cover the paper loss, at the request of the lender, who is usually the brokerage house.

Let us review an example. XYZ Company is selling at $50 a share. The investor thinks XYZ is going to decline, so he borrows stock from the brokerage house, and shorts the stock, that is, sells the brokerage house stock at $50 a share. Since this stock is really the property of the brokerage house, the investor has to pay interest on the value of the stock, he has to pay the dividend of the stock, since he now "owns" the stock on a temporary basis, and he has to pay commission for the short sale transaction. Any time after a short sale (a day or a year later) an unfavorable report for XYZ comes out, and the stock drops to $40 a share. The investor buys XYZ at $40 a share, "covers his short," and makes $10 a share, less his interest costs, any dividends which occurred during the time of the short, and another commission for covering the short.

There is a difference between shorting a stock and selling a stock. In a shorting situation, an investor "borrows" stock from the brokerage house to cover a short. The brokerage house charges a loan fee. Generally, the investor has to repurchase the stock to pay back the brokerage house (hopefully at a lower price). In a sales situation, an investor owns shares in a stock. The investor sells the shares of the stock. The investor delivers the stock certificate to the brokerage house. The brokerage house pays the investor within three days (the legal settlement time in the United States).

However, there can be problems with a short sale. If the stock the investor borrowed and sold goes up in price, the investor has to cover the difference with real money, or repurchase the stock at a loss, to repay the brokerage house. If the investor "shorts" XYZ at $50 a share but the stock goes to $60 a share, the investor has to produce $10 a share to cover the potential loss (a "margin call") or buy the stock to cover the short. A margin call is the demand for money to cover potential losses, so that the brokerage house can be reassured that the investor will have the funds to cover any losses.

The entire short transaction process is pretty straightforward. This differs from a little known but highly prevalent (and illegal) practice of "naked short selling." In this naked short sale transaction, the investor does a "naked short" of a stock. The brokerage house never delivers any security to collateralize the loan, and the broker knows that this is in violation of Financial Industry Regulatory Authority (FINRA) rules. However, the penalties are not enforced. Hypothetically, the investor can sell more than the issued shares of a company. Even though there is a FINRA Reg. T requirement to "locate" shares of stock in the company, the brokerage houses often ignore this, resulting in a failure to deliver.

Let us examine this in more detail, to try to understand the nuances of a naked short sale. In order to execute a short sale, a brokerage house had to lend a stock to an investor who was executing a short sale, that is, identify that the brokerage house had the stock it was going to lend in its inventory of stock holdings. However, in 1993, the Securities and Exchange Commission (SEC) changed their wording from "an investor may <u>borrow</u> stock from the brokerage house to cover the short sale" to "the brokerage house has to <u>locate</u> stock to cover the short sale."

This change of regulations led to a marked increase in brokerage houses failing to deliver. A failure to deliver occurs when a naked short seller shorts a stock. The investor must post collateral to cover this short. But if the brokerage house doesn't deliver stock to cover the short, then there is a failure to deliver. There are regulatory penalties for failure to deliver, but they are not enforced. This failure to deliver situation can lead to many abuses, since a brokerage house can sell shorts without having stocks in their inventory to cover these shorts. Then, if a market correction occurs, the brokerage house is not in a position to cover all the outstanding shorts.

There are some practical implications to the naked short sell situation. As an example, say XYZ Company is selling at $50 a share. The investor thinks XYZ is going to decline. Naked shorts are executed on the stock by an investor, that is, stock is sold at $50 a share, but the brokerage house never locates stock to cover the short sale. Hence this is a naked short. A month later, or a year later, an unfavorable report for XYZ comes out, and the stock drops to $40 a share. The investor buys XYZ at $40 a share, covers his short, and makes $10 a share, less commissions, dividends, and interest payments. There is no problem in this situation, other than the fact that the transaction is actually illegal, due to the absence of collateral to cover the short.

Let us compare and contrast a short sale and a naked short sale. For a short sale, an investor borrows stock from the brokerage house to sell short. The brokerage house charges a stock loan fee and a commission on the transaction, and the investor is liable to pay the dividend due from the stock. When the investor decides to repurchase the stock to cover the short sale (hopefully at a lower price), he also pays a commission on the transaction, and the transaction is completed. This differs from a naked short sale. In this situation, the brokerage house allows an investor to short a stock before the stock is located, which creates the naked short. This failure to deliver may remain open for weeks or months. More importantly, there is no limit on the quantity of stock that can be shorted in this naked fashion, since there is no need to have actual stock in the brokerage house account.

This begs the question, How do the brokerage houses get away with this? Historically, stock certificates were actually counterfeited and used to support short sales. After the 1929 market crash, the Securities Acts of 1933 and 1934 were created in the United States. These acts created the Securities and Exchange Commission (SEC) and National Association of Securities Dealers (NASD, now FINRA). A letter ruling by the SEC in 1993 dropped the word "borrow" from the short seller's lexicon/rules, and substituted the word "locate" for the collateral stock. This same letter ruling created exemptions from even this rule for three kinds of traders: market makers, arbitrageurs, and hedged (fund) accounts. Once freed from the enforcement of Reg T, and using "ex clearing" (unreported trading hidden from regulators), brokerage houses began naked short selling. It is estimated that over the next 10- to 15-year period, 80% of NASD (now FINRA) member firms' profits came from naked shorting. The member firms primarily focused on small public companies on the OTC Bulletin Board and the Pink Sheets, which are in development stage. In 2002, one syndicate operator, Amir "Anthony" Elgindy, was arrested in connection with his activities surrounding terrorism, bribes of FBI agents, and money-laundering issues. His syndicate consisted of 650 members, including many large hedge funds.

The most troubling aspect of naked short selling is from the imputed "contra account" effect. Every time a share is shorted naked, a counterfeit long is created, but never registered by, known to, or accounted for by the targeted company. Some interesting twists in Financial Accounting Standards Board (FASB) and generally accepted accounting principles (GAAP) also entered into the naked short sellers' tactical equation. If naked short sellers bankrupt or cause the deregistration of a targeted company, they can avoid a revenue recognition event under GAAP, because the short needn't be covered. Therefore, since there was no revenue recognition event, according to GAAP, there was no taxable event. Because of this, naked short sellers often pursue their targets with unbridled aggression, always hoping for either (1) an involuntary deregistration of the company or (2) its actual bankruptcy. If either (1) or (2) occurred, according to the SEC rules, the shorts never had to be covered. The naked short seller could essentially launder money without tax consequence. It was tax-free income. These are backroom games, hidden from the public. Brokerage houses can avoid a traceable clearing and settlement of securities by using direct "broker to broker" clearings of securities, called "ex-clearing" (dark pools). Shorts and counterfeit longs can sit in "ex-clearing" and remain unreported. This tricks an investor into thinking he has bought (long) real shares in a company, but these are counterfeit shares.

C. Austin (Bud) Burrell, former executive vice-president of Shearson-American Express Lehman Brothers, is now one of the leading experts for prosecutors of naked-short selling crimes. According to Burrell, in a presentation at the Harvard Club in New York, the biggest perpetrators of the "crime" of naked short selling are the brokerage houses themselves, trading between each other using "ex clearing." Burrell reports that naked short selling is a money-laundering scheme for organized crime and terrorist groups, and market manipulation. He recommends outlawing naked short selling.

There have been feeble attempts at this control. FINRA 4320 mandates 13-day buy-ins for open delivery failures. FINRA 2010-043 requires any short sale exempt trade to be reported. Market makers now must formally acknowledge that they are not locating stocks before a short sell, thereby creating a naked short sell. The third rule requires that offers and bids be approximately the same size, thereby preventing the control of stock movement using small trades to offset large ones.

While naked short selling is per se an illegal, criminal activity (although rarely prosecuted), short selling is a legitimate investment tool. Short selling allows an investor to make money even in a falling market. This is a valuable tool, because stock prices do not always go up. Stocks fluctuate in price, sometimes with reason and sometimes without reason. Shorts can be used to protect a long position or to hedge against a temporary drop in price. Conventional shorts are a tool for adding liquidity in the market, due to purchasing of the stocks, when the shorts are covered.

Since there are natural fluctuations in the price of a stock, the shorts are used to take advantage of this fluctuation. The proceeds of the short sale are used to increase the long side of the positions by the investors. This investment strategy covers all aspects of market fluctuations, where investment can be construed as 130/30. This means that the net market exposure remains 100% (130% long and 30% short).

When money managers use shorts as part of an investment philosophy, they focus on in-house company research, fundamentals, technical analysis, and cash flow to evaluate superior opportunities for long and short investments. Strategies may include sector balancing, growth, cash flow, bonds, income, short selling, dividend capture, risk aversion, and other investment techniques. However, astute money managers do not use short selling alone, but only as a tool to augment all investment activity.

I strongly believe that in-house company research is the most important aspect of successful investing. Research purchased from large brokerage houses often suffers from a persistent time lag. By the time an investor receives research, it is "old news," and the market has already adjusted to the information. Often, the "research" is not considered objective; it advances the self-interest of the brokerage house.

[After my presentation concluded, I was deluged with questions about my approach. I tried to record these questions, and I have shared the answers I gave to the questions later in this book. I hope this book will prove to be a useful guide to the use of shorts for the long term as part of an investment philosophy.]

3

Portfolio Management—General Principles

I am responsible for supplying private and institutional clients with practical investment advice. I have experience across a broad array of industries with a special focus on growth companies and short-selling strategies.

Even though I mentioned the bottom-up approach in a previous chapter, it is important enough to warrant repetition. The proprietary bottom-up approach to investing that I use places a strong emphasis on company research, fundamentals, technical analysis, and cash flow to evaluate greater opportunities for long and short investments. Incorporating sector balancing, growth, cash flow, bonds, income, short selling, risk aversion, and other investment strategies can lead to a more comprehensive understanding of the positions. I find it of paramount importance to develop in-house company research in order to incorporate objective and subjective information. This leads to a focus on company fundamentals, technical analysis, and cash flow in order to mitigate the potential biases held by large institutional investors, which often have questionable amounts of holdings in the companies which are then recommended for purchase.

Again let me reiterate that the aggregate portfolio of a client always varies, subject to one's risk tolerance, investment objective, and the monetary size of the portfolio. It is imperative to review the positions, movements, corrections, and retractions of each issue.

Near-term objectives, intermediate objectives, and stop losses are set and reassessed on each issue to avoid being "stopped out." For individual issues, one must take notice of the 10-day, 50-day, and 200-day moving averages (referred to in most financial publications as 10 dma, 50 dma, and 200 dma). These are commonly viewed as a reputable tool to analyze their inseparable relationship with deviations, plunges, and down-gaps in conjunction with institutional, hedge fund, or mutual fund investors taking or disposing these positions. When the momentum of a stock overextends its respective movements above the set barriers or resistance line, it is time to seriously reevaluate that holding. In regard to long positions, the critical factors to consider are the relative strength as well as flow movements and the holding of short positions by institutional investors due to their need to potentially cover.

The same technique I use to create a stop loss for a long position is applied to the short positions. The majority of the spikes in short position prices are created by short sellers covering their positions. Often, these spikes will be eliminated, and the declining pattern will continue to lower prices, especially if the fundamentals of a company are not strong. Most institutional investors take advantage of the short-term rebound in price, because they know that the price rise is not sustainable due to the inherent flaws in the fundamentals of a company they have shorted.

It is imperative that one understand the value of incorporating the 130/30 model technique where proceeds from shorts are subsequently applied to other selected issues for their long-term growth rate higher than the 25–30% level. It is the apparent long-term appreciation found in the value of these growth stocks that makes up for the cost, fees, and interest charges levied by the short position lenders.

The long and short positions are tracked on various factors, especially on the technical formation of the 50-day moving average (50 dma) and the 200-day moving average (200 dma), relative strengths, and daily trading volume. Efforts are made to discard the positions that are not meeting the set standards. Violation of these settings results in the disposal of an issue.

My investment style is to create customized portfolios. I believe this strategy can be successively applied to a much broader range of sectors, styles, and market caps. While one's personal investment methodology is subjective, here it is based on the assumption of allocating 10% to 20% fixed income, 20% to 30% big caps, 20% to 30%

growth-oriented equities, and 15% to 20% short positions. These allocations and apportionments are fundamentally based on internal company research that evaluates fundamentals, technical analysis, and cash flow to identify candidates for long and short holdings. Remember, as I said before, taking all these factors into account, my focus is on sector balancing, growth, cash flow, bonds, income, short-selling, dividend capture, risk aversion, and other investment techniques. My primary experience is based on working mostly with high-net-worth individuals as well as select institutional entities. I have found that the seemingly different nature of these two forms of clients can be reconciled by their unified desire for more sustainable and/or less volatile portfolio allocations. Normally, my strategy is to try to increase the asset value of portfolios by double and triple digits, in a time frame of one to five years. I have never seen myself as a trader and it is not my natural instinct to exit the market or sell during perceived corrections. Experience has shown that it's very difficult to be consistently profitable by continuously trading. Furthermore, I believe that my decision to work as an advisor precludes any financial incentive from commissions procured from trading and instead has put more interest in fulfilling my fiduciary responsibility to my clients' portfolios. Since I do not make money on commissions, I subsequently focus on finding value. For example, some recent opportunities are growth companies in biotechnology, pharmaceutical, health-oriented areas, and technology fields. There is also significance in some high-quality companies' corporate bonds, inclusive of short-term and reverse convertible bonds, often averaging returns of 9% to 11%. In a reverse convertible bond, if the price of the stock falls below a certain barrier from the stock price at the time of the purchase of the bond, the client will be given stock in the company in lieu of a return of the principal. However, if the stock price stays the same or goes higher than the original purchase price of the bond, the client will be given the principal back, plus interest. For example, if I buy $10,000 worth of a company's reverse convertible bonds at a designated interest rate of 9.5% at today's stock price of 15, and if next year the price stays at 15, I'll get back my $10,000 plus 9.5% interest. If the price falls 20% or more below the original purchase price of $15, say $3 below the original price of $15, then the investor will be given stock in the company at the current price of the stock, that is, $12 a share, equal to the original purchase price of the bond, and not be given any interest.

It is apparent that there are many factors that determine whether or not to take a long position on the stock. It is inevitable that every company price has hiccups. However, while today's artificial intelligence (AI) environment is often seen as a lucrative method for a particular stock selection, both programmable and self-learning systems are not as precise as a well-trained human mind. Although self-driving cars could prove very lucrative, the use of AI for stock selections is not quite that simple.

Please understand that I don't intend to sell short with the idea just to have a short position. Rather, I try to use shorts as a hedge against the market. I try to sell short companies where I feel the growth rate is stalled or will not be what it had been before, or that the average investor has pushed the stock up excessively and it's overpriced.

What triggers an exit from the stock is the reduction of money flow into the stock. I value the idea of fundamentals, but really the basic appreciation of the stock or the decline of the stock is related to its fundamental and technical picture augmented by money flow. Once the movement of these stocks has deteriorated from a technical point of view, it's time to exit. I always try to be ahead of the market, but that is difficult. I use technical assessments and pictures as tools, because there are corrections and retractions for each one of the stocks that I mentioned that sometimes go beyond certain percentage points. For example, there are a lot of traders who maintain that when the stock drops 8% to 10%, it should be exited. I do not feel this is good judgment, because each stock or each equity has its own deviation and its own retraction. Sometimes there may be a percentage of volatility so high on these particular stocks that the slide retraction could be much more severe than 8% to 10%, yet on the rebound it will be quickly aided by short covering, to the point that the stock will make new highs. It is very important to treat each stock separately and to follow that procedure of individual assessment. I believe large brokerage houses do not have this luxury because they are compelled to follow so many issues. Since I limit the number of issues I track, and I follow them very closely, I have the ability to take advantage of market fluctuations.

On a technical basis, I value the movement of the stocks on two main averages, the 50-day moving average and the 200-day moving average. I follow pattern fluctuations to make sure that there is a systematic advance going on for, say, a few months to a year, and other factors, such as volume and relative strength. These are the objective parameters I follow on each particular equity. I try to diversify as much as possible, by industry sector, market capitalization, and geography, but the most important factor is the risk tolerance of each client. One of the most important factors is diversification within selected sectors. It is important to not have too much of a particular type of stock and to invest for the long term. My advice to most investors is to limit their trading tendencies. Do not jump in and out of an issue. In a volatile environment, it is extremely difficult to be consistent utilizing the mentality of trading. I have found that it is invaluable to study companies and treat each one very much like its own investment rather than simply a trade. Therefore, if the technical aspects of a stock have been properly selected, the positions should be maintained four to eight quarters before the stock appreciates to its full potential, unless there is a dramatic dropoff or loss of market share or loss of money.

I also suggest looking for companies with very little to no debt. Most of the companies I mention in my portfolios do not carry much debt with them, and that is vital. It is rare for a company to have consistent and continued earnings growth at a certain percentage rate. There will always be hitches, and there will always be articles predicting pending doom for said company, such as downgrades and negative news. You just have to ride out all these fluctuations. Remember, if it is a good company, with sound fundamentals, and is ill-positioned, there are many fluctuations or retractions on the downside—but the company should rebound and you should be able to build up on these fluctuations. If the company has positive essentials, it can sustain itself against the natural amount of retractions and setbacks.

In addition to looking at individual stocks, one must look at market conditions. I look at the CBOE Volatility Index (VIX), the Arms Index, and major indices such as the Dow Jones Industrial Average, the S&P 500, the NASDAQ Composite, and of course the Dow Jones Transportation Index. Based on the expected earnings and the P/E ratio from the major indices, I can give you one bit of advice. Short for the long term. Never trade. Rather, only invest.

You must appreciate how much the market has changed since 2008. As of 2019, the United States now produces about 10 to 12 million barrels of oil a day, which represents about half of what it consumes. This is a far better production ratio than in the past and makes the economy far less vulnerable to supply shocks resulting from any potential crisis in the Middle East or South America or West Africa, or any of the OPEC nations.

My professional history has trained me to focus on performance, as my income is derived from the success of the clients' portfolio. It has also led me to advocate a strong aversion to the use of allocating clients' positions in a similar and/or grouped mentality. Although a lump-style account or a branded fund would arguably be easier to manage, it has never appealed to my sensibilities. Additionally, the level of transparency based on never functioning as a custodian and the option to use a multitude of insured SIPC custodian firms has had a direct effect on focusing on the primary issues in developing these portfolios.

I believe that this strategy differs substantially from that of other financial advisors, investment advisors, and traders due to the unique incorporation of shorts as a form of building wealth. It is no surprise to hear that shorts are very difficult to master, but from my years of experience I found that some stocks flourished while others withered, and I believe I have developed a more reliable selection method. I often created a stop loss to protect clients' positions, which means that if the stock moved against me, I would absorb only so much of the loss before covering the short position or selling the long ones. I also recognize that market fluctuations are driven by the sheer volume of shares that institutions hold. It is for this reason that I strongly resist the "word" on the Street as I feel that these institutions tend to have a sheep mentality. Simply put, if one brokerage house buys a stock, they seemingly all rush to buy that stock. On the other hand, if they take note that a stock is overpriced, or there's the least bit of reported bad news, they panic and liquidate the stock. What is most fascinating is that you can usually detect these kinds of market movements by looking toward the volume of shares traded.

One perfect example of the "sheep mentality" due to "institutional jitters" leading to an unwarranted sell of a position was Quality Systems. I am mentioning this stock only for informational purposes and do not recommend buying or selling it. This company made information management software, mainly for medical and dental companies. Quality Systems delivered a disappointing earnings report and the stock fell to $45. Again, this fall in stock price was the result of massive sell-offs by institutional investors. In my estimation, the company had good values, a good cash position, and great management. Months later, the stock was trading at $71. There was nothing wrong with the company's growth except in the minds of the analysts, who overresponded to a single earnings report in which the earnings missed the projections. I call this a "single earnings-consensus miss." This scared off the institutions, as usual. Too much of what happens in the market is a result of an emotional reaction to the ordinary volatility of stocks as interpreted by shareholders based on the comments of analysts. Too many investors, including professional money managers, do what analysts tell them to do, without rhyme or reason. I have learned to not simply read what people have to say about a company but rather read the market's reactions to analysts' reports. Most importantly, doing my own research has freed me from potentially uninformed or biased general information. This information is often so seductive because of the ease with which one can readily access it and the sheer volume of material offered. Thus I focus only on a small number of issues to research, providing me with both a more in-depth evaluation of each issue and the positive mental reinforcement as a result of forming my own analysis.

Additionally, by the time most research reports done for institutions reach the press, they are old news. Moreover, by the time the research reports are published and available to the public it is likely that the insiders have already taken a position in a stock which has discounted its movement in the marketplace. It can be said that a negative report has a larger short-term impact on the price of a stock, causing it to fall precipitously, compared to a positive report where the advances on its price take longer to manifest. Simply stated, if a stock price falls due to a negative report, it plunges quickly, while a positive report creates a slower and smaller increase in price (up gap).

Throughout this book, I share with you the parameters I use for selecting securities to purchase, short, hold, or sell. By now, it should be obvious that this requires a multifactorial analysis, taking into account considerations ranging from the price of oil and trade barriers and tariffs, to legal barriers, to the behavior of the C suite executives, to interest rates, to unforeseen events such as political crises anywhere in the world. Anything from earthquakes to insect infestations of crops or food poisoning in a restaurant chain can have a substantial effect. I will explore individual issues in depth, using them as examples for selecting the parameters I use for measuring performance. Then, using pattern recognition and predictive analytic techniques, I am going to examine which of these parameters appeared in stocks that I have selected for purchase or shorting. From this, I will offer the reader an analytic model that I feel confident can be followed.

My Asset Allocation of a Portfolio

The average stockbroker or portfolio manager often bases their investment philosophy in relationship to days, weeks, or months. While some may make returns off of their investment, I have found that both for long and short positions one should be in it for the long haul—years. I do not advocate the concept of selling as soon as a profit is present or if there is a setback in the stock price. If properly selected, a stock will handle these corrections. Therefore it is not about being in and out of a stock. One must take into account the investor tolerance of volatility, which is called the "beta" of the stock. Some investors want a beta of less than 1, with a stable stock price. Others can tolerate swings in stock prices. I purchase stocks with the idea of sustainability. Through self-analysis I feel that one can in fact provide information that an investor can use with his own stockbroker. Once it has been established that the elimination of commissions, either straight, draw, or residual, discounts any inherent motivation to buy and sell stock, preservation takes over as a primary factor. A number of investment firms make efforts to stabilize the investments of their clients and have asset preservation as a goal. Many clients like this risk-averse method of investing, which actually is a very prudent approach if preserving capital is essential and central to the investment philosophy of a client. Unfortunately, statistically, this method of capital preservation is not foolproof. One has only to look at the 2008 stock market crash, which produced 35% to 50% losses. By 2017, many investment counselors and investment advisors had yet to recover the capital that they lost in 2008. This had a profound effect on many investors.

The failure of these investment advisors can be summarized succinctly: they do not have the power of the short sell. There is no way to take advantage of a loss or drop in the market without utilizing shorts. If you look at the overall price of the stock, it may take six months to a year to increase in price, but it can precipitously drop 30% or 40% within a week. Without the ability to make money during the falling phase of the stock, an investment counselor is left only with increasing funds in an up market.

Let me clarify that shorts are completely different from puts and calls or other options. The major distinction is that puts and calls, the so-called options market, have a time limit associated with the option. In effect, a put or call is a bet that the stock will go up or down in a certain period of time (https://www.optionsanimal.com/how-often-do-options-get-exercised-early/). One commonly held belief is that only one time out of 10 does the fluctuation of the price of the stock make it worthwhile to exercise a put or call. Some investors have taken advantage of this and sell puts and calls, using the rationale that 9 times out of 10 they're going to make money because the put or call will never be exercised. The reason so many venues present this statement as truth is because only 10% of option contracts are exercised. That is true (https://www.thebluecollarinvestor.com/percentage-of-options-expiring-worthless-debunking-a-myth/). However, 55–60% of option contracts are closed out prior to expiration, which accounts for the trading in the options themselves. In the volatile market of today, the majority of the puts sold to generate money for an account resulted in large losses for institutional investors. Investors who wrote calls, hoping to take minimum earnings, often had the stock taken away, and they never realized its full appreciation.

Again it is invaluable to develop one's own research. I start by examining the company in depth. For example, I explore all the factors that could contribute to the profitability of the company, the longevity of the company, the ability to maintain its position in the marketplace, and a host of other factors, all of which are examined by other investment advisors. However, my goal is to invest in a company for the long term. I do not want to have my investment dependent on the inherent fluctuations in the market. I want to invest in the stock that has the ability to sustain market swings and recover from them. A double- or even triple-digit increase in asset value on the money consistently, usually in a time frame of one to five years, is not unreasonable. Key to my long-term investments is the degree of appreciation. I have can absorb the market fluctuations and still show a long-term gain.

I allocate the assets in three broad categories of investments: growth stocks, anchor stocks, and fixed income or index investments. I typically invest 30–40% of an account into growth stocks, 25–40% into anchor stocks, and 25–30% to fixed income stocks, bonds, or other investment vehicles.

In the growth stocks I look for a growth rate of 20% to 30%, or more, a year that is sustainable for six to eight quarters. I focus on the fundamentals of the triple E's (earnings, earnings, and earnings), based on the expected price-to-earnings ratio (P/E) on major indices, with replacement earnings. Stocks that have these characteristics have a very high P/E, depending on the growth of earnings.

Everyone recognizes that the market will have both its ups and downs. My goal is to pick companies that can survive these setbacks and, if the price drops, recover their value within a reasonable period of time. To fit into this category, I avoid what I define as single item producers, which may have a product that is good for one year but not for the next five years. I'm looking for sustainability and am keeping my eyes open for companies with enough cash reserves to purchase competitors should some company be in position to challenge their current leadership position in the industry.

For the anchor stocks, I look to the old standbys, which are diversified and have consistent sales. These companies have lots of cash, with the ability to buy new products. They have a high percentage of the market share. They have a positive cash dividend. Stocks that are clearly diversified and consistently increase their dividends are attractive. Most importantly, they have high market share in their segment of the market.

For the fixed income portion of my portfolio, I look for exchange-traded funds (ETF) indexes, preferred stocks paying a dividend, Treasury bills, and convertible bonds.

As you can see, these three segments of the market account for 100% of a portfolio's investments, in various ratios, depending on my client's investment philosophy and risk tolerance.

The final piece of the investment puzzle comes in the form of shorts. I may have 10% to 40% of an investment portfolio in short positions, depending on market conditions and volatility. A short is used as a hedge for the accounts. Short sales can generate income. Using this technique, the proceeds are applied to other selected issues, for their long-term growth rate of 25–30%. Apparent long-term appreciation in the value of these growth stocks makes up for the costs/fees being levied by the lenders for the short positions selected. I look for companies with a large float on their stock or larger companies to avoid the possibility of acquisition, being squeezed by scarcity of float, the brokerage house or lender calling the short, margin calls, an overmature company, or growth on a sliding scale. For the average investor and even for the average financial/investment advisor, shorts are avoided because of their seemingly inherent level of difficulty to practice. They must be reviewed daily. A spike on the positive side could trigger an unsophisticated investor to cover the short, rather than accumulation of the stock by an investor. In fact, it's not uncommon that a price jump in the stock could be an institutional investor covering a short. Again, it is worth emphasizing that it may take 6 to 12 months for a stock price to increase into double digits, and that declines can occur within a much shorter time. Institutional investors trade stocks frequently, and high-frequency investors do the same. They don't want to hold the stock too long and try to time their investments to the minuscule market fluctuations, rather than the long-term big picture.

In summary, I diversify the accounts I manage into 18 to 24 positions or more in holdings that I've researched myself, and the aggregate depends on the risk tolerance of the client. I divide the portfolios into the three segments mentioned earlier while using the short income to add to the long positions in the growth stocks. This gives me the 130/30 model.

Explanation of the Use of the 50-Day Moving Average and 200-Day Moving Average

A number of stock analysts use a stock market performance measurement called a "moving average." Moving averages can be used to gauge the direction of price movement in a stock. The simple moving average of a security or a commodity calculates its average price for a set length of time, usually 50 days or 200 days, to the present and then each successive day, drops the price from the earliest date, and adds the one from the latest day. This creates a smoothed price trend line, which is an indicator used in technical analysis.

If the moving average is headed down and the stock price drops below the moving average, this may signal that it's time to sell. Alternately, if the moving average is headed up and the stock price rises above the moving average price, this may be a buy signal. However, analysts use other indicators to verify the direction of stock movement to prevent them from acting on a misleading signal.

Frequent time spans of moving averages for stocks are 10, 30, 50, 100, and 200 days. Shorter time periods are more sensitive to price changes. Longer periods are less sensitive and smooth the moving average out more.

The daily price to be used in the calculation must also be defined. Closing price is the most common, but technicians may choose a variation, such as the sum of the day's high and low prices divided by 2 [(daily high price + daily low price)/2].

A weighted moving average gives more importance, or weight, to data closer to the present. It will change direction faster than the simple moving average.

Whether an investor uses the 50-day, 100-day, or 200-day moving average (which I subsequently refer to as 50 dma, 100 dma, or 200 dma), the method of calculation and the manner in which the moving average is interpreted remain the same. A moving average is simply an arithmetic mean of a certain number of data points. The only difference between a 50 dma and a 200 dma is the number of time periods used in the calculation. The 50 dma is calculated by summing up the past 50 data points and then dividing the result by 50, whereas the 200 dma is calculated by summing the past 200 days and dividing the result by 200.

Many technical traders ("quants") use these averages as an aid to determine when to enter or exit a certain position, which then causes these levels to act as a strong support or resistance point. Therefore, this almost becomes a self-fulfilling prophecy.

Simple moving averages (SMAs) are often viewed as a low-risk area to place transactions, since they correspond to the average price that all traders have paid over a given time frame. For example, a 50 dma is equal to the average price that all investors have paid to obtain the asset over the past 10 trading weeks (that is, over the past two and a half months), making it a commonly used support level. Similarly, the 200 dma represents the average price over the past 40 weeks, which is used to suggest a relatively cheap price compared to the price range over most of the past year. Once the price falls below the 200 dma, a support line has been broken. Individuals who have already taken a position may consider closing the position to ensure that they do not suffer a larger loss.

William O'Neil, the founder of *Investor's Business Daily*, and Gil Morales are very successful investors. They rely heavily on 50 dma and 200 dma to decide when to short stocks. In their book *How to Make Money Selling Stock Short* (John Wiley & Sons, 2005), they show graph after graph of inflection points and crossing points in the 50 dma and 200 dma as examples of timing short selling. Their book offers fantastic historical examples of great short plays, which have value in a retrospective sense.

Critics of technical analysis say that moving averages act as support and resistance because so many traders use these indicators to influence their trading decisions.

I differ from most stock analysts because I do not rely on just a single moving average. I use the relationship between the 50 dma

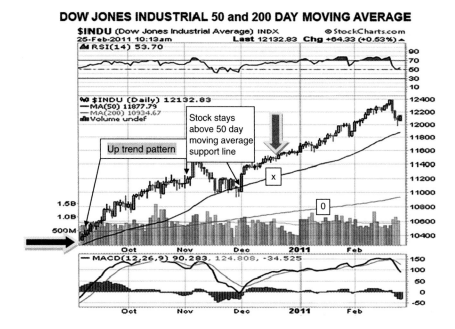

Figure 4.1 This stock was in death cross territory, and then switched to golden cross.

Chart courtesy of StockCharts.com.

and 200 dma. Markets fluctuate, with so many variables contributing to the fluctuation that it is nearly impossible to predict and track market movements. However, individual stocks and indices have a natural cycle that can be tracked. This cycle is tracked using a moving average. Again, I most often use the 50 dma and 200 dma. I give you an example in Figure 4.1.

Staying Above the 50-Day Moving Average

The reader is cautioned not to rely on any information provided in this example for making decisions about trading any security. Please refer to the **Caution—Limitations and Difficulties** section found at the end of Chapter 1.

Figure 4.1 is a copy of a 2011 Dow Jones Industrial Average (^DJI) 50-day moving average and 200-day moving average chart for INDU (Dow Jones Industrial Average). In this chart, the line with an "x" mark on it is the 50-day moving average and the line with an "o" on it is 200-day moving average. The bar graphs on the bottom are daily volume (black arrow). The mixed light and dark lines, which appear above the 50-day moving average, are the daily closing price of the Dow Jones Index.

The "up-trend pattern" is defined when the daily closing of the index is above the 50 dma, as is shown in this graph. When a sell-off occurs, as happened in the month of November, the 50 dma is the primary "support line," meaning that the stock didn't dip below this line.

This same type of pattern is shown on the Standard & Poor 500 (50 dma and 200 dma chart) for SPX (^GSPC) (the old and new stock symbol), and the NASDAQ 50 dma and 200 dma chart for the COMPQ NASDAQ Composite (^IXIC) (the old and new stock symbol). See Figures 4.2 and 4.3.

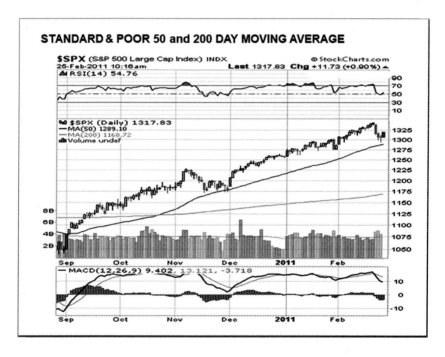

Figure 4.2   Standard & Poor 50 dma and 200 dma.

Chart courtesy of StockCharts.com.

The reader is cautioned not to rely on any information provided in this example for making decisions about trading any security. Please refer to the **Caution—Limitations and Difficulties** section found at the end of Chapter 1.

NASDAQ 50 and 200 DAY MOVING AVERAGE

Figure 4.3   NASDAQ 50 dma and 200 dma.

Chart courtesy of StockCharts.com.

The reader is cautioned not to rely on any information provided in this example for making decisions about trading any security. Please refer to the **Caution—Limitations and Difficulties** section found at the end of Chapter 1.

All three of these indices had sell-offs in November, but none of them had the price of the index drop below the 50 dma support price. Therefore they continued the upward pattern with another sell-off in late February.

The Golden Cross

There is also one other common feature these three indices share. In addition to having the price of the index stay above the 50 dma, they all have the "golden cross." This is the point on their graphs where the 50 dma crosses the 200 dma. At this point in time, it is recommended that these indices be purchased and held in a long position. For INDU (^DJI), this crossing point occurred on the first of October

2010. From the date of the crossover point, when the stock was selling at 108, the index rose to a high of 124 (up 14.8%) by the end of February. For SPX (^GSPC), this crossover occurred in late October 2010, when the index was 1200, and by the end of February, the high price of the index was 1325 (up 10.4%). For COMPQ (^IXIC), the crossover occurred in the latter half of October 2010, when the index was 2500 and by the end of February the high price was 2850 (up 14%).

These graphs illustrate the first component of predictive analytics applied to the stock market. They are a reflection of earnings, mergers or acquisitions, changes in leadership, changes in economic factors, trade tariffs, changes in taxes, or any other variables that could impact the price of the indices. All of this important information has already been analyzed by the major brokerage houses, major research centers, other financial institutions, and by their traders.

The Dow Jones Industrial Average (^DJI) is comprised of 30 major companies, and the S&P 500 (^GSPC) is reflective of 500 companies in eleven sectors. The NASDAQ (^IXIC) is comprised of a number of various companies listed in NASDAQ, several of which are also listed on New York Stock Exchange.

This led to the purchase of the various stocks, and the continued support of the price, compatible with their price-to-earnings ratio within their industry, and their projected earnings. The only thing we are doing is reading the trend of the trading in these stocks. I could never hope to gather all of the important information that would determine whether a stock should be purchased or sold, and if I did, the information would probably be too old to be of any value. However, the brokerage houses have far greater resources than most investors and they make their money by the spread in trading, so this is really a case of "follow the leader." It is also an example of pattern recognition. I noticed the formation of the golden cross in certain issues and began taking long positions in those stocks. In four months, a number of the stocks were up 10.4% to 14.8%. On an annualized basis, this could mean a 30% to 45% growth in the value of the stock in a year.

Staying Between the Parallel Tracks

However, things are not always that simple. Let's look at the case of Core Lab (CLB) from the year 2010 to 2011. Please note that I am not recommending this stock for purchase or shorting. This sample

CHART of 50 DAY and 200 DAY MOVING AVERAGE for a BUY SCENARIO

Figure 4.4   Chart of 50-day and 200-day moving averages for a buy scenario.

Chart courtesy of StockCharts.com.

is for illustration purposes only. The chart is shown in Figure 4.4. The 50 dma and 200 dma for CLB have not had a crossover, so this ideal pattern wasn't present in the stock. On top of that, negative news in mid-October 2010, with heavy volume, resulted in a sell-off. When the price dropped below its 50 dma, this suggested a short. However, the price of the stock never dropped below the 200 dma. After the rebound, it continued above the 50 dma. Even though the stock fell from 90 to 75, it never fell below the 200 dma, and it rebounded to 90 in less than a month. By the end of February it was selling at 103, for a gain of 14.4% in four months. So we now have another pattern to recognize. In this pattern, the 50 dma remains above the 200 dma, and the price of the stock remains above the 200 dma, indicating that the stock is a candidate for a long position. Note that both of these features must occur for the stock to be a long position candidate—the 50 dma remains above the 200 dma, *and* the price of the stock never drops below the 200 dma. This pattern suggests that institutional buyers are supporting this stock, and that the stock has a good fundamental base, so it was able to rebound from negative news. It takes a healthy company to weather a storm. The 50 dma and 200 dma help to interpret this information. Remember, these averages reflect the market in general and institutional buyers in general, so by understanding the relationship of these 50 dma and 200 dma, small investors are just reading what big investors are thinking.

> The reader is cautioned not to rely on any information provided in this example for making decisions about trading any security. Please refer to the **Caution—Limitations and Difficulties** section found at the end of Chapter 1.

The Double Dip

Another factor in analyzing buy and sell decisions on stock is the price of the stock in relationship to its 50 dma and 200 dma. When a stock does a "double dip," it is time to short it, regardless of the position of the 50 dma day and 200 dma. If the price of the stock dips below the 50 dma, and then again dips below the 200 dma, it is time to consider a short of the stock. This is clearly demonstrated by Figure 4.5, which shows Nutraceutical International (NUTR) from 2010 to 2011. In late November, and by December 1, NUTR crashed below the 50 dma day and the 200 dma. It dropped from $17 a share, below its 50 dma, falling to $15 a share. It rebounded to $16 a share, but never got above the 50 dma. It again fell below the 200 dma, to $13.50 a share, remained there for a month, and then the "death cross" happened: (see below for explanation of "Death Cross."). On January 28, 2011, the 50 dma dropped below the 200 dma, forming the death cross. Even though the price of the stock rebounded slightly, the presence of the death cross was not good. Since the 50 dma fell below the 200 dma, there was less chance for a sharp rebound unless a takeover offer or other positive announcements occurred.

> The reader is cautioned not to rely on any information provided in this example for making decisions about trading any security. Please refer to the **Caution—Limitations and Difficulties** section found at the end of Chapter 1.

CHART of 50 and 200 MOVING AVERAGE for SHORT SALE SCENARIO

Figure 4.5   Chart of 50- and 200-day moving averages for a short sale scenario.

Chart courtesy of StockCharts.com.

The Death Cross

A clear sign that the technical pattern of the stock is deteriorating is when the 50 dma drops below the 200 dma. This indicates that market forces are not supporting the price of the stock, and for whatever reason, there's been a selloff of this equity. In Figure 4.5, NUTR exhibited a death cross in late January of 2011.

The Support Line

When you evaluate the graph of a chart, sometimes you can draw a line of consecutive days of a stock price, and the stock price never drops below that line. This suggests that the market and traders feel that the stock is still attractive and has enough value to warrant trading at the particular support line price. If the stock is still attractive at a certain price, more shares are traded at that price, and there is market confirmation of the value of the stock, as reflected in a "support price line." An example is shown in Figure 4.6. From December of 2016 to June of 2017, Intel had a support line ranging from $33 to $36 a share, as shown by the horizontal black arrow in the stock chart.

> The reader is cautioned not to rely on any information provided in this example for making decisions about trading any security. Please refer to the **Caution—Limitations and Difficulties** section found at the end of Chapter 1.

The Resistance Line

When you evaluate the graph of a chart, sometimes you can draw a line of consecutive days of a stock price, and the stock price never rises above that line. Often this "resistance line" is created by institutional traders selling the stock. When the resistance line is "penetrated,"

Figure 4.6   Example of a support price line.

Chart courtesy of StockCharts.com.

this breakout signals that it may be time to buy the stock. Network Appliance had a resistance line between $40 and $42 from May to July 2017, as shown by the black arrow in Figure 4.7. The price broke through the resistance line in July and had a hiccup, but then broke through resistance in November 2017, with rather impressive results. Note the golden cross that occurred in May 2017. The golden cross coupled with breaking through the resistance line suggested that the stock was going to climb.

> The reader is cautioned not to rely on any information provided in this example for making decisions about trading any security. Please refer to the **Caution—Limitations and Difficulties** section found at the end of Chapter 1.

There are other technical patterns that are important indicators, but they are difficult to predict, and reliance on these indicators can

Figure 4.7   Example of a resistance line.

Chart courtesy of StockCharts.com.

lead to disappointment. Examples of these are the "head and shoulders" and the "cup with a handle" patterns. Unfortunately, most investors can only recognize them after the fact, and not as they are developing. Once they have clearly manifested this limits their usefulness as an aid to further stock selection. There are very few events that occur systematically after these patterns are recognized, so using these to determine a stock purchase is best left in the hands of experts.

5

The Theory Behind the "Parnes Parameters": Using Pattern Recognition, Retrospective Analysis, and Bayesian Analytics

The Parnes Parameters are a set of generalized observations of investment practices; they are not a chart or device related to any particular security, nor do they provide any predictive capabilities, nor are they represented as having predictive value. These are the factors I examine when I decide to buy or short or sell a stock. However, no matter what type of investing you do, the more successful you are in predicting the future, the more successful you will be with your investing. There are various ways to predict the future. Aside from the average fortuneteller with a crystal ball, or palm reader, the most primitive form of prediction for the sake of making money takes the form of gambling. For gambling, which involves inanimate objects such as cards and dice, there are a certain set of statistics, mathematically derived, that allows you to predict what the odds are for a certain event occurring. Even playing the lottery has clearly defined odds, astronomical as they may be. The amount of just plain dumb luck that is involved in betting allows someone to pick a winner against huge odds. Almost for certain, when someone wins a gambling bet, hits the slot machine, picks the 35-to-1 number on the roulette wheel (the odds of picking a winning single number at roulette winning are 38 to 1, but the house only pays 35 to 1, and is guaranteed to make money consistently on at least 3 of all 38 or 7.89% of all bets made), or hits the lottery, the person will only tell you about how much money he made on that spectacular bet. You never hear how much money he lost on his way to that big win, or subsequent losses after the big win.

When the object on which you bet is a living organism, a whole new set of variables arise, but they nonetheless follow the same statistical process. These can involve horse racing, dog racing, car racing, tennis, and, to really complicate matters, team sports, such as football and baseball. Very often, the odds makers consider factors such as the injury of a player, the type of field on which the game is played, and even the referee. The more variables involved, the more difficult it becomes to predict future outcomes. It is curious that people use the same terminology when it comes to playing the market as they do when playing the ponies. But I don't want you to bet on the market or play the market. I want you to invest in the market, not by making bets, but by following a well-defined set of rules.

In financial situations, such as the stock market, the number of variables increases geometrically. Therefore, the chance of picking a winner increases exponentially. And, just like picking a winning horse, if an investor picks a winning stock and makes 10 or 20 times on his invested capital, you are certainly going to hear about it. We all get a little jealous when we hear of those "home runs." However, we really don't know the amount of money lost before or since the spectacular investment. Was it the result of a lucky selection, or a part of an investment strategy? The purpose of this book is to help you interject a scientific basis of stock selection into what often seems like an impossible predictive situation. Let me reassure you, picking a good stock is not just dumb luck. I want you to make money slowly and methodically and, most importantly, consistently. The purpose of this book is to help an investor recognize the trends that are emerging as the result of the instructional traders' involvement in the market. Using specialized analytic techniques, this book will help investors spot trends that are indicative of institutional trading, and allow the individual investor to trade as if he is part of the institutional cartel. The investor is taught how to recognize when the institutions are trading and why, and how to address this.

The individual investor will never be on the inside of these trades, but he can learn to recognize the trend of these trades and cash in on it. This is just like learning how to cheat at poker, not so you can cheat, but so you can recognize when the other players are trying to cheat you.

There are many ways to pick stocks. People rely on research generated by brokerage houses, research institutions, recommendations from the broker, reading annual reports, and even tips from their barber or brother-in-law. However, this book offers a scientific and reproducible methodology with proven, consistent results. These results are obtained as a result of scientific principles called "pattern recognition" and "predictive analytics."

Essentially, predictive analytics is defined as a methodology that allows you to predict the future with some degree of accuracy. An example of this can be demonstrated by a group of physicians at the Johns Hopkins University School of Medicine. They developed an Internet-based questionnaire that predicts, with a purported 95% accuracy, which patient will have abnormalities on medical testing, and predicts with 85% to 100% accuracy who will not have abnormalities on medical testing.[1,2] Additionally, this group developed a diagnostic paradigm for the 40% to 80% of chronic pain patients who were misdiagnosed, which renders diagnoses with a 96% correlation with diagnoses of Johns Hopkins Hospital doctors, and predicts surgical findings with 100% accuracy.[3,4]

If this methodology could be used to evaluate medical cases, I surmised that this same methodology could be applied to picking a stock, with some degree of predictive value. Since my background was engineering and mathematics, I quickly recognized the technique that was used in these medical settings as a technique that was transferable to the world of finance. I devised such a methodology for the stock market, which is called Parnes Parameters. Basically, the Johns Hopkins Hospital doctors developed a model for predictive analytics that can be used in any setting that benefits from the ability to attempt to anticipate outcomes.

Unlike other so-called expert systems that use Boolean logic to try to solve a problem, my system uses Bayesian logic, which produces much more accurate results. A number of people have tried predictive models for the stock market, but their major failing has been the use of Boolean logic instead of Bayesian logic. Boolean logic is the standard "branching diagram" that is often used as part of a decision tree. There are several flaws with Boolean logic. First and foremost, there is no weight assigned to each of the variables. Second, the outcome of each variable has a 50–50 chance of influencing the outcome, because the event can either occur or not occur. Last, because of the very nature of branching diagrams, there is no provision for multiple events occurring at the same time. This has led to the failure of Boolean logic to provide a useful predictive analytic model in medicine, with accuracy rates running between 64% and 85%, unlike the test developed by the Johns Hopkins Hospital group, which uses Bayesian logic and has a reported accuracy rate of 95%.[5]

Probably the easiest way to understand the difference between Boolean and Bayesian logic is to consider a flat tire on your car. If you use Boolean logic to analyze this problem, you would walk out and look at your car to determine whether or not you had a flat tire. When you look at your car, you have two possibilities: (1) you do not have a flat tire and (2) you do have a flat tire. This is the start of a Boolean logic branching diagram. Once you determine that you do have a flat tire, you then would say, "My gosh, I have a flat tire." Then, using Boolean logic, you begin to assess the problem. The first question to be asked would be "Is there a leaky valve stem?" If the answer is yes, then you would repair the valve stem. If the answer is no, you would progress to the next arm of the branching diagram: "Do I have a cut side wall?" If the answer is yes, then you have to replace the tire. However, if the answer is no, then you would progress to the next item on the list, which would be "Do I have a nail in the tread?" If there is a nail in the tread, then you would repair the hole caused by the nail. If there is no nail in the tread, you would continue through the rest of the branching diagram until you found a positive answer. You'll quickly note that there are three flaws with this type of logic. The sequence of the possible choices seems to be random. Moreover, at each juncture point between the choices, you have the option of determining whether a problem is present or not, that is, a classic on-off, open-shut, 0-1, binary logic choice of Boolean logic. There is no ability to grade the severity of the event. The event is either present or not. The third failure of Boolean logic is the absence of the possibility of multiple etiologies causing the same problem. Clearly, you can have a leaky valve stem and a nail in the tread of a tire, both of which will result in a flat tire. Using Boolean logic, you would first have to try one repair process, and would be puzzled that it did not correct the problem. Only if you went back to the branching diagram would you succeed in finding another process that required repair.

Boolean logic, however, is not how we solve problems. We solve problems using Bayesian logic. Bayesian logic is experiential. In our lifetime, we know certain things that happened, and we quantify the frequency of these events. So, in the case of the flat tire, we would say, "My tire is flat. I've had 22 flat tires in my lifetime, and 19 of those have been due to a nail in the tread. (Your numbers might vary.) However, I've had two flat tires that were caused by a leaky valve stem, and one flat tire that was caused by the loss of bead between the tire and the rim." Based on these experiences, you can assign a weight to the likelihood of a problem occurring. In the case of the flat tire, 19 of the 22 flat tires, or 86%, have been due to a nail in the tread. However, two of your flat tires, or 9%, have been due to a leaky valve stem. Only one of your flat tires has been due to the loss of bead between the tire and the wheel rim, which accounts for only 4.5% of all your flat tires. So if you went to a tire repair store, you are most likely going to buy a tire patch that allows puncture repair, and you might also buy the replacement valve stem to save yourself a trip back to the same store. As you can see, Bayesian logic requires determining what factors are involved in causing a problem and assigning a weight or likelihood to these problems arising. The only way you get a weight or percentage likelihood is experiential. You've become your own life's actuary, just a sure as an actuary determines odds for the insurance company. Now let's see how this applies to the stock market.

There are four elements in developing an "expert system." The first and most important element is the *results*, or *outcome studies*. There is no sense in following a system that gives you poor results. If you are pleased with the positive results of the system, then it is worthwhile to pursue a method of duplicating the system on a consistent basis.

The second component of developing an expert system is the *pattern recognition*. In this method, you look for clusters of events that occur in a situation for which you already have positive results. Restated, if you know that a stock has produced impressive growth after you've purchased it, you retrospectively examine the factors that led you to purchase the stock in the first place. If you do this enough times, you will find that a pattern of factors emerges, which consistently appeared in the historical data. This pattern more often than not led you to purchase the stock, with the positive results that you have. This pattern recognition can be determined only by *retrospective analysis.*

This third component of developing an expert system, the retrospective analysis of various stocks with which you've had positive results, is purely *evidence based.* If you retrospectively analyze enough stocks, you will develop a statistically significant set of data that will allow you to select recurring components used in your selection process.

One question becomes "How many stocks do I need to review to be statistically significant?" Sample size is a critical element in research. Most statisticians say that a minimum of 33 samples is needed to have a statistically valid sample, which can be analyzed with the *t*-test (which is explained in more detail later), and that the power of the probability score becomes asymptotic at 33 samples. This means that increasing the sample size beyond 33 stocks does not increase the value of the significance of the probability by a great deal.

Table 5.1 shows this concept clearly. It is commonly accepted that a set of data with less than 5 chances in 100 of occurring by chance alone is considered a statistically significant outcome.

If you have 100 children in a summer camp, in the 9- to 12-year-old age group, 2 or 3 of them will be four feet tall, and two or three of them will be six feet tall. Most will be about five feet tall. This

Table 5.1   Probability of an Event Based on _T_-Test Calculation

	Degrees of freedom	Odds of chance occurrence	Odds of chance occurrence	Odds of chance occurrence	Odds of chance occurrence	Odds of chance occurrence
Probability		0.10	0.05	0.02	0.01	0.0001
	1	6.314	12.706	31.821	63.657	636.619
	15	1.753	2.131	2.602	2.947	4.073
	24	1.711	2.064	2.492	2.797	3.745
	30	1.697	2.042	2.457	2.750	3.646
	40	1.684	2.021	2.423	2.704	3.551
	60	1.671	2.000	2.390	2.660	3.46
	120	1.658	1.980	2.358	2.617	3.373
	infinity	1.645	1.960	2.326	2.576	3.291

would be a random distribution, since there are no definitions of the type of population, just children 9 to 12 years old. This definition of the population does not define the population further than that. If this were a summer camp for children of professional basketball players, then a researcher might expect a less random distribution. If you were to graphically represent the random distribution, most of the height measurements would cluster around the middle, and, as shown in Figure 5.1, only 2.1% of the sample falls at either side, representing very short or very tall children.

If a physician blindly chose a child from this sample, there would be a 2.1% chance the physician would select a very tall child and a 2.1% chance he would select a very short child. But the chance of the physician picking either a very tall or very short child would be 4.2%. All statistics work in this fashion. The various statistical tests tell the likelihood of an event occurring just by chance or because there is a significant finding in the data from the research. After the various statistical tests are calculated, the number that is generated from the calculation is then compared to a probability table, like the one shown in Table 5.1. In Figure 5.2, if the calculation of the *t*-test score for a given number of subjects gives a number greater than the amount shown for a given probability, then the data are considered significant. The factors to consider in this calculation are the size of

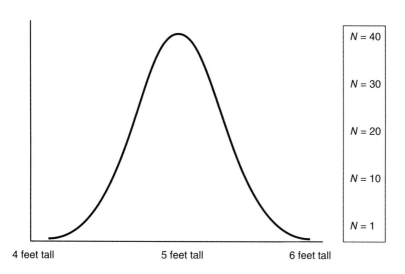

	N = 40
	N = 30
	N = 20
	N = 10
	N = 1

4 feet tall   5 feet tall   6 feet tall

Figure 5.1   Gaussian distribution, the bell-shaped curve.

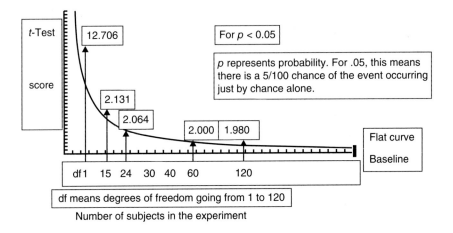

Figure 5.2   Probability curve.

the sample, shown in the left-sided "df" column, which represents the degrees of freedom (usually the number of subjects minus 1, which means the number of variables in a sample size which are not constant, i.e. free to vary), and the rows of the probability of the event occurring, shown in the top row, starting with .10, or one chance in 10, and ending with .001, meaning one chance in 1,000. The numbers in the table represent the actual calculated t score and allow a person to determine if the data are significant. Note that in the highlighted .05 column, the t score needed for data to be considered significant is 12.706 for 2 items (2 – 1 = 1 df), 2.131 for 16 items (16 – 1 = 15 df), and 2.064 for 25 items (25 – 1 = 24 df). The difference between 1 df and 15 df is a t score difference of 10.575. Increasing the number of items from 16 to 25 requires only a change in the value of the t score of .067 to be considered significant. If the number of stocks is increased to 31, the t score change needs be only .022 to be significant, and increasing to 41 stocks, the t score need change only .021. The progression is obvious. Without doing a number of laborious calculations, after approximately 30 stocks, the change in the t score needed to be considered significant is about .022 to .021 with an increase of 10 stocks. If the number of stocks changes from 41 to 61, the change in the t-test score needs to be .021 to be considered significant. These data gave rise to the thought that the t-test score becomes "asymptotic" (an asymptotic line gets closer to a flat line on a curve as the distance gets closer to infinity) at 33 subjects, and increasing the size of the sample after 33 patients is not really going to increase the chance of getting a significant set of data. So from a statistical point of view, using 33 stocks in a study is almost as good as using 61 stocks.

The next paragraph requires knowledge of the "Rule of 72," which says that to find the number of years required to double your money at a given interest rate, you just divide the interest rate into 72. For example, if you want to know how long it will take to double your money at 7% interest, divide 7 into 72 and you will get a little more than 10 years. I am assuming the interest is annually compounded (http://moneychimp.com/features/compound_interest .htm). This rule is remarkably accurate, as long as the interest rate is less than about 20%. At higher rates the error starts to become significant. For a more academic discussion of the mathematics associated with the Rule of 72, I refer you to http://moneychimp.com/ features/rule72_why.htm.

After selecting the appropriate number of stocks to evaluate, the fourth component of developing the expert system is the *prospective testing* of your theory. If you have good results, you did a retrospective analysis to look for significant and recurring patterns as part of your pattern recognition. Now you're going to take the components that occur most frequently to see if they have a reliable predictive value. So if I randomly select investments that collectively increase 12% in value, compounded, it would take roughly 6 years to double the value of the investments. If I randomly select investments that collectively increase 7% in value, compounded, it would take roughly 10 years to double the value of the investments. Therefore, for the purposes of our research, by selecting stocks that doubled in value in five years or less, I am selecting stocks that consistently give a double-digit or more increase in asset value over the period of time for which they are held. The "selection system" analysis focuses on these stocks.

How does predictive analytics work? At the risk of being labeled a quant (someone who performs quantitative analyses of companies) I shall explain the methods I use. The first thing to do is identify the various factors that contribute to outcome. This is analogous to predicting the outcome of rolls of the dice and involves probability and statistics. Let's consider two dice, with six numbers on each die. Multiplying 6 × 6, we arrive at the number of possible combinations, which is 36. This means that there are six items that can occur at any one time, multiplied by another six items that can occur at any given time. Since each die has only one pip (the name for the dots on a die) with the number 1, there is only one way to roll 2, which is to have the pip with number 1 show up on each die. Since there are 36 possible combinations, that means your chance of rolling a 2 is 1 out of 36. The same rationale applies to the chances of rolling a 12, since there is only one way to make the number 12, which is to have the side with six pips show up on each die. The statistics involved in rolling dice are very simple, because you have a finite number of variables. This makes the odds easy to calculate.

Unfortunately, picking a stock is not quite so simple. It involves a multifactorial analysis. The first step in pursuing the predictive analytic model is picking a system that has good outcome results. As I said before, there is no sense in trying to develop a system that does not have good predictive strength. So the most important starting point is examining a system that has a proven track record. If you already have good results, then the task becomes understanding how you got those good results. Most people are not able to verbalize the techniques they use. So, I began to apply my engineering and mathematics experience to analyze and verbalize what I actually do when I pick a stock.

Once you have found a system that has good outcomes, the next step is defining which variables contribute to the price of the stock in the future. The list is excruciatingly long and just when you think you have it all figured out, an unpredicted variable occurs. I call this the Barbaro effect, based on an event that occurred at the Pimlico Race Course, when the horse that won the 2006 Kentucky Derby, the first race of the Triple Crown, was favored to win the second race of the Triple Crown, the Preakness at Pimlico. Then an event that had never previously occurred in Triple Crown racing (nor has it ever occurred since) actually did occur. Barbaro got about 70 yards from the starting gate and his leg snapped, with an audible crack heard in the grandstand. Because this event was so unusual, and so unpredictable, a lot of people lost a lot of money that day (see Figure 5.3).

What were the odds of this happening? Statistically, you would need to tally the number of horses that raced in the Kentucky Derby, Preakness at Pimlico, and the Belmont Stakes. Even if a single horse raced in all three races, it would count as three events, because there were three chances for the horse to break its leg in those races in that year. Then, add up the number of horses in each year for the

Figure 5.3   Preakness at Pimlico.

number of years the Triple Crown has been run, and this becomes your denominator. Put 1 over the denominator, since there is only been one broken-leg event in all the history of all those races, and you now have the odds of a superior racehorse breaking its leg in a Triple Crown race.

Some factors that influence the price for stock are the obvious: earnings per share, the price-to-earnings ratio, past performance, actual sales, projected sales, one-time occurring expense or one-time occurring income, change in leadership of the company, "force majeure" (a term that appears often in contracts, meaning "acts of God" such as hurricanes, earthquakes, or fires), geopolitical turmoil, the price of oil, acquiring a patent on a new product or expiration of the patent of an old product, market fluctuations, stock manipulation by various parties, corporate raiding, takeover bids, mergers, failure of competitive products manufactured by the companies, retraction, corrections, and so on. As you can see from this partial list, the factors are extensive. Each of these events can have a short-term or long-term effect on the performance of the company.

Once you've established a list of potential factors that influence the price of the stock in the future, you have to assign a weight to each one of the factors. What this means is how likely the occurrence of a single factor will be in influencing the price of the stock in the future. Some factors will have no influence over the future price of the stock while others will have a dramatic influence. Assigning a weight to each factor is a matter of experience and retrospective analysis. Retrospective analysis is the other essential part of predictive analytics; it means evaluating each of the factors from a historical perspective to see how that particular factor influenced the price of the stock in the past. From these data, you can notice certain patterns that emerge. This pattern recognition then can be used to create a predictive analytic model. Then you have to test this analysis to see if the factor you picked has any value for determining the price of the stock in the future. This is called a prospective analysis.

This entire process serves as the basis of Bayesian logic or Bayesian analysis. This is often termed "past is prologue," meaning past historical events allow you to predict future events. If you sat for three days at the Old Faithful geyser in Yellowstone Park, you would note that there is a highly predictable pattern to the eruption. The geyser has erupted every 44 to 125 minutes since 2000. Therefore, you could safely say that the geyser will erupt at least once in two and a quarter hours. However, like all things in life, past performance is no indication of future performance.

In order to test the value and statistical significance of the various factors and weights you assigned to these factors, you must construct a matrix that lists all of the factors, the weight assigned to each of the factors, and the outcome of each weighted factor. Remember, assigning a weight is determining how likely the occurrence of a single factor will be in influencing an event outcome. An underinflated football has less of a weight in determining the outcome of a football game than the star quarterback breaking his leg just before the game.

The skill comes in determining how much of a weight should be assigned to each factor. This comes only from experience and historical data. This is why insurance companies have the "rule of big numbers." Unlike a dice game with a known number of outcomes, insurance companies insure against the events, which have an enormous number of variables. It is difficult to predict the outcome of an event when you're trying to determine the likelihood of a house fire, a car accident, or someone slipping on ice in front of your building.

Insurance companies use the rule of big numbers to determine these odds, which allows them to set rates for their insureds. This means using the analysis of hundreds of thousands or even millions of events to examine the likelihood of an accident occurring. The insurance companies gather as much information as they can about a particular event, which allows them to accurately set their rates. Clearly, the tail that wags the dog in the insurance industry is the actuary, the individual who gathers all this data and then assembles a predictive analytic model that allows the insurance companies to determine the likelihood of an event. If the chance of a house burning down is 1 house in 100, then calculate your breakeven point as if 1 house in 20 burns down. This works quite well for the insurance companies, who now know what the odds are of an event happening and charge accordingly higher than your anticipated payout (which is considerably more than the 7.89% at the roulette table).

Once you have a vast amount of data, you then can determine the statistical value and accuracy of your predictive model by a series of statistical tests, such as analysis of variance, the R test, or the F test. The statistical test allows you to determine how reliable your matrix is for determining the future. This is expressed as a "p value," which expresses the chance of an event happening merely by chance, or if there is a cause-and-effect relationship between an item and the predicted outcome. Clearly, the larger the number of events that you analyze, the more likely you are to have accurate predictive models.

What factors do I consider, and what weight do I assign to them? I recognize that stock market conditions influence the price of the stock as much as, if not more than, the performance of an individual company. We should focus on the external factors that influence the price of the stock as well as on the internal factors pertaining to a company. All of these factors have to be evaluated simultaneously, and each has its own predictive impact or weight on the price of the stock.

There is a basic underlying principle to consider. Less than one-third of all investors in the stock market are individual investors. Commissioner Luis Aguilar of the Securities and Exchange Commission, in a 2013 speech before an audience at Georgia State University (https://www.sec.gov/news/speech/2013-spch041913laahtm), reported that in 2010, institutional investors controlled 67% of the market, and in 2009, 73% of the stock of the 1,000 largest corporations was controlled by institutional investors. In 1990, the average daily volume on the NYSE was 162 million shares. In 2013, that average daily volume was approximately 2.6 billion shares. The universe of institutional investors includes mutual funds and ETFs (exchange-traded funds), regulated by the SEC, as well as pension funds, insurance companies, and a wide variety of hedge funds and managed accounts, many of which are unregulated. Due to the sheer volume of trades, the nanosecond time needed for the electronic trades, as well as subquote unexecuted trades and naked short sales, the individual investor hasn't got a chance in the market. He is betting against the house as surely as if he went to a casino and bet at various games. He may win one, once in a while, and, like all gamblers, that is the one he chooses to remember. But taken over a 10- or 15-year stretch, it is a rare individual investor who makes any money in the market. So, the purpose of this book is not to teach an investor how to pick a stock, or how to evaluate a company, or how to do day trades, or trade puts and calls, or other options; those factors are all analyzed by the institutional investors. By the time the research reaches the private investor it is old, outdated, and often no longer applicable.

It is an invaluable skill for an investor to recognize the trends that are emerging as the result of the institutional traders' power of the market. The predictive value of these factors often has more weight in predicting the value of a stock than the actual internal workings of the company. Using predictive analytic techniques, investors will gain insight into identifying trends that are indicative of institutional trading tactics, which allows the individual to invest or trade as if he is part of the institutional cartel. While the individual investor will never be on the inside of these trades, he can learn to recognize the formulation and tendencies of these trades in order to cash in on it.

The first step in understanding institutional investor activities is understanding "short sales." A short sale is nothing more than a bet. There are the occasional unexpected events that defy all odds, and skew the predictive value of all systems, but for the most part, there are certain consistent events. Let us examine a typical short sale transaction. An investor thinks a stock will go down. He may have heard rumors that a company was going to lose one of its biggest customers, or that the CEO was going to be indicted for insider trading, or he had a bad meal at one of the restaurants of the company, or his brother, a truck driver for a supply company, told him that sales of a company must be down because he is making only two deliveries a week instead of the usual five. For whatever reason, the investor thinks the company will be in financial trouble. So this investor wants to make money on this assessment of the company. The investor approaches the brokerage house to bet against the company by selling a short.

The first step is to have a margin account, and to see if brokerage houses or lending institutions have the stock you want to short available. This last consideration is important to avoid a "short squeeze," which occurs due to several events. One event is when the lender of the stock demands his stock be returned, or the second may be when the number of shorted positions exceeds the availability of the stock. A third factor may be the acquisition of the shorted stock. A fourth event may be an event triggered by a regulatory agency, preventing the trading of the stock. Short sales cannot be made in IRA accounts, 401(k) accounts, or trust funds.

The brokerage house lends shares to the short seller and charges a fee, and interest changes per month on shares lent, with the hope of buying the stock back at a lower price. The brokerage house "lending" the investor stock in this company, if available from the lender, allows the investor to sell the stock short. The short seller can use the proceeds from the sale of the stock to buy stocks long or sell other stocks short. The investor pays a stock borrowing fee. The contract remains open as long as the investor wants—for years, until covered or called by owner. This is when the investor buys back the stock he doesn't own but has borrowed from the brokerage house, hoping to cover his short by purchasing the stock at a lower price. The difference between the short price and purchase (buy-back) price is profit (or loss, if the investor covers the short at a higher price). The caveat is that the short seller could be squeezed by the brokerage house if the stock price increases, or the company could be acquired by another company, which would result in a loss to the short seller.

Again, here is an example of a short sale:

XYZ Company is selling at $50 a share. The investor thinks XYZ is going to decline, based on information he has, and he shorts the stock (i.e., sells the stock at $50 a share). At this point in time, he has proceeds from the sale of the stock, less the brokerage fee for selling the short, and the meter is running on the amount of interest he will have to pay the brokerage house for borrowing the stock. The longer he keeps the short open, that is, uncovered, the more interest he will have to pay for maintaining that short position.

Any time after a short sale (a day, a month, or a year later) an unfavorable report for XYZ comes out, and the stock drops to $40 a share.

The investor buys XYZ at $40 a share, covers the short, and makes $10 a share. From this profit, the investor has to deduct the cost of the brokerage fees for selling the short and deduct the brokerage fee for buying back the short, pay back dividends to the lender if the stock paid dividends while he had shorted it, plus the cost of the interest he has to pay for borrowing the stock.

There is other one important consideration. Any profit or losses from short transactions are treated as short-term gains or losses for tax purposes. Also, there is a "wash sale rule." If investor sells a stock for a loss, they may not repurchase it for 30 days. This prevents the investors from applying the short-term loss against their income. This is the simple version of a short transaction. However, in reality, there are three possibilities:

1. The investor shorts 100 shares of XYZ Company at $50 a share and receives $5,000 from the sale, less the commission of $10. The investor now has $4,990 in his account, but owes the brokerage house $5,000 plus interest of $$ of $2 a day as an example. Ten days later, the stock of XYZ falls to $40 a share, so the investor covers the short by buying back 100 shares of XYZ for $4,000. This leaves $990 in the account. The investor owes the brokerage house $20 in interest for the 10-day loan, leaving $970 in the account, and $10 in commission for buying XYZ at $40 a share, leaving $960 in the account. The stock went "ex-dividend" while it was shorted, so the investor has to pay $1 a share, which is another $100 deducted from the account, leaving $860. This is not a bad return in 10 days for trading stock which was never owned.

2. The investor shorts 100 shares of XYZ Company at $50 a share and receives $5,000 from the sale, less the commission of $25. There now is $4,975 in the account, but owes the brokerage house $5,000 plus interest of $2 a day. It takes 100 days for the stock of XYZ to fall to $40 a share, so the investor covers the short by buying back 100 shares of XYZ for $4,000. This leaves $975 in the account. He owes the brokerage house $200 in interest for the 100-day loan, leaving $775 in the account, and $25 in commission for buying XYZ at $40 a share, leaving

$750 in the account. The stock went "ex-dividend" while it was shorted, so the investor had to pay $1 a share, which is another $100 deducted from the account, leaving $650. This is still not a bad return for trading stock which was never owned, but less than the investor might have received if the stock price had fallen sooner than 100 days.

3. The investor shorts 100 shares of XYZ Company at $50 a share and receives $5,000 from the sale, less the commission of $25. There is now $4,975 in the account, but the investor owes the brokerage house $5,000 plus interest of $2 a day. Over the next 100 days the stock of XYZ rises to $60 a share, which reaches the threshold of concern for the brokerage house. The brokerage house wants to be protected from any loss, and informs the investor that there is a margin call. This means the investor has a choice. As a first option, the investor can cover the short by buying back 100 shares of XYZ for $6,000, plus the $25 commission. This creates an expense of $6,025, against which there is only $4,975 in the account. The investor still owes the brokerage house $200 in interest for the 100-day loan, for a total expense of $6,225, but has only $4,975 to pay this expense. This means that the investor must give the brokerage house $1,250 to close out the transaction. The second option is to meet the margin call and add another $1,250 to the account to keep the transaction open, in the hopes that XYZ stock will drop below 60, eventually drop below 50, and fall to the range where the short transaction will be profitable. Of course, the longer this short is kept open, the lower the stock needs to drop to make the transaction profitable, because the investor is still paying interest every day on the loan he made when the short sale was first created.

It is important to note that any capital gains from a short sale are treated as ordinary income, and the long-term capital gains reduction is not applicable.

Short sellers were blamed for the Wall Street Crash of 1929. In fact, there is some evidence that the short sellers actually printed fake stock certificates so they could use them as collateral to cover their short. Political fallout from the 1929 crash led the 1938 Congress to enact a law banning short sellers from shorting shares on a "downtick," which meant that an investor could not short a stock if the most immediate trade prior to the proposed short reflected a downturn in the price of the stock. This was known as the "uptick rule." The US Securities and Exchange Commission (SEC) called this Rule 10a-1(a)(1). Essentially, it stated that a listed security could be sold short only at a price above the price at which the immediately preceding sale was made. This is called a "plus tick," which means the stock was trading higher, even just 1/8 of a point higher, than the previous trade. There was a second option: a stock could be shorted at the last sale price at which it traded if that sales price was higher than the last different price. Short sales were not permitted on minus ticks or zero-minus ticks. In 1994, the National Association of Security Dealers (NASD) and National Association of Securities Dealers Automated Quotations (NASDAQ) adopted their own short sale rules, known as NASD Rule 3350, which was based on the price of the last bid rather than on the last sale to be reported. On July 3, 2007, rules regarding the shorting of stock were removed by the SEC (SEC Release No. 34-55970).

In the face of unregulated short selling, speculators took uncontrolled risks in the stock market and in real estate, which led to the 2008 market collapse. This was especially true in the realm of mortgage-backed securities. These securities were financial instruments created by brokerage houses, which were secured by mortgages. The investment philosophy at the time was that this was a secure investment because people would always want to hold on to their homes, and therefore they would always pay their mortgages, which provided the income for these mortgage-backed securities. However, there was one flaw in this widely held belief. For a variety of reasons, the Affordable Housing Act allowed noncreditworthy individuals to acquire mortgages, and the banking rules were further relaxed so that these mortgage loans were made on an undocumented basis. These loans became known as "no-doc" loans, meaning that the financial status of the borrower was never verified and no due diligence was ever put into place. Essentially, if a borrower stated that they had a certain amount of income on their mortgage loan application, there was no mechanism in place to verify that this was true. There was no requirement for income tax returns or even W-2 forms from the place of employment; hence the term "no doc." Prior to this relaxation of rules, banks had "red-lined" certain areas of a city, meaning that the bank would not make any mortgage loans within certain areas because the risk of not getting repaid was too high, or the value of the property suggested that the people who lived there were not credit-worthy. Essentially, it blocked out people wanting to purchase low-priced housing from receiving mortgage loans. This practice was outlawed, for a variety of reasons, and then the pendulum swung the other way. Banks were willing to make loans to anyone, without regard to their ability to repay the loan. What created the invest-ment frenzy in mortgage-backed securities was the aggregation of loans. All types of loans were packaged together, and investors would look at this loan package as a whole, rather than taking the time to do the due diligence to examine each of the loans within the package. This type of behavior was best portrayed in the movie *The Big Short.* The price of these mortgage-backed securities kept rising, and this type of investment vehicle became the darling of the investment community.

Let us examine some of the factors that suggest a stock should be shorted. Do I think a stock is overvalued? What were the predictive analytic factors I considered? As an example, let us look at the bank-ing industry as a whole. I considered the relaxation of banking regu-lations, allowing loans to noncreditworthy individuals. Additionally, I considered the relaxation of qualifying the mortgagees with no-doc loans. Then I took into account that there was a mass hysteria to rush into the housing market. I considered that the housing market is always cyclical. I considered the rapid rise in value of certain stocks. There were stocks that exceeded the normal price-to-earnings (P/E) ratio for mortgage companies and banking companies. They were out of line with industry averages, with a far higher P/E ratio than their peer group. I noted the trading volume of certain stocks, which was far higher than they had been in the preceding years. I consid-ered the 50 dma and 200 dma. So regardless of the company, it was the external factors which led me to be cautious.

As you can see, there are numerous components to the develop-ment of a predictive analytic model. For the Parnes Parameters, I had to mentally assign weights to each of the variables in order to determine the course I should take with certain real estate and bank-ing stocks.

Notes

1. Hendler, N., Mollett, A., Viernstein, M., Schroeder, D., Rybock, J., Campbell, J., Levin, S., and Long, D (1985). A Comparison Between the MMPI and the "Hendler Back Pain Test" for Validating the Complaint of Chronic Back Pain in Men. *The Journal of Neurological & Orthopedic Medicine & Surgery* 6 (4, December): 333–337.
2. Hendler, N., Cashen, A., Hendler, S., Brigham, C., Osborne, P., LeRoy, P., Graybill, T, Catlett, L., and Gronblad, M. (2005). A Multi-Center Study for Validating The Complaint of Chronic Back, Neck and Limb Pain Using "The Mensana Clinic Pain Validity Test." *Forensic Examiner* 14 (2, Summer): 41–49.
3. Davis, R.D., Hendler, N., and Baker, A. (2016). Predicting Medical Test Results and Intra-Operative Findings in Chronic Pain Patients Using the On-Line "Pain Validity Test." *Journal of Anesthesia & Critical Care Open Access* 5 (1): 00174. doi:10.15406/jaccoa.2016.05.00174.
4. Landi, A., Davis, R., Hendler, N., and Tailor, A. (2016). Diagnoses from an On-Line Expert System for Chronic Pain Confirmed by Intra-Operative Findings. *Journal of Anesthesia & Pain Medicine* 1 (1): 1–7.
5. Hendler, N., Berzoksky, C., and Davis, R.J. (2007) Comparison of Clinical Diagnoses versus Computerized Test Diagnoses Using the Mensana Clinic Diagnostic Paradigm (Expert System) for Diagnosing Chronic Pain in the Neck, Back and Limbs. *Pan Arab Journal of Neurosurgery*: 8–17.

CHAPTER 6

Variables to Consider for the Parnes Parameters

There are a number of Wall Street advisors who make recommendations to purchase stock or sell stock. They cite remarkable returns, or a single stock they picked that had 500% returns in two years. Or they will report an incredible return using a system that worked in a rising market, but fails in a falling market. One of my acquaintances knew Jack LaPorte, a very fine fellow, who ran one of the T. Rowe Price funds. One year, Jack made 52% in the market, and was written up in almost every financial publication in the country. When I congratulated him on his performance, Jack, in his typically modest fashion, thanked me, and cautioned me that his method worked in the current market, but not to expect those types of returns in the future, since his investment philosophy didn't work in all markets. His modesty led to a most prescient statement. The next year his returns were toward the bottom third of those of money managers in the United States. However, Jack was smart enough to recognize the shortcomings of a single investment philosophy for stock purchases.

On the other hand, some investment advisors have done quite well with a single investment philosophy approach, such as shorting. While Gil Morales was at William O'Neil + Company, Inc. as a vice president and manager of the Institutional Services Division, from 1997 to 2005 he achieved a return of approximately 2100% in his portion of the firm's proprietary account and co-authored, with Bill O'Neil, *How to Make Money Selling Stocks Short* (John Wiley & Sons, 2005). Subsequently, in 2009, he and Dr. Chris Kacher launched the investment advisory firm MoKa Investors, LLC and in 2010 authored the top-selling investment books *Trade Like an O'Neil Disciple: How We Made 18,000% in the Stock Market* (John Wiley & Sons, 2010), *In the Trading Cockpit with the O'Neil Disciples* (John Wiley & Sons, 2012), and *Short-Selling with the O'Neil Disciples: Turn to the Dark Side of Trading* (John Wiley & Sons, 2015).

It is tough for an individual investor to rely on market newsletters or newspapers as a source of information about any company. By the time any small investor has valuable information about a company, large brokerage houses have already digested this information and acted on it. Even if information is only 12 hours old, it is already too old for the individual investor to take full advantage of it.

I assembled the various elements that were consistently found in three categories of investments I make for my clients:

1. Securities in which I took a long position:
   a. Growth stocks
   b. Anchor stocks
   c. Fixed income securities
2. Stocks I shorted
3. Securities I sold

This analysis provides us with five categories of securities for a retrospective analysis. Of these five categories, I sold too few securities to provide a statistically significant analysis. Of the remaining four categories, the anchor stocks and fixed income securities seemed to be less exciting to the average investor. Therefore, I developed the Parnes Parameters for the growth stocks in my long position and the stocks I shorted over a one to three-year period of time.

I focused on defining the factors I considered before purchasing a stock. Other financial advisors may choose other factors, but the ones I am listing were scientifically derived from observations of my own selection processes in picking high-growth stocks. This was the result of a retrospective analysis of these stocks.

These growth stocks fit within my investment philosophy, which has been to evaluate a company that has good basic fundamentals and stay with that company throughout the ups and downs, corrections, and other market fluctuations. I decided to focus the development of the Parnes Parameters on this category of stocks, since this group of stocks presented the most challenging and most rewarding aspect of an investment portfolio.

Additionally, I reviewed stocks I shorted over the same one to three-year period. Finally, I looked at stocks I had sold. Please note the distinction between selling a stock and covering a short. When you short a stock, you in effect borrow stock and sell it at a given price, with the expectation that the stock will drop in value. When you cover your short, you are repurchasing stock. That is different than selling the stock. Once you sell a stock, you have relinquished ownership in that equity and no longer have an investment in that company. In general, I sell a stock when I feel it has reached its growth potential. On the other hand I sell a stock when I lose faith in the management, there is bad news about the company, the product doesn't seem to be sustainable, if the price of the stock falls below both the 50 dma and the 200 dma, and if there is a death cross of the 50 dma through the 200 dma. In my experience, once someone sells a stock, very few people have the discipline to repurchase it at a lower price, or even as it increases in price.

I use two components to evaluate a stock—sometimes sequentially and sometimes concurrently. These are the *fundamental components* of a company, such as sales, earnings, P/E ratio, and so on, and the *technical pattern*, which is how the security performs in the market, using graphs and charts to track market trends. This is done using 50 dma and 200 dma and comparing the stock to its peer group and to the market in general.

Sometimes the fundamentals are completely different from one issue to another. Some stocks have a typical 12 to 1 P/E ratio, and sometimes there are no earnings but the stock is worth buying because the debt is declining. An example of the latter consideration would be Tesla, which has no earnings but has a brand.

Sometimes the technical picture is subject to error. One case in point is calculating the beta of a stock. The beta coefficient is a measure of the volatility of the price of a stock compared to a market benchmark. A higher beta indicates greater volatility than the market as a whole, and a lower beta means less volatility. A number of reports indicate that the beta ratings available for free contain errors in their calculations. Additionally, the length of time for evaluating the beta of a stock results in different betas. For our purposes, since we invest for the long term, we use a longer time period to calculate beta, maybe five or even 10 years. On the other hand, brokers who buy and sell frequently use a beta over a much shorter time frame.

When I evaluate stock using both the fundamental and technical techniques, I do so concurrently. These two broad general elements cannot be evaluated in a vacuum. They interrelate with one another. I shall try to explain the various considerations under each heading of fundamentals and technical assessment. To tell the truth, these are difficult components to evaluate, and they have a large subjective component to them. I use my judgment to assign weights to each component of the elements, and this carries a large experiential component. However, I shall try as best I can to convey to you my thought process for each of the elements. Please remember that your experiences are not the same as mine, and my subjective assessment of values to assign to the parameters may differ from yours. Therefore, there is no way to guarantee that you will get the same results using the Parnes Parameters as I do. I am working on a technique to reduce interrater reliability issues, that is, the difference in scores on the Parnes Parameters between analysts, but this will take a larger number of stocks and much more time before this is complete. So, for now, I hope that you and I evaluate things in the same way so that your results will approximate mine. But there is no guarantee that past performance can be repeated. What follows is a list of the parameters I evaluated for selecting stocks to purchase. This list of parameters was retrospectively derived from stocks that met the criteria I outlined earlier. Not all of the stocks have all of the elements of the list of parameters, but these elements are present in many of the selected stocks. From this list, I created the Parnes Parameters, which assist me in selecting stocks to purchase on a scientific basis. This technique was experimentally derived from my successful selection of stocks that met the criteria. Recognizing similar patterns of these productive stocks, using the pattern recognition technique, allows for the parameters to be developed—the Parnes Parameters.

> The reader is cautioned not to rely on any information provided in this example for making decisions about trading any security. Please refer to the **Caution—Limitations and Difficulties** section found at the end of the first chapter.

Let us examine the two components of evaluating stocks: fundamental and technical.

Fundamentals: Getting Down to Basics

This exercise may seem pedestrian to the reader, but it is imperative to keep sight of the basic principles that make a successful company.

In the excitement of the moment, these principles often get over-looked. After many of the major headings, I list three broad possible categories for each one. Some headings have only one choice, such as the expiration of a patent. The thought is that this list should cover the range of possibilities for each company.

1. **Management**
   a. If the management is in turmoil and there are lots of changes in the C suite, this typically conveys that a company is in trouble. When companies undergo this type of management experience, they are not good securities to purchase.
   b. If management is new and has untested executives with good history elsewhere, this suggests that the board is looking toward the future. The results need to be seen, but at least new executives with a good track record interject a note of hope into a company.
   c. If the executives have a good track record and a consistent performance history, or if executives have been promoted from within, this suggests that the company is looking to develop continuity of management. This makes for a stable company, and a good investment opportunity.
2. **P/E Ratio**
   a. If a company has a price-to-earnings (P/E) ratio comparable to its peers, this means it is neither ahead of nor behind the pack. This is a good sign of stability. The parameters for this type of element would be a 1 to 1–1.5 P/E ratio compared to peers (i.e. 20/1 P/E ratio for company vs. 20/1 P/E ratio for the peer group).
   b. If a company has a P/E ratio of 1.5 to 4 compared to peers (i.e. 60/1 P/E ratio the company vs. 20/1 P/E ratio for the peer group), there's a chance that the market has overvalued this company, especially when compared to its peers. There may be some factors that contribute to this high rating, and it's conceivable that the rating may be deserved. This is where in-depth investigation into the operation of the company becomes very valuable. The stock may have the potential for great appreciation.
   c. If a company has a price-to-earnings (P/E) ratio four times or more higher compared to its peers (i.e. 90/1 P/E for the company, vs. 20/1 P/E for the peer group), the market

is betting on unfulfilled promises. The market may be right, and the institutional investors may know something I don't, or the market may be caught up in a frenzy about a trendy new product and unjustifiably overvalue a company. Again, in-depth evaluation of the company and its competition is essential to determine whether or not this company is a good buy or a good short.

3. Price of Product versus Competitors'

   a. If the price of a company's product is comparable to that of competitors (e.g., Toshiba vs. HP computers), then I consider other factors, such as service, reputation, longevity of the product, and other considerations that may differentiate this company's product from others.

   b. There is a middle ground, where prices nearly match, but some features are standard on one company's item and optional on the competitor's item. It would be like comparing the base price of one car, which is lower than that of a competing car, but the latter has standard air conditioning, Sirius radio, backup screen, and self-parking while these are expensive options on the first car.

   c. If the price of a product is two times or more the price of its competitor, (e.g. Apple vs. another cell/computer company), I have to analyze the company more thoroughly. Is the more expensive product worth it? Can the more expensive product do things that the less expensive product cannot? Certainly, Apple has a great reputation for graphics and music, compared to its peer group. Additionally, Apple has made great inroads into schools, so that a whole generation of students have learned to compute using Apples rather than computers with some other operating system. Are these advantages worth the price differential? Consider this as a piece of the puzzle.

4. Percentage of Penetration in Market and Market Share

   a. Does a company have 50% market penetration and greater than 50% market share? These are two different questions. As an example, Tesla does not have greater than 50% of the automotive market share in the United States, but it certainly has more than 50% of the electric car sales. This kind of dominance makes Tesla the company to watch for electric cars, since it has greater than 50% market penetration. Will this translate into cars in general?

   b. If a company has 30–50% market share and there is a small amount of market penetration, then this company has good potential for growth. An example of this would be a company that manufactures solar panels. The central market is nearly every household in the United States, but the amount of market penetration at this point in time is less than 2%. However, if a company has 30–50% of the market share, that is, 30–50% of the 2%, then the potential for the growth of this company is huge. If the company can maintain its market share as this type of product increases in market penetration, the company will ride a huge wave of profitability.

   c. If a company has 20–30% market share and the product has good market penetration, on the order of 50% or more of the potential customers, then the only way that this company can grow is by increasing its market share. This is a harder proposition than increasing market penetration. However, there is still potential to invest in this company if all of the parameters look good, that is, management, cash position, and so on.

5. **Diversifying in Different Fields**

   a. If a company has 10 or more products, it can better survive the vicissitudes of the marketplace than a company with fewer products. This may present a good investment opportunity, since the ebb and flow of sales would offset any ebb and flow in sales of another product.

   b. Using the same logic, a company with 5 to 10 products has less flexibility than a company with more than 10 products, but certainly more flexibility than a company with only three products.

   c. Finally, a company with fewer than three products or in some cases only one product is highly vulnerable to competition and fluctuations in the market. Unless it is a rare instance, this may not be a good company to purchase.

6. **Cyclical Industry Like Housing or Picnic Plates**

   a. Toilet paper is a great example of a nonseasonal item. Clearly, the housing market is cyclical, with peaks and valleys occurring every 5 to 15 years, but it is not seasonal. An investor can be easily be fooled by the steady progress of increase in sales in housing, only to receive a nasty surprise when the market takes a downturn. Timing the cycles is a real skill that can help with long-term investments.

    b. Ice cream is a year-round treat, but sales do peak in the summer months.

    c. There are other companies that have their sales cycle with peaks and valleys on an annual basis. A company that makes picnic plates or Christmas ornaments is an example of such a company. Any comparison of sales in this company has to be done on a same-month to same-month comparison from one year to the next to get any useful data.

7. Volume of Stock Traded

    a. There are many ways to evaluate the volume of stock traded. Since I trade for the long term, I look at stock trades for the previous three months. If the trading is more than 100,000 shares a day on a regular basis, the institutional buyers are clearly interested in this security. This is a good sign but also a cautionary one, since the stock could be subject to either a trading frenzy or a trading sell-off. For any stock with this volume of shares traded, I also look at market conditions, which are covered under the technical section below.

    b. For stock that trades less than 100,000 shares a day but greater than 50,000 shares, I examine the basic fundamentals of the company more closely. The stock is less likely to fluctuate with the market and may carry good investment opportunities. For stock in this range, I look at the return on revenue compared to competitors'.

    c. For stocks trading less than 50,000 shares a day, I really focus on the basics of the company. There can be some great buys with stocks that are thinly traded, unlike everything I've mentioned. However, this requires individual evaluation of the company.

8. Return on Revenue versus Competitors'

    a. There are several factors that influence return on revenue. Cost of goods and overhead are chief among these. Earnings before income tax, depreciation, and amortization (EBITDA) evaluations do not always tell the full story of the health of a company, especially when companies can manipulate generally accepted accounting practices (GAAP) and book as income sales for which they have yet to receive money. If a company is on a par with peers within the industry, this is a favorable sign for the company.

    b. Some companies have cut back on overhead or found a different source of raw goods, which increases their revenue compared to competitors.

    c. Some companies have updated manufacturing facilities or switched to robotics compared to their competitors. After the initial capital expenditure, which probably occurred in the previous year, their cash flow and return on revenue may improve dramatically compared to competitors'. Consider a fully automated, electronically fired blast furnace with 7 men running a cold-rolled steel plant, compared to 150 men operating a coal-fired furnace using 100 year old technology of Bessemer convertors to make steel.

9. **Outdated Product**

    I suspect that most investors would shy away from investing in companies that produce photographic film and film cameras instead of digital cameras. Likewise, a company that did nothing but rent VHS videos would not fare well against Netflix.

10. **Cash on Hand to Current Debt Ratio**

    a. "Current debt" is the amount of money owed within a one-year period of time. If a company has enough cash to meet its current debt, regardless of sales, the company is in good shape on a cash basis. Unfortunately, due to the accrual accounting system, most people either do not look at the cash basis of a company or have difficulty determining the cash available. A company with a 2-to-1 cash to current debt ratio is strong financially and a good candidate for an investment. No one could harm the company by calling the debt.

    b. A company with a 1-to-1 cash to current debt ratio is solid and, all things being equal, a good choice for an investment.

    c. A company with a 0.5-to-1 or less cash to debt ratio has to rely on profits or borrowing to pay current debt. While a lot of companies fall into this category, there is some risk in investing in this type of company.

11. **Fully Developed and Marketable Disruptive Technology**

    a. While this type of situation is the stuff dreams are made of, there is no guarantee that a disruptive technology can penetrate the market. Xerox did. Apple did. Amazon did. But for every one of these gigantic home runs, there is a string of failures. One way to assess the potential of a company with a disruptive technology is the early sales it may have.

    b. The number of orders received is another variable.

    c. If the product is ready to market, with the product in production, this is better than working prototypes or blueprints.

12. **Growth in Earnings**

    a. If a company has increased earnings for eight consecutive quarters, this is a good indication that they have strong management, a good product, and a great marketing and sales team.

    b. If a company has increased earnings for five or more consecutive quarters, this is a good indication that they have a young but strong management, a good product, and a great marketing and sales team just realizing its full potential.

    c. If a company has increased earnings for three or more consecutive quarters, this is a good indication that they have a young but strong management, a good product, and a great marketing and sales team just realizing its full potential, with enormous growth opportunities if all other factors (debt, P/E ratio, etc.) are equal to or better than same-industry companies.

13. **Growth in Revenue**

    a. If a company has increased revenues for eight consecutive quarters, this is a good indication that they have strong management, a good product, and a great marketing and sales team. They have potential for increasing earnings, but they have the first step of the equation correct: they are getting money in the door. Amazon is such a spectacular example. They consistently have grown revenue, with little or no earnings. But they had 52% of all retail sales in the United States in 2018. A small reduction in overhead would propel them into the ranks of unstoppable.

    b. If a company has increased revenue for five or more consecutive quarters, this is a good indication that they have a young but strong management, a good product, and a great marketing and sales team just realizing its full potential. A new source of raw goods or automation could make them very profitable.

    c. If a company has increased revenue for three or more consecutive quarters, this is a good indication that they have a young but strong management, a good product, and a great marketing and sales team just realizing its full potential, with enormous growth opportunities if all other factors (debt, P/E ratio, etc.) are equal to or better than same-industry companies.

14. **Type of Product**
   a. If the company manufactures a product with diverse uses, then it has the ability to resist market vicissitudes and fluctuations. One example would be silver, which is used to coat electrodes, but is also used in infection control, and even in wiring. With diverse markets, the company can resist swings due to a decline in one market segment or another.
   b. An example of this is a supplier to multiple manufacturers. There is only one company in the United States that makes the tiny little screws for eyeglass frames. This was also true for the manufacturer of disc drives, and, at one time, the computer chip.
   c. Single-product companies are less desirable.

The reader is cautioned not to rely on any information provided in this example for making decisions about trading any security. Please refer to the **Caution—Limitations and Difficulties** section found at the end of the first chapter.

Assessments Using Technicals

This is a way of understanding and tracking the movements of institutional investors in a particular stock and comparing them to the market as a whole. The most commonly used technicals are the 50-day and 200-day moving averages. These measure the responses of the institutional investors. There are also factors external to the company operation that need to be considered.

15. **Brokerage House Recommendation**
   a. Brokerage house upgrades produce a short-term uptick in the stock.
   b. A buy recommendation has the same short-term effect.
   c. A hold recommendation means that there is still some growth left in the company.
   d. A sell recommendation will have institutional investors dumping the stock.

16. **Price Relative to 50-Day and 200-Day Moving Averages**
    a. If you look at the moving average charts and the 50 dma is consistently above the 200 dma and the stock price is consistently higher than the 50 dma, this is a good sign. The stock is outperforming the historical of the past 200 days.
    b. If the stock price seems to be moving higher and higher from the 50 dma, this is a great sign. Something is happening to drive the stock price higher than it has been in the past.

17. **Death Cross (50-day moving average falls below the 200-day moving average)**
    a. If there is no death cross, this is a good sign for a stock.
    b. However, the 50-day moving average dropping below the 200-day moving average within 10 days represents a retraction in the price of the stock compared to past performance and could be several things. There may have been an institutional sell-off of the stock, or bad news about the company product or management. On the other hand, if the fundamentals of the company are sound, this may represent a temporary hiccup and may actually be a buying opportunity.
    c. If the death cross occurred 11 to 25 days ago, this is not a hiccup, but a sustained retraction.
    d. If the death cross lasts for more than 25 days, the company has some problems that bear exploration.

18. **Golden Cross (50-day moving average crosses the 200-day moving average)**
    a. If the golden cross occurred less than 10 days ago, the stock is on the move up, compared to past performance. The institutional buyers are getting interested.
    b. If the golden cross occurred 11 to 25 days ago, the stock is maintaining its gains and maturing.
    c. If the golden cross occurred more than 25 days ago, the word is out. Lots of people are looking at this stock as a buy.

19. **Resistance Line**
    This is a line on the graph of the stock price, at a certain price. When a stock price does not rise above this line, the line is termed a resistance line.

    a. Obviously, when a stock price penetrates the resistance line, it means that it is no longer stalled at the resistance line, and this is a good thing for the stock.

    b. If the resistance line is steady, it means that the market doesn't feel that there is much immediate growth potential, but it is not a bad sign.

    c. It is not good if a stock price falls below the resistance line and cannot rise above it. This means that the market feels the stock has less potential for growth.

20. **Support Line**

Again, this is a line on a graph of the stock price, at a certain price. It suggests that the stock should not fall below this price.

    a. When the price of the stock has been steady for 10 days or more, this is indicative of a solid performance of the company and a declining beta. It is a less volatile stock.

    b. When the price of the stock has been steady for five days or more, this is indicative of a good performance of the company, and it is on its way to a well-accepted market price.

    c. If there is no obvious support line, the price of the stock can vary.

21. **Takeover Bid**

There are a thousand things that can happen to derail a takeover, from stockholder revolts to SEC rulings to violations of monopoly rules to failure to get financing. Therefore, the further along a takeover is in the process, the more likely it is to occur, unless the Barbero effect takes over . . . a totally unexpected event. So I have considered these factors when I evaluate the stages of the takeover. Remember, the company that purchases another will have a decline in its stock price while the company that is being acquired will have an increase in its stock price.

    a. When payment is made for a takeover and regulatory hurdles are overcome, then the benefit of the conjoined companies will become evident in a month or two.

    b. When a date is set for takeover, this makes the likelihood of a merger closer to reality.

    c. When a takeover bid is made, the takeover candidate will have a jump in stock price.

    d. Very often, the mere rumor of a takeover will make a stock price jump.

22. **Beta Value of Stock (at least a three-year record) and Relative Strength**

The beta value is an indication of the volatility of the stock price. If a stock price is volatile, it can fluctuate 20% to 50% over the course of the years, which makes investing in the stock a bit like riding a rollercoaster.

a. With a beta less than 1, there is a solid price base for the stock, and stock movement is more predictable.

b. With a beta between 1 and 1.5, there are some hiccups and fluctuations.

c. With a beta more than 1.5, there are many corrections and hiccups to the stock price, and the timing of purchasing and sales is hard to predict.

23. **Change in Industry**

a. The company has emerged with a disruptive technology, which impacts their industrial segment or even the market as a whole. Amazon, which is changing the face of retailing, is a perfect example of this.

b. If the company has an innovative product, then market penetration and sales are paramount.

c. If the company is eclipsed by a new product in their market segment, it now faces some major problems to overcome.

External Factors

24. **Favorable Legislation**

a. If regulations change that favor a company, the impact can be tremendous. If the government opens up an area with huge potential and allows an oil company to drill oil in parklands, for example, there is a huge impact on the company.

b. Changes in tax structure can have an impact on a company. With a revised tax bracket and depreciation allowance increase, EBITDA improves.

c. If onerous restrictions are changed, then this might benefit a company. A change in labeling or packaging requirements may increase the bottom line.

25. **Change in Prime Rate**

a. If a company is debt free or is less dependent on external funds for operation, then the impact of a rise in prime rate has little to no impact on it.

   b. As the level of debt increases, the prime rate impacts on the bottom line more.

   c. If a company is carrying large debt, a significant rise in prime rate can sink it.

26. **Change in Oil Prices**

   a. If the company is not dependent on the transport of a product, such as an Internet-based product, oil prices have little to no effect on the company. If the company is an oil producer . . . well—need I say more?

   b. Most companies have some reliance on transportation, shipping of goods, and even manufacture of goods from petroleum products, so these companies will feel the effect of increased oil prices.

   c. Airlines, trucking companies, bus companies, and so on can take a real beating as oil prices increase.

27. **Change in Tariffs**

   a. If a company has no dependence on any imported goods or raw material, tariff increases have little impact. Conversely, if the tariffs raise prices on imported competing products, then they can be helpful.

   b. The impact on a company depends on the ratio of imported to exported products.

   c. Companies that export can be hurt by retaliatory increases in tariffs abroad, just as companies that import can be hurt by tariffs on goods they typically bring into the country.

28. **Negative Regulatory Changes**

   a. If a company escapes regulatory controls, then there is no impact on the company.

   b. There are instances where the regulatory impact is moderate.

   c. Other companies come under complicated regulatory controls, such as pharmaceutical manufacturers and gun manufacturers.

29. **Change in the Stock Market in General**

   a. Some stocks are impervious to the general stock market fluctuations.

   b. Some companies may respond to market fluctuations less severely than others.

   c. A number of companies are susceptible to bull and bear markets, which is no reflection on the performance of the company, but rather the overall market conditions.

30. Force Majeure, Acts of God—Floods, Fires, Earthquakes
   a. Sad to say, there are some companies that benefit from natural disasters. After several hurricanes destroyed the Boardwalk in Atlantic City, the price of lumber rose 200% in the local area, as the city rushed to rebuild. Trailer sales and temporary housing may benefit as well.
   b. The effect of natural disasters on the flow of traffic and commerce can directly and indirectly impact companies to various degrees.
   c. Clearly, the companies most harmed by natural disasters are those in the insurance industry. One liability company was on the verge of bankruptcy after a hurricane wiped out large parts of Mississippi because the company had more than 5% of its business in this single state. A forest fire in California was harmful to Pacific Gas and Electric.

31. Relative Strength Line
   This compares the stock price performance to that of the S&P 500.
   a. If the slope of the line is sloping higher than the S&P 500, then the stock is outperforming the S&P 500.
   b. If the slope of the line is parallel with the S&P 500, it is performing at the level of the S&P 500.
   c. If the slope of the line is lower (sloping downward), then the stock is underperforming compared to the S&P 500.

32. Cup with Handle Breakout
   A "cup with handle" typically forms after a stock reaches a new 52-week high, falls in price, and regains its old high price. When the graph of the stock price forms a cup with handle configuration, usually within a 30- to 60-day period, this anticipates an upward breakout, higher than the previous high.
   a. If the handle is higher than the previous high, then this indicates a buy situation.
   b. If the handle falls 7–10% from the all-time high, then this is a downward pattern breakout.

33. Common Sense and Discipline
   After reviewing all these parameters, I recognize that common sense and discipline prevail. Excessive trading, in addition to the short-term capital gains tax burden it produces, negates the potential gains.

    a. Market retraction: If a stock has good fundamentals, do not respond to short-term market retractions. Have the discipline to add to an existing position or initiate one.

    b. If a stock has good fundamentals, do not respond to short-term market gains. Hold the stock. Do not sell.

34. Put-Call Ratio

This describes the market as a whole and is determined by puts and calls in the entire market. The ratio is bullish when the indicator moves above 1–1.2. As an example, on August 21, 2015, the ratio was 1.48. The contrary indicator is bearish when the ratio drops below 0.60–0.55.

    a. When the ratio is above 1.2, this is a buy signal.

    b. When the ratio is below 0.60–0.55, the investor should consider profit taking.

> The reader is cautioned not to rely on any information provided in this example for making decisions about trading any security. Please refer to the **Caution—Limitations and Difficulties** section found at the end of the first chapter.

Based on these Parnes Parameters, I have a framework for evaluating a stock. By evaluating each parameter, I can more objectively determine which stock to purchase.

It is highly unlikely that any results you obtain will be the same as mine, since almost all of the ratings in these parameters are subjective. You and I are going to subjectively evaluate things differently. You should not rely on the Parnes Parameters to make any decisions about buying or selling stock. Past performance is no guarantee of the same performance in the future. The Parnes Parameters are for informational purposes only and should not be regarded as investment advice. They are merely one of the methods I use for selecting stocks.

> The reader is cautioned not to rely on any information provided in this example for making decisions about trading any security. Please refer to the **Caution—Limitations and Difficulties** section found at the end of the first chapter.

Shorting for the Long Term

The way I differentiate myself from other investors/traders or other short sellers is directly related to the way I use short sales. There have been some investors/traders who have done quite well using shorts on occasion and have reaped huge returns. These are very clever investors/traders, but my approach differs from theirs: I consistently use shorts as part of my investment strategy. It is this consistent use of short selling that sets me apart from other investors/traders/short sellers.

Let me share with you why I selected short selling as part of my investment strategy.

1. Shorts don't expire, unlike puts and calls and other options. I have held some shorts open for two or three years. I am not under time constraints in order to evaluate my position, and more importantly, I don't have a ticking clock running against me. If I have made the correct decision, I don't have to worry about the variable of making the correct decision within a certain period of time. Once I have eliminated the element of time, my decision stands on its own merit. If you think a stock is going to go down, then short it. Why would you add the other variable of having the stock go down within a certain period of time? If you made a good choice in the first place, there is no sense in hampering yourself by interjecting the element of time. This allows

me to trade securities without looking over my shoulder at the clock. My short selling is removed from one major element in the investment equation—the element of time. This allows me to make rational, thoughtful decisions about my position in the stock without feeling pressured. This is the very rationale I use when I tell my clients "don't put money in the market if you need this money to live." When you need to take money out of the market because your child wants a new car or is going to college, you make decisions about investments that are not business decisions. They are decisions of necessity.

2. I use the proceeds from the shorts to leverage my long position, enhancing my opportunity in the long side of the market. I recognize that this is a little like buying stock on margin, but if I choose the shorts wisely, the associated borrowing costs for shorting the stock are less than I would pay in interest when buying a stock on margin. Moreover, the anticipated return is well worth the risk. So, if everything goes the way I hope it will, I actually make money in three ways: (1) an increase in value in my long position, (2) an increase in value in my short position, and (3) saving money on the cost of borrowing to purchase more long positions. This acts as a hedge, which helps to stabilize an account.

3. I purchase shorts as a long-term investment, much the same as I would purchase a long position in a stock. If a stock that I shorted is up 15–20%, I keep the short open if I firmly believe the company is in trouble, A typical investor would cover a short when a stock has jumped this much in price. I have been out of the money as much as 20%, met the margin call, and two months later made money covering the short when the stock dropped back down. This is shorting for the long term. This is important, since I am not responding to short-term market fluctuations. I shorted the stock since it had less than favorable fundamentals, and if these fundamentals haven't changed, I don't panic; I maintain my discipline of shorting for the long term. This approach takes discipline and faith in your decisions.

4. I strike a balance in the portfolios I manage by trying to have up to 100% of my long investments augmented by up to 30% of their value from proceeds from short sales. This is what I call the 130/30 model. Sometimes, the portfolios may have market variables from 120/20 to 200/100. Using a 130/30 model

I select long positions that equal up to 130% of the nominal capital invested and short positions that equal up to 30% of the nominal capital net market exposure. Under this technique, the proceeds are diverted/applied to other selected issues for their long-term growth rate of earnings and revenue above 25%–30% or higher. The apparent long-term appreciation in value of these growth stocks makes up for the costs/fees being levied by the lenders for the short positions selected. I mention this model elsewhere in the book, but it bears repetition. Essentially, if I think a stock is worth taking a long position, I wish I had more money to invest in the stock. The way I get this extra money is by shorting a different stock. So I am leveraging the amount of stock I have in my long positions by using the proceeds from the short position. But rather than just borrowing money in order to increase the number of shares in my long position, I'm using a technique that actually generates money, that is, selling the short position. For a number of my clients, I try to use 130% of the value of their portfolio in the long positions while 30% of the value is in shorts. This gives the overall 100% portfolio value. The ratio can vary from 110%/10% to 200%/100%, depending on market conditions and the risk tolerance of my clients.

5. A number of investors/traders are "sheep." They follow the trends in the market, or they are in the market for short-term gains. They panic when the market responds in a certain fashion and sell positions that could be profitable if they had been held longer. In this respect, I am a "goat." I do not follow the herd. I do not panic. I avoid participating in mass hysteria.

6. I make use of the Relative Strength (RS) line. This is a difficult and not often used parameter. Most services do not carry information on this quantifier. Very simply stated, the RS line compares the performance of the price of a stock against the S&P 500 performance as a whole. Like any stock, the S&P performance can be charted and the relative slope of the performance line can be observed. The performance line of any stock can be compared to the S&P performance. If the slope of the graph of a particular stock is better than the S&P's (the distance between the lines of the stock compared to the S&P keeps increasing, as both of the lines slope upward),

then investors say that the stock is outperforming the S&P. Obviously, if the slope of the stock performance line gets closer and closer to the S&P line, and in extreme instances crosses below the S&P line (reminiscent of a death cross of the 50-day moving average cross to the 200-day moving average), then the stock is underperforming. The interpretation of the RS line is relatively simple. If a stock is outperforming the market, then there are some unusual circumstances that institutional investors recognize, leading to increased performance compared to the market as a whole. The old expression "a rising tide floats all boats" comes to mind. As the indices of the market rise, then one would expect the price of stocks to rise as well, since, after all, the index is comprised of various stocks. If a stock moves counter to the index (falls below the pricing), this is not a good sign. It is underperforming.

7. I engage in a bottom-up approach. I focus on company research conducted in-house, fundamentals of the company, technical analysis of the various parameters, and cash flow to evaluate superior opportunities for both long and short positions. I use short selling as just one of many investment strategies, which may include sector balancing, growth, cash flow, bonds, income, risk aversion, hedging, and other investment strategies. This differs from other short experts who focus on short selling by itself without integrating it into an overall investment plan.

8. I focus on contrarian objectives, which can be realized throughout various market cycles based on three simple factors: (1) I am a disciplined absolutist in my investment and trading management, (2) I offset and mitigate industry and sector driving volatility with generalist selections, and (3) I am growth oriented, with my preference for a long position bias with industry-known short-selling capabilities.

9. I use the short positions (in certain accounts) to neutralize the portfolios in a bull market and to maximize performance in the bear market. For the long positions, the fundamentals, technical considerations, and earnings growth rate are the hallmark of my selection processes. Naturally, general market conditions and accumulation with high volume by institutional investors play a large role in the selection of long issues.

10. I customize my portfolios so they include a mixture of fixed income, anchor positions, growth-oriented positions, and short positions. My strategy can be successfully applied to a wide range of sectors, styles, and market caps. While the specific percentages of these groupings may fluctuate, depending on market conditions and average holding, they include 10%–20% fixed income, 20%–30% large-caps, 20%–30% growth-oriented equities, and 15%–20% short positions. Please note the role of short positions in the overall portfolio mixture. Short positions augment my investment philosophy; they do not overwhelm it. Each portfolio may contain 18–24 long positions and 1 to 10 short positions that are held on average (dependent on the client's risk tolerance) between one and three years, subject to market conditions.

11. Using both long and short positions gives an unprecedented advantage in maximizing the profit capabilities in both bull and bear markets. I would focus on selecting momentum equities for long positions augmented by fundamental and technical characteristics. Short selling takes into account equities that are viewed as technically mature, compounded with foreseen deterioration but a decline in the future fundamental status.

12. I allocate the majority of my investors' capital in US-based securities, American depository receipts (ADRs), which represent foreign companies trade within the United States as a security instrument, and bonds. By focusing primarily on US basic equities and ADRs or significant companies that are traded on established global exchanges, I'm picking well-established companies. I avoid high-risk foreign companies, regardless of the yield potential, because of so many unpredictable variables that can occur, such as nationalization of the company, civil war, devaluation of currency, and imposition of tariffs. Recent global influences prompted me to try one or two foreign stocks, but it is only my toe in the water, and not even my whole foot.

13. My contrarian philosophy separates me from other money managers, since I often take an opposing viewpoint from the majority of investors. One fundamental principle to recognize is that "behind smart money there is loose money," indicating

that the time for me to exit will soon follow. These factors help select positions for short-selling opportunities. Let me explain this a bit further. Institutional investors represent smart money. By the time individual investors recognize that a certain stock has great value and decide it's time to buy, the institutional investors are ready to take profits in this stock. It is important to understand when the institutional investors are ready to divest themselves of positions in a certain stock.

14. Since I build segmented portfolios and segregated portfolios for each client, I must keep abreast of current market conditions. Ideally, a portfolio will be diverse enough so that it is significantly noncorrelated to the volatility of the stock market. I would call this investment philosophy a hedge-style diversified strategy, which has been created to maintain a potential for lower volatility and higher sustainability compared to typical stock market risk. I attribute this to my macro view across asset classes, industries, and time sequences. It is a global conceptual viewpoint of the stock market, which many money managers do not utilize.

15. I invest based on market value exposure and duration-weighted exposure, relative to hot and cold sectors, in an attempt to limit risk by basing my understanding on the technical aspects of a stock and its respective status regarding the overall market.

16. On occasion, I will use stop losses (limiting losses or protecting profits specific to the business once you have a profit) to mitigate risk. However, they are not applied to a single portfolio as a whole, only to specific equity positions. The stop losses are overridden expressly when the position fundamental supports a shift in stop placement. Sometimes, the fundamental of a stock movement warrants no stop loss. I do not want to risk losing my long-term potential in a company that has good fundamentals and institutional support.

17. In the event of a market downturn, I utilize my proprietary volatility analytical model (Parnes Parameters) to determine if adjustments are fully supportable. The Parnes Parameters lend a strong degree of objectivity to what sometimes can be subjective decision-making. The Parnes Parameters help me review risk capital allocations when significant increases in equity accumulation occur. They allow me to adjust portfolio composition through cash repositioning, disbursements, and new acquisitions.

18. I use the proceeds from shorts to enhance my long position instead of buying more long positions on margin. People ask me why I do this. For many accounts, such as trusts, IRAs, 401(k)s, or any other deferred compensation accounts, the law does not permit margin accounts and short selling. However, for accounts that permit this activity, this process becomes useful. With either a margin or a short, I am going to pay interest charges and other fees. I avoid margin fees on long positions by using the proceeds from the short to increase long positions. However, by maintaining shorts, I have developed a hedge in a portfolio account, which helps the account in the case of a market drop due to geopolitical events, external events, market corrections or retractions, recessions, actions by the Federal Reserve regarding interest rates, and fluctuations in the price of commodities such as oil, gas, and basic materials, depending on the global supply and demand. The percentage of short positions in the portfolios varies with the risk tolerance of the clients, as well as market conditions and volatility. During 2007–2008 through 2012, the volatility of the market increased, so high-frequency traders and institutional traders increased their short positions dramatically, which alarmed regulatory agencies. This led to more regulations to limit short selling by certain groups from certain sectors. This resulted in my invitation to be a keynote speaker before the Financial Market Legal Committee of the Supreme Court of the UK, hosted by the Bank of England. During this era, the number of stock exchanges increased dramatically as a result of the spread of the Internet, computers, and algorithm trading. I pointed out that regulation within the well-known exchanges was futile, because a trader could move his operation to Timbuktu and bypass any legislation to limit short selling.

These 18 concepts are not exhaustive but do cover most of the salient features of my investment philosophy. Obviously, individual needs will require modification of these features to provide a customized portfolio. However, for the most part, I tend to follow these precepts.

The reader is cautioned not to rely on any information provided in this example for making decisions about trading any security. Please refer to the **Caution—Limitations and Difficulties** section found at the end of the first chapter.

Case Studies for Long Positions

Long Position Stocks

When I take a long position, I emphasize the management of a company, the business plan, the interest of investors who are accumulating positions for the long haul, growth rate of revenue and earnings, profit margins, cost of doing business, amount of taxes paid, and so on. These involve assessing both fundamentals and technical considerations.

The portfolios I manage are customized into a variety of categories depending on risk tolerance and investors' objectives. There are growth accounts, income accounts, risk-tolerant accounts, risk-intolerant accounts, fixed income accounts, regulated accounts (IRAs and 401(k)s), where my investment choices are limited by law, trust accounts, and so on.

Large Portfolios

For large portfolios, I emphasize market movement to establish positions. For growth portfolios, I put up to 30% of a portfolio into growth companies, 30% into anchors, and 20% into fixed income stocks, with 20% in cash or reserved for short positions. Some accounts, such as IRAs and 401(k)s, are not permitted to hold margins or short positions, and some accounts do not warrant short positions. Percentages vary with movement of the market and the risk tolerance of the clients. The percentage of growth and anchors will increase to more than 30% in bull markets. The remaining percentage of 10%–20% is allocated to short positions. The dollar amount of long positions (not number of shares) varies between $15,000 and over $100,000 in each category, depending on the client's objective. I create diversified portfolios across a variety of industries, and I look for new technologies that enhance earnings and growth rate with sustainability. My investments are for the long term (at least eight quarters, or two or five years or even longer) based on sustainability of earnings and products, despite hiccups. I try to avoid stocks below $10– $15 and avoid single-product companies, unless the capital requirement to enter the marketplace is very large and the R&D is very advanced. I look for takeover candidates. I avoid companies involved in the development of a medical product in the early stages, because this is too risky, since government approval is required for a success. FDA approval for pharmaceuticals and even devices can take 3 to 10 years and drain a company's resources. An adverse event can sink the company, such as the Dalkon Shield problems did to Parker-Davis. Since it takes $1,000,000,000 and 10 to 12 years from date of discovery to FDA approval for most pharmaceuticals, there is a lot riding on FDA approval, and even then the testing on 2,000 or 3,000 subjects needed to get FDA approval does not have the same level of detection of risk factors as a pharmaceutical in use with 1,500,000 patients, which occurs after a product is released. Then, of course, there is the issue of concealing adverse events. As an example, this occurred when 90 deaths in the UK from a nonsteroidal anti-inflammatory product were not reported.

In my large portfolio accounts, I hold a variety of stocks, some of which are growth stocks, some are anchor stocks, and some are both growth and anchor. There is no emphasis on number of shares in any single stock. My investment is done by dollar amount, not the number of shares. I am sure other investment advisors use other allocation methods. I am just sharing mine.

Rationale for Buying and Holding Apple

Let me share with you some of my thought processes. As an example, I am picking a single stock, one that many investment advisors recommended—Apple. I am not saying that my selection of this stock is unique. I am only going to explain why I recommended buying Apple. Other investment advisors also recommended buying this stock. You would need to check their investment philosophy to understand why they recommended Apple. At present, I am neither recommending nor dismissing Apple as an investment. You would need to contact your own investment advisor to determine whether Apple is suitable for you.

In 2001, the price was 18 to 22 before the split, and then there was a 7 to 1 split. So multiply 167 by 7 and the 2001 share at $18 is now worth $1,169, as of March 2018. In retrospect, why I bought Apple is pretty obvious. Apple started with computers to compete with Compaq, Toshiba, Dell, and so on, but then entered into the cell phone market for consumers and kept upgrading to keep consumers updating their phone every one to two years. Apple targeted the younger generation. I remember going to the Apple retail store in New York and seeing the long lines outside the store, and the two-hour wait to be served by a salesperson. I was one of the few people in the store over the age of 30. Clearly, Apple had reached the younger market at an unprecedented level. One differentiation from other companies was using company stores, rather than the model used by BlackBerry, which had stagnant, older business customers using their cell phone services without new developments. In general, large business is resistant to change, but the consumers were susceptible to it. The phone product increased in complexity and its services were able to challenge other services. Eventually the smartphone challenged the computers. The addition of the ability to take pictures and then send them to friends, above and beyond the standard telecommunication options, resulted in superior acceptance by consumers. So I held on to the stock for the long term. As of 2018, Apple had $300,000,000,000 in cash, which enhances R&D, allowing the company to keep its market share and penetrate previously blocked markets such as China, Iran, and the Middle East. On the black market, an Apple iPhone can even bypass the blockage of networks. The apps, upgrades, and iTunes also supplement monthly rentals. Even at $3 a month, these add up when compounded by hundreds of millions of customers. Despite negative comments, I held on. Look at the 50 dma and 200 dma. The 50 dma is consistently above the 200 dma, and recently the 50 dma has a faster upward slope than the 200 dma's. Even at $90 a share, accumulation and distribution were positive.

Look at Figure 7.1 to see Apple from September 2017 to January 28, 2018.

The reader is cautioned not to rely on any information provided in this example for making decisions about trading any security. Please refer to the **Caution—Limitations and Difficulties** section found at the end of the first chapter.

Retrospective Analysis versus Backtesting

I am going to present examples of stocks that made money, an example of stocks that were selected to short, and examples of stocks where both the long position and short position lost money.

Now let's apply the list of parameters that was retrospectively derived from stocks I had selected to purchase. Since the Securities

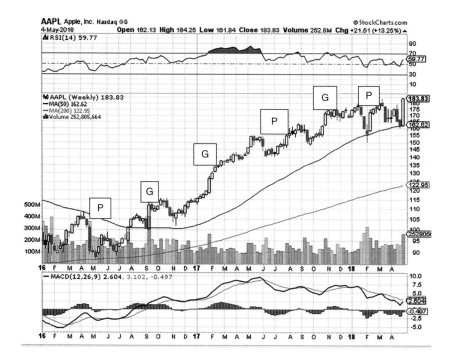

Figure 7.1   Apple 50 dma and 200 dma chart (this is not a recommendation to buy or sell). Chart courtesy of StockCharts.com.

P = plunge = shows traders are selling.
G = gapped up = shows traders are buying.

and Exchange Commission (SEC) scrutinizes backtesting very carefully, let me make a distinction between backtesting and a retrospective analysis. Backtesting involves the use of theoretical performance developed by applying a particular investment strategy to historical financial data. Investment advisors create a theory and then look back on selected stocks to try to prove their theory. An advisor has a particular point of view, unsubstantiated by any facts, and then goes back to identify stocks that fit the theory. This is not science; this is salesmanship, which is why the SEC does not approve of this technique. Backtesting sees how well a strategy would have done ex-post facto. Backtesting assesses the viability of a trading strategy by selecting securities that support the theory and then sees if it would work using historical data. If backtesting works, traders then employ it going forward. Often, automated trading systems rely on backtesting to prove their value. One of the great fallacies of back-testing is the bias that creeps into data selection. If a backtesting theory is to be considered valid, it must be comprehensive in evaluating all companies that should be covered by the theoretical consideration. However, it is often the case that the investor who advanced the backtesting theory under consideration wants to look good. He wants people to see how clever he is. Therefore, these advisors often disregard companies that disprove their theory and create a bias in the interpretation of the results.

I am not doing that. I am doing case studies that are retrospective analyses of stock that performed well. I am doing the reverse of backtesting. I am taking historical financial data from stocks that are doing well and deriving the factors that made this stock attractive to me when I first bought it. This is called pattern recognition, which means determining what factors were consistently present in stocks that did well. This is done by retrospective analysis, which was described in detail in Chapter 5.

In the case of backtesting, an investment advisor takes his investment strategy, looks back on historical performance, and tries to make his investment strategy fit into stocks that performed well while ignoring stocks that fit into his theory but didn't do well. The key words here are "theoretical performance." In effect, theoretical performance is another term for prediction. Another definition of backtesting is the process of testing a trading strategy on relevant historical data to ensure its viability before the trader risks any actual capital. A trader can simulate the trading of a strategy over an appropriate period of time and analyze the results for the levels of profitability and risk (https://www.investopedia.com/terms/b/backtesting.asp#ixzz5JOfoAvPE).

There are other elements of backtesting to be considered, such as duration of the backtesting period so that fluctuations in market conditions are considered (which allows uptrends and downtrends to be taken into consideration), sample size, too long or too short a period of time, and "robustness." A measure of robustness is accomplished by comparing the results of an optimized backtest in a specific sample time period (referred to as in-sample) with the results of a backtest with the same strategy and settings in a different sample time period (referred to as out-of-sample). If the results are similarly profitable, then the strategy can be deemed to be valid and robust and it is ready to be implemented in real-time markets. If the strategy fails in out-of-sample comparisons, then the strategy needs further development, or it should be abandoned altogether (https://www .investopedia.com/terms/b/backtesting.asp#ixzz5JOiN6fes, https:// www.investopedia.com/terms/b/backtesting.asp#ixzz5JOfoAvPE).

In summary, backtesting consists of developing a theory and trying to find examples that support the theory. This is the complete reverse of what I am doing with the Parnes Parameters. I have selected a variety of stocks, made a series of observations, looked for a pattern that consistently appeared in these stocks (pattern recognition), and from these observations I have developed a method of selecting stocks, which I use. I selected stocks that performed well as well as stocks that performed poorly and tried to tease out the factors that separated these two groups of stocks. However, there is a great degree of overlap in some factors. If you use Venn diagram terms, there is a large union set. This is graphically represented in Figure 7.2. It would be foolish to say that there is a foolproof pattern of stock selection due to all of the variables involved.

Case Study Method

Most textbooks for law school and business school use case studies to try to convey the concepts of how business is conducted. I think this is a valuable format, as long as it is organized properly. A recitation of historical events has far less value if the concepts used in the

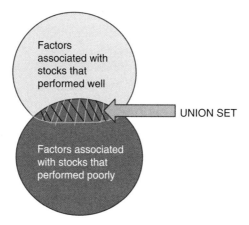

Figure 7.2   Venn diagram of factors influencing stock performance.

decision-making process are not explored. So with this thought in mind, I offer a conceptual framework on which we can hang historical facts. If you will, we're going to build a financial Christmas tree. The tree will be the same for all stocks, but the ornaments we hang on the tree will be different. By maintaining the same format for each stock, the differences between the stocks will become immediately apparent and easily differentiated.

Not all of the stocks have all of the elements of the list of parameters, but these elements are present in many of the selected stocks. To create this list, I looked at fundamentals and technical evaluation. These are the factors I used to construct the list for the Parnes Parameters technique, which assists me in selecting stocks to purchase on a scientific basis. This technique was experimentally derived from my successful selection of stocks. Recognizing similar patterns of these productive stocks using the pattern recognition technique allows for the parameters to be developed—the Parnes Parameters. This will identify which stocks have sustainability and growth potential.

I provide a detailed evaluation of Amazon as an example of a "buy opportunity" to show the depth of evaluations I normally perform when I do my own market research. Then, in Chapter 8, I will use Chipotle as an example of another in-depth evaluation, but this time on the short side. I am providing you with real evidence-based examples of my decision-making process and documenting my statements with historical data. I am not making wild claims; rather I am presenting scientific and historical evidence, from which the Parnes Parameters technique was constructed, to prove its accuracy. Please remember, there is a lot of subjective assessment of the values of the Parnes Parameters, so there is no guarantee, either stated or implied, that your results will duplicate mine. But hopefully you will see that the Parnes Parameters have some value, and certainly beats a monkey with a dartboard. (Maybe I shouldn't say that, since I haven't tried the monkey yet.)

Amazon—An Example of a Long Purchase Held for 18 Years (This Is Not a Recommendation to Buy or Sell or Short)

Amazon is a perfect example of my philosophy for a long purchase. I first purchased the stock in 2000, and I continue to hold it. I even add to the position in any correction or retraction of the market. So, we should analyze why I purchased the stock in the first place and why I held it through a series of rollercoaster ups and downs over the years. I was intrigued by the business model of Amazon from the onset. Even though the company initially had no earnings, the business model attracted mutual funds, institutions, exchange-traded funds (ETFs), and, most importantly, high-frequency traders (HFTs). This was the new model for retail sales over the Internet. The management was excellent and the business model made sense. The stock had the potential for high-percentage market penetration, not only in retail but through the projected introduction of Alexa and Echo, Amazon movies, Amazon Prime, and the potential for various new businesses. The stock had positive revenue growth in the 20%–30% range, even though it had a negative triple-digit price-to-earnings ratio. The technical picture was intriguing because the measure of outflow and inflow was in the positive mode, and the correction-retraction fell many times below the 50 dma and 200 dma. The plunges created short positions that would be a plus on any reversals, because they had to be covered by the short sellers, and on many occasions created a "short squeeze." In October 2016, when Amazon dropped from 430 to 360, it then rebounded and created a V-shaped graph, and broke out through its primary resistance (425–435) in early February 2017. The trend line (volume) continued to trade above a flat line, indicating heavy trading on the buy side. As a result of penetration through primary resistance, above 435, a new upside pattern developed through stages with sustainable uptrends. At this time there was no need to maintain a stop loss. Also, I added to the long position for the upward stepper.

The sustainable upward movement brought the price to the 830–840 area, creating a temporary overextended pattern where the correction-retraction was imminent, augmented by the election of President Trump. After the election, the price plummeted to 680–690. That correction created a short position with an expectation of reversal to challenge the primary resistance of 730–740 and secondary resistance of 770–780. By this time, investors, traders, and analysts were mesmerized by the power of Amazon's market penetration, with an expected revenue increase for the November–December 2017 holiday season from the negative P/E ratio of triple digits to a double- or single-digit negative or even a positive P/E, which had not been seen since its inception. The positive earnings reports squeezed short sellers, bringing the Amazon stock to a new high of 856. Since the election of President Trump, Amazon has grown from 680 to a price of 1,050–1,650 in late April 2018.

The reason I held the stock was the technology, since Amazon was way ahead in cloud computing, retail models, and search engine optimization (SEO). I never sold this stock because of the amazing potential of Amazon. Amazon was embryonic in 2000, and many investors kept it in their portfolios to show a growth stock; that is, institutional investors and smart investors held on to the stock. Any retraction was a real attraction for a new buyer, doubling up on the downside. The vision of the management was to develop a new product and rid themselves of failed products. They were always ahead of their competitors. They went after the entire Internet retail trade, not just books. To this end, over the Christmas season of 2017, Amazon had 52% of retail trade in the United States and 2% globally.

I wrote about Amazon in *Modern Trader* in October 2017. At that time, Amazon had a pending acquisition of Whole Foods (WFM). Some investors thought that it was time to short their Amazon (AMZN) positions. I thought they were short-sighted and failed to see the opportunity to accumulate a position for solid long-term growth. I thought that Amazon's downward momentum was not fundamentally sustainable, and its upward movements would be generated by high volatility within bid-ask prices, resulting in a short squeeze.

Amazon, with a stock capitalization of nearly $500 billion, was founded in 1994 and headquartered in Seattle. The company engages in the retail sale of consumer products and service subscriptions in North America and internationally. From its humble inception focusing expressly on books, Amazon expanded into unanticipated retail segments such as artificial intelligence, food, music, media content, publishing, manufacturing electronic devices, and consumer products.

In June 2017, the quarterly report for Amazon indicated a 25% increase in its revenue to $38 billion while its operating income slid 51% to $628 million (adjusting for periods of earning expansion with increased investing). Amazon's recorded capital investment comprised of its yearly capital expenditure of $2.5 billion (up 46%) and its capital leases such as property and equipment—up 50% to $2.7 billion—has astonished the Street. These numbers are indicative of Amazon's demonstrative efforts to reinvest and refine its shipping capacity, digital video segment, Echo device, and affordable cloud services solutions.

Those companies that hold on to traditional methodologies and try applying them to Amazon fail to understand that Amazon never followed a traditional business model. They are expecting corrections and retractions similar to other stocks, rather than embracing Amazon's 20-year proven model as sufficient evidence that Amazon is different and has a unique growth metric. Amazon's surprising acquisition of Whole Foods only serves to provide further support that the company has not topped off and will continue with its forward momentum.

This all has implications that will boost Amazon's bottom line. Even in the face of a potential failure to acquire Whole Foods and expand its physical offerings, Amazon has proven itself capable of handling defeat, as it has with other failed expansion attempts (i.e. Amazon's Fire phone). The window for investors to purchase Amazon will eventually shut as the company continues to evolve and reshape the future for both its shareholders and the world. Therefore, I would consider keeping Amazon as a long-term growth solution and a lucrative future investment.

Amazon has broken the traditional valuation model since 1995 from its sporadic profitable quarters versus the belief of sacrificing profitability for growth. Its technical outlook indicates a status of reinforcement rather than divestment due to its P/E ratio dropping to low triple digits from commanding high triple digits and has been on a clear pattern of ascension since 2016.

Continually trading above its 50 dma and 200 dma, Amazon has been a picture of consistency, leading to its rise through early June 2017, when its price temporarily breached $1,000. A sell-off created its July low near $950. Sporadic correction and retraction operating above the 50-day moving average may challenge support below this level, perhaps testing down to $910. Shorts in general are difficult to master because of the scarcity of float/liquidity, requiring a contrarian sense of objectivity. Amazon's business model is equally contrarian by its nature. In the context of the market, Amazon is most solidly a long position and provides a unique opportunity for any portfolio accumulation. Amazon may not have reached the low of this correction, but there is more room on the upside.

I recommend buying Amazon at between $970 and $988 with a near-term objective of $1,108. In October 2017, I thought that, long term, Amazon could reach $1,250. A drop below $903 would indicate further weakness, but Amazon will be back above the $1,000 mark relatively shortly. As of late April 2018, Amazon is hovering between $1,500 and $1,650, with a potential of hitting $2,000 and beyond.

The reader is cautioned not to rely on any information provided in this example for making decisions about trading any security. Please refer to the **Caution—Limitations and Difficulties** section found at the end of the first chapter.

Amazon—Using the Evaluation Parameters

The reader is cautioned not to rely on any information provided in this example for making decisions about trading any security. Please refer to the **Caution—Limitations and Difficulties** section found at the end of the first chapter.

These factors are often difficult to evaluate and they have a large subjective component to them. I use my judgment to assign weights to each component of the elements, and this carries a large experiential component. Remember, this list of parameters is not back-testing. It is a multifactorial review of the various features, retrospectively derived, that led me to buy a stock. Doing this for a significant number of stocks leads to pattern recognition—seeing what factors consistently appear in stocks that do well. The Parnes Parameters technique is presented to help the reader gain some insight into my thought processes.

Please remember that your experiences are not the same as mine, and my subjective assessment of values to assign to the parameters may differ from yours. Therefore, there is no way to guarantee that you will get the same results I do when you use the Parnes Parameters.

Assessment of Amazon Using Fundamentals

Internal Factors

1. **Management**
   The management of Amazon is one of the most creative in the country. They are flexible and highly responsive to changes in the market. Most importantly, they anticipate the market and plan accordingly. The management of Amazon gets the highest grades.
2. **P/E Ratio**
   This is the exception that proves the rule. Amazon has a negative triple-digit price-to-earnings ratio, and therefore should

not have a place on the "buy" list. However, the stock had positive revenue growth of 20%–30% annually. This is a situation where I had to weigh the value of a positive price-to-earnings ratio against the spectacular growth rate. I eventually decided that the growth rate was much more important than the price-to-earnings ratio. However, if I remain true to my Parnes Parameters, with a price-to-earnings ratio of 250/1 (compared to the market average of 18/1), Amazon would get very low marks in this category.

3. **Price of Product versus Competitors'**
   There are very few direct competitors to Amazon, so the pricing that Amazon created was less important than its market penetration. Amazon gets high marks in this category.

4. **Percentage of Penetration in Market and Market Share**
   Over the Christmas season of 2017, Amazon had 52% of retail trade in the United States and 2% of the retail trade globally. These are astounding figures. Any company that has more than 50% market penetration and greater than 50% of market share is unstoppable. Actually, these are two different questions, and Amazon answers them quite well. This kind of dominance makes Amazon the company to watch. Amazon gets the highest marks in this category.

5. **Diversifying in Different Fields**
   Certainly, Amazon is not a one-trick pony. It no longer sells just books; that business model disappeared a long time ago. Amazon expanded into Alexa and Echo, Amazon movies, and Amazon Prime. Although they initially started by selling books, the management quickly realized that they could use this model to expand into the entire retail trade market. The recent takeover negotiations for Whole Foods demonstrate that diversification is a valuable component to Amazon. Amazon gets high marks in this category.

6. **Cyclical Industry Like Housing or Picnic Plates**
   Technically, one could say that the retail industry is a cyclical and seasonal market. Most trade publications indicate that 20%–25% of all retail sales occur in the month of December, because of the holiday season. In the case of Amazon, the incursions into all retail markets, not just books, allows the company to weather any slumps in one retail segment or the other. Just like any retailer, Amazon has its best quarter in the last quarter.

However, unlike other retailers, Amazon is not burdened by bricks and mortar, with the attendant problems of real estate. Therefore, compared to its peer group of retail marketers, Amazon gets moderately high marks in this category.

7. **Volume of Stock Traded**

It is important to repeat that there are many ways to evaluate the volume of stock traded. Since I trade for the long term in mind, I look at stock trades for the previous three months. If the trading is more than 100,000 shares a day on a regular basis, it is suggestive that the institutional buyers are clearly interested in this security. This is a decent sign but also a cautionary one, since the stock could be subject to either a trading frenzy or a trading selloff. For stock with this volume of shares traded, I also look at market conditions, which are covered under the technical section below.

8. **Return on Revenue versus Competitors'**

In the absence of a brick-and-mortar sales model, Amazon's return on revenues is far better than other competitors in the retail space. There are no real competitors, on a direct sales model over the Internet, other than some small competition for dog food, human food, some dresses, and so on. But compared to a brick-and-mortar store, Amazon is doing far better than its competitors.

9. **Outdated Product**

Certainly, the business model that Amazon follows is cutting-edge compared to its competitors. So, in this category, it is not so much a product, but the business model that comes into consideration. Maintaining a website is a lot cheaper than maintaining real estate. In this category, Amazon gets high marks.

10. **Cash on Hand to Current Debt Ratio**

At the time I first recommended Amazon, it had a more than 0.5-to-1 cash to current debt ratio and had to rely on increasing sales to pay current debt. While a lot of companies fall into this category, there is some risk in investing in this type of company. Amazon was on an upward growth pattern, but when I first bought it, the cash to current debt ratio was not good.

11. **Fully Developed and Marketable Disruptive Technology**

While this type of situation is the stuff dreams are made of, there is no guarantee that a disruptive technology can penetrate the market. Xerox did. Apple did. Amazon did. One way to assess the potential of company with a disruptive technology is the early sales it may have. The number of orders received is another variable. Amazon's product was ready to market, with the product in production.

12. **Growth in Earnings**

Amazon's operating income slid 51% to $628 million (adjusted for periods of earning expansion with increased investing). This is tricky to evaluate. On an absolute basis, a decline in earnings is clearly undesirable. But a company's funding expansion and investments with its earnings is a sign of a forward-thinking management group. Taking all these factors into account, even though the income is used for expansion, it reduces available cash for the company. Therefore, this decline in cash has an element of risk in terms of meeting debt service, and especially if an investment proves nonproductive. Therefore, Amazon gets a low score in this category. Amazon has no earnings.

13. **Growth in Revenues**

Revenues were $88.99 billion at the end of 2014, with a steady progression to $107 billion at the end of 2015, $136 billion in 2016, and $177.8 billion by the end of 2017. That represented a trend in increased revenues for eight or more quarters. Based on the criteria of the Parnes Parameters, the company gets a high ranking in this category.

14. **Type of Product**

Amazon has many and diverse products for sale. This diversity allows Amazon flexibility in the marketplace and doesn't tie the company to a single product. Amazon expanded from books to everything, with this company accounting for 52% of all retail sales in the United States in 2017. Even if one considers Internet marketing as a product, Amazon has diversified beyond that segment as well. Amazon gets high marks in this category.

The reader is cautioned not to rely on any information provided in this example for making decisions about trading any security. Please refer to the **Caution—Limitations and Difficulties** section found at the end of the first chapter.

Assessments Using Technicals

This is a way of understanding and tracking the movements of institutional investors for a particular stock and comparing them to the market as a whole. The most commonly used technicals are the 50-day and 200-day moving averages, which measure the responses of institutional investors and are the factors external to the operation of the company, which need to be considered, and essentially convey to the investor the way institutional investors are responding to the company.

Assessment of Amazon Using Technicals at the Time I Recommended Purchase

15. **Brokerage House Recommendation**
    Brokerage house upgrade recommendations have been all over the place. Some say Amazon is overpriced; others say the company has no earnings, so sell it. Others have issued hold recommendations. I would have to agree with the latter.
16. **Price Relative to 50 dma and 200 dma**
    There has been an ascending pattern to the price of the stock, which has stayed above the 50 dma and 200 dma.
17. **Death Cross**
    Despite wild market fluctuations, the five-year 50 dma and 200 dma of Amazon had only one death cross. It was close in April 2016, but not profound. The five-year chart is shown in Figure 7.3. There was a death cross in May 2014, but this was 14 years after I had purchased the stock. I thought it was worth holding Amazon because of the other factors. I felt the death cross was insignificant.
18. **Golden Cross (50 dma crosses the 200 dma)**
    In March 2015, Amazon had a golden cross after its previous death cross in May 2014. I have long advocated buying on a golden cross only after a previous death cross, but the time frame was too long between these two events to have any predictive value.
19. **Resistance Line**
    This parameter has more of a short-term value than a stock being held for the long term. When the resistance line is steady or when the stock price declines below the resistance line, then I become concerned. For a six-month period in 2014 Amazon's stock price dipped below the 200 dma, but not

to a significant degree. I decided to hold the stock, but realistically, the score for this parameter was negative.

20. **Support Line**

Amazon has a support line that had been steady for more than 10 days when I recommended buying the stock.

21. **Takeover Bid**

There was no active takeover bid for Amazon. Actually, it was quite the opposite. Amazon was the hunter and began looking at other companies. Usually, the price of a stock will go down if it is actively looking to purchase another company, and the company price drops even more if it buys another company.

22. **Beta Value of Stock (three-year level)** (Morningstar, Google Finance, and Yahoo Finance)

The beta value for Amazon has been high, indicating stock price volatility.

23. **Change in Industry**

This is one area where Amazon shines. It has repeatedly emerged with disruptive technology and is always developing or acquiring innovative products. Amazon gets high scores in this category.

The reader is cautioned not to rely on any information provided in this example for making decisions about trading any security. Please refer to the **Caution—Limitations and Difficulties** section found at the end of the first chapter.

Assessment of Amazon Using External Factors

These are factors that are out of the control of the company and the market, so they should not be considered under either fundamentals or technicals. Often, these factors can arise in an unpredicted fashion (the Barbero effect mentioned earlier). As an example, in 2010, if you had had a shipment of highly perishable lobsters from Maine that needed to reach France in 12 hours, you would have been blindsided by the unexpected eruption of the volcano Eyjafjallajökull in Iceland, which paralyzed air traffic over the northern Atlantic for six days due to volcanic ash. From April 14 to 20, 2010, about 20 countries closed their airspace, impacting approximately 10 million travelers and 200 lobsters.

24. **Favorable Legislation**

There are several recent rulings that may impact Amazon's bottom line. The government has debated and enforced the ruling that Internet companies must charge sales tax in each state in which the company operates, defined as shipping to a state, as opposed to where the company was domiciled. The idea to use drones to deliver packages may run afoul of pending drone regulations. The Whole Foods merger requires regulatory approval. The problems facing Amazon are no better or worse than those facing other companies in the same market segment. Amazon gets a moderate rating in this category.

25. **Change in Prime Rate**

Prime rate has no effect on Amazon. The company has debt, but is paying down the debt with increased revenue.

26. **Change in Oil Prices**

Most shipping is done by truck or air, and the shippers will pass on increased fuel costs. So this will have a moderate effect on the company.

27. **Change in Tariffs**

Tariffs may have a limited impact on sales of Amazon, but that remains to be seen.

28. **Negative Regulatory Change**

Being required to collect sales tax in each state, as opposed to just the state where the company is domiciled, could impact sales a bit.

29. **Change in the Stock Market in General**

Amazon does move with the market, so there is a moderate effect on the company.

30. **Force Majeure, Acts of God—Floods, Fires, Earthquakes**

Like all force majeure events, none are anticipated. I imagine if the electric grid were sabotaged, or the Internet went down, it would hurt Amazon. Both are unlikely.

31. **Relative Strength Line**

The slope of the line representing the stock price remains higher than the S&P 500 Industrial Average, with occasional dips into a parallel path. Being conservative, I would say that Amazon is performing at the level of the S&P 500.

32. **Cup with Handle Breakout (after a 52-week high)**

Look at the 50 dma and 200 dma graph in Figure 7.3 (see O in figure 7.3). The handle being higher than the previous high indicates a buy situation. However, there really was never a cup with handle pattern, so this technical is not applicable.

33. **Common Sense and Discipline**

    Common sense says that Amazon has brilliant leadership, a good business model that is getting better, increased sales to help reduce debt, an expanding product base, and has become a household word. This category is my ultimate "fudge factor." My gut instincts tell me to buy and hold Amazon.

34. **Put-Call Ratio**

    The put-call ratio for Amazon was about average for a retailer. But this is not a brick-and-mortar retailer, since it is an Internet company retailing goods with a huge market share. The market may not be fully appreciating Amazon.

The reader is cautioned not to rely on any information provided in this example for making decisions about trading any security. Please refer to the **Caution—Limitations and Difficulties** section found at the end of the first chapter.

My analysis of Amazon convinced me to buy and hold the stock. In fact, I was convinced that if I had the opportunity to buy more Amazon, on a brief dip in the price due to institutional sell-offs or short sale coverage, I probably would do so. I did end up buying more. As of the end of 2017, Amazon was selling for $1,600. See Figure 7.3. (This is not a recommendation to buy or sell.)

The reader is cautioned not to rely on any information provided in this example for making decisions about trading any security. Please refer to the **Caution—Limitations and Difficulties** section found at the end of the first chapter.

I offer this detailed evaluation of Amazon to give an example of the thought processes I use in order to make a recommendation to purchase a stock.

Some of the websites I used to obtain market information are:

https://www.marketwatch.com/investing/stock
http://www.stockcharts.com/freecharts/
http://www.buyupside.com/movingaveragechart/
    5yearmoveaveinput.php

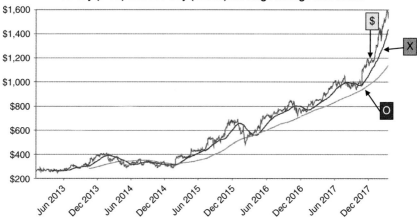

Figure 7.3   Amazon Five-Year 50 dma and 200 dma.

Amzn = Amazon five-year graph of 50 dma (line marked by x), 200 dma (line marked by o), and stock price (line marked by $).

Source: http://www.buyupside.com/movingaveragechart/movavechartdisplay.php?symbol=amzn&.

A Case Study for a Stock I Shorted for the Long Term—Chipotle

(This is not a recommendation to buy, sell, short, or cover a short.)

> The reader is cautioned not to rely on any information provided in this example for making decisions about trading any security. Please refer to the **Caution—Limitations and Difficulties** section found at the end of the first chapter.

Just as I explained in the chapter on picking a stock for a long position, I use two components to evaluate a stock to short, sometimes sequentially and sometimes concurrently. These are the *fundamental components* of a company (sales, earnings, P/E ratio, etc.) and the *technical pattern*, which is how the security performs in the market, using graphs and charts to track market trends. This is done using 50 dma and 200 dma and comparing the stock to its peer group and to the market in general.

Sometimes the fundamentals are completely different from one issue to another. Some stocks I wish to short have a typical P/E ratio, and sometimes there are earnings so far out of line with their peer group that the stock price seems artificially inflated. An example of the latter consideration would be many of the dot-com companies of the 1990s, which had no earnings but were being sold on the prospect of dramatic earnings and expected astronomical growth in the absence of good fundamentals. Shorts may go against me, but we try not to be stopped out. I continue holding and increasing short positions at times, since the proceeds from the shorts are placed into high-growth stocks. As long as these growth stocks keep increasing in value, I am not concerned about the movement of the short position. *This gives me the ability to hold shorts for the long term.* If the increase in value of the long positions outpaces the potential paper loss in the shorts, then the shorts are not of immediate concern, for the following reasons:

1. The short sellers may have been squeezed by favorable news, with an upgrade in the rating of the stock, or some new development.
2. These increases are short term, but the fundamentals of the company do not warrant sustainability of the increase in price.
3. Eventually, in the long term, a reversal of price will occur, due to poor fundamentals of the company, and it will continue to lose value. Also, external factors, such as Chipotle's *E. coli* scare, will drive the stock lower.
4. The behavior of hedge funds, institutional traders, and other large holders is to look for an exit strategy as soon as possible. This is what I call the "herd mentality."

Case Presentation (This is not a recommendation to buy, sell, short, or cover the short)

> The reader is cautioned not to rely on any information provided in this example for making decisions about trading any security. Please refer to the **Caution—Limitations and Difficulties** section found at the end of the first chapter.

One classic example of the philosophy of shorting for the long term is Chipotle (CMG). Since the parameters of this company were bad, even when stock price increased, I didn't cover the short. When the stock went up to 600 to 700 or more, I kept increasing my shorts, because the fundamentals of the company would reverse the extreme ascent pattern of the stock. I kept the short position, anticipating more negative news, producing reversals, with the plunging pattern occurring over a much shorter time course than any ascent. Remember, I have found that stocks decline much faster than they recover. When I evaluate any stock using both the fundamental and technical techniques, I do so concurrently. These two broad general elements cannot be evaluated in a vacuum. They interrelate with one another. I shall try to explain the various considerations under each heading of fundamentals and technical assessment. To tell the truth, these are difficult components to evaluate and they have a large subjective component to them. I use my judgment to assign weights to each component of the elements, and this carries a large experiential component. However, I shall try as best I can to convey my thought process for each of the elements.

What follows is a list of the Parnes Parameters that I use to evaluate for selecting stocks to short for the long term. This list of parameters was retrospectively derived from stocks that met the criteria of a projected decline in price over the next year or longer. These are stocks that typically have appreciated rapidly but do not have sustainable fundamentals that warrant their inflated price. Not all of the stocks have all of the elements of the list of parameters, but these elements are present in many of the selected stocks. From this list, I created the Parnes Parameters for Stocks to Short, which assists me in selecting stocks to short on a scientific basis. This technique was experimentally derived from my selection of stocks that met my criteria to decline in the next year or more. Recognizing similar patterns of these overvalued stocks, using the pattern recognition technique, allows for the parameters to be developed—the Parnes Parameters for Stocks to Short.

Case Study for Shorting a Stock for the Long Term

Chipotle—An Example of a Short Held for Two Years

(Note: Proceeds from this short were used to purchase Amazon. I covered the short at $295–$300, when management changed. Chipotle had fallen from the $700–$750 range several years earlier.)

The reader is cautioned not to rely on any information provided in this example for making decisions about trading any security. Please refer to the **Caution—Limitations and Difficulties** section found at the end of the first chapter.

Chipotle Mexican Grill (CMG) is a trendy Mexican-style restaurant chain founded in 1993. It has developed and operates more than 198 restaurants in the United States, with 29 international restaurants, and 23 restaurants that do not conform to the Mexican-style menu. The Denver-based CMG has become famous for its unique food services, also becoming infamous as a long-term short position.

Fundamentals

Since 2015, CMG has signaled its short-selling potential and has been continuously recommended as a short by me. CMG relished its notoriety and its growth rate in 2015, sending the equity at an all-time high of $758.61 a share, with a market cap of $15.19 billion and earnings per share of $16.76, resulting in a price-to-earnings ratio of 29.07.

In the fall of 2015, an *E. coli* outbreak at various stores in multiple locations across the United States created a major problem for Chipotle. In 2016, the Centers for Disease Control (CDC) issued a formal declaration of the direct association between food handling at Chipotle and the *E. coli* outbreak, which generated extensive negative media coverage. This negative press led Chipotle to slash its sales and earnings forecast, which set the stock price plunging from its 52-week high of $521.52. Subsequently the stock had a market cap of $12.82 billion, earnings per share of .77, and a price-to-earnings ratio of 524.84, as of March 8, 2017. This P/E ratio clearly was unsustainable. During the same period, Chipotle was faced with a secondary offering of 2.9 million shares by prominent shareholder activists, which further reduced the market's trust in Chipotle.

To further compound its woes, an additional foodborne contamination was reported. In July 2017 it was confirmed that 130 customers in Sterling, Virginia were infected with a norovirus from contaminated food from a Chipotle restaurant. This made it even more difficult for Chipotle to distance itself from its reputation of food poisoning. In an effort to avoid further problems, Chipotle increased its standards of food handling and food supply, which increased its operating costs, and funded an extensive promotional and advertising campaign to offset the bad press it had received. Despite these efforts, the loss of goodwill and the lingering bad press and food poisoning reputation stigmatized Chipotle. As a result of this, Chipotle stock has continued to decline, and the earnings have suffered. Its continuous disappointing earnings have reinforced it as a volatile short position, with more declines in the offing.

The reader is cautioned not to rely on any information provided in this example for making decisions about trading any security. Please refer to the **Caution—Limitations and Difficulties** section found at the end of the first chapter.

Technical Picture

In the October 2017 issue of *Modern Trader,* on page 14, I wrote "CMG warrants lower P/E multiples to reflect today's slower growth rate versus its competitors. It is plunged with the downed gap with multiple plunge milestones."

I was intrigued with its 50 dma and 200 dma in late March 2017; after straddling those averages for most of the year, it established a clear reverse head-and-shoulder pattern before topping at $499 on May 16.

After the norovirus outbreak in July 2016, further sell-offs accelerated in that month and subsequent months, taking Chipotle to its 3½-year low in October 2016. This indicated that the next clear technical support level was the 2012 low of $240 a share. The continued weakness pushed Chipotle into a death cross on August 2, 2016, with the 50 dma crossing below the 200 dma while the market traded below both of these moving averages. CMG again entered a death cross in late November 2016 and subsequently dropped from $576 a share to just below $400 a share in six weeks. In March 2017, Chipotle entered a golden cross and rebounded 25%.

In October 2017, I wrote in *Modern Trader,* on page 15, "CMG's troubles are clearly not over, and the recent fundamental weakness following the known norovirus outbreak has created extreme technical damage."

It wasn't until the change of management in 2018 that Chipotle again regained some of its momentum. However, I still feel that all the fundamentals necessary to produce a sustainable company are not in place. At present, I maintain a wait-and-see attitude.

The reader is cautioned not to rely on any information provided in this example for making decisions about trading any security. Please refer to the **Caution—Limitations and Difficulties** section found at the end of the first chapter.

Evaluating Chipotle

The factors in the Parnes Parameters are often difficult to evaluate and have a large subjective component to them. I use my judgment to assign weights to each component of the elements and this carries a large experiential component. Please remember that your experiences are not the same as mine, and my subjective assessment of values to assign to the parameters may differ from yours. Therefore, there is no way to guarantee that you will get the same results I do when you use the Parnes Parameters.

Assessment of Chipotle Using Fundamentals (I recommended shorting in 2015)

Internal Factors for the 2016–2017 period

1. **Management**
   The management of Chipotle was not able to erase the stigma of the *E. coli* poisoning of various customers in a number of locations across the United States in the fall of 2015. The ruling of the Center for Disease Control in 2016, declaring a direct association of the poisonings to Chipotle, further impacted the stock.
2. **P/E Ratio**
   The P/E ratio of 525.84 (on March 8, 2017) was unsustainable and would warrant a reduction. There are a number of casual restaurants with P/E ratios hovering between 18 and 25 to 1. Chipotle would get very low marks in this category.
3. **Price of Product versus Competitors'**
   There are a number of casual restaurants and theme restaurants. The prices of meals at Chipotle initially were low compared to those of other restaurants, but management had to raise prices to compensate for improved quality control and advertising to offset the negative press.
4. **Percentage of Penetration in Market and Market Share**
   After the *E. coli* scare, Chipotle lost a significant percentage of its market share. Market share further eroded after the norovirus outbreak.
5. **Diversifying in Different Fields**
   Certainly, Chipotle is a one-trick pony. Current management is trying to change this, but at the time of my multiple recommended shorts, it had not diversified. In fact, attempts

at diversification, adding hamburgers to the Mexican fare, failed. Chipotle does have a small percentage of non-Mexican-food restaurants, but not enough to shore up the major focus.

6. **Cyclical Industry Like Housing or Picnic Plates**
   People always have to eat. This is not a cyclical industry.

7. **Volume of Stock Traded**
   Chipotle traded between 1,000,000 and 2,000,000 shares a day, indicating high volatility, which invited day traders, high-frequency traders, and computer-driven trading programs.

8. **Return on Revenue versus Competitors'**
   The brick-and-mortar restaurant model, with most real estate owned by the company, leads to tied-up capital, real estate debt, and an undervalued stock price because of the treatment of real estate by generally accepted accounting practices (GAAP). Real estate must be carried at a fully depreciated level rather than "marked to market." This negatively impacts earnings.

9. **Outdated Product**
   Mexican food is a trendy product, and the increase in the Hispanic population further enhances the appeal of a specialty restaurant of this type.

10. **Cash on Hand to Current Debt Ratio**
    At the time I first shorted Chipotle, it had a more than 0.5-to-1 cash to current debt ratio and had to rely on increasing sales to pay current debt. While a lot of companies fall into this category, there is some risk in investing in this type of company. Chipotle was on an upward growth pattern, but after the two health scares, the cash to current debt ratio was not good.

11. **Fully Developed and Marketable Disruptive Technology**
    Chipotle had a fully developed market concept with a readily duplicated restaurant model.

12. **Growth in Earnings**
    Since 2015, earnings have declined dramatically, from $16.76 a share with a P/E ratio of 29.07 to $0.77 with a P/E ratio of 525.84 (circa March 8, 2017). The drop after the *E. coli* and norovirus scares, with subsequent negative press, was responsible.

13. **Growth in Revenues**
    Revenues for Chipotle ranged from a high of $4.57 billion in September 2015 to a low of $3.87 billion on September 16, 2016. This decline in revenue represents a more than 15% decline. See Figure 8.1.

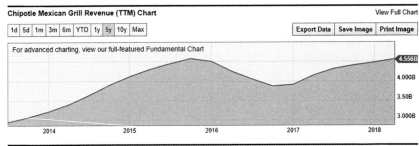

Figure 8.1   Chipotle Mexican Grill Revenue (TTM) chart.

Source: www.ycharts.com.

Note: I highly recommend YCharts for historic data (see https://ycharts.com/companies/).

14. Type of Product

Again, Chipotle has primarily Mexican food as its product. This lack of diversity limits Chipotle's flexibility in the marketplace and ties the company to a single product. Chipotle tried to expand from Mexican food into hamburgers, but this was not well received.

The reader is cautioned not to rely on any information provided in this example for making decisions about trading any security. Please refer to the **Caution—Limitations and Difficulties** section found at the end of the first chapter.

Assessments Using Technicals

This is a way of understanding and tracking the movements of institutional investors for a particular stock and comparing them to the market as a whole. The most commonly used technicals are the 50 dma and 200 dma, which measure the responses of institutional investors. These are the factors external to the operation of the company, which need to be considered, and essentially convey to the investor the way institutional investors are responding to the company.

Assessment of Chipotle Using Technicals at the Time I Recommended Purchase

15. **Brokerage House Recommendation**

    Brokerage houses upgraded recommendations when activist interest pushed prices up. Since the company experienced not one, but two food poisoning scares, recommendations have fallen off.

16. **Price Relative to 50 dma and 200 dma**

    There has been a descending pattern to the price of the stock, which declined below the 50-day and 200-day moving averages for all of 2016. See Figure 8.2.

17. **Death Cross**

    The death cross occurred in August 2016, as shown in Figure 8.2.

18. **Golden Cross (the 50 dma crosses the 200 dma)**

    In mid-March 2016, there was a golden cross, but it reversed itself in August 2016 to a death cross. See Figure 8.2.

Figure 8.2   Golden cross reverses to death cross. Chart courtesy of StockCharts.com.

19. **Resistance Line**
    For short positions, a support line is more important than a resistance line.
20. **Support Line**
    Chipotle has a primary support line at 416–410 and a secondary support line at 381–370. See Figure 8.2.
21. **Takeover Bid**
    There was no active takeover bid for Chipotle.
22. **Beta Value of Stock (three-year level)** (Morningstar, Google Finance and Yahoo Finance)
    The beta value for Chipotle has been low, indicating stock price decline and decreased performance.
23. **Change in Industry**
    The restaurant industry change is best measured by the number of new restaurants opened rather than a change in product. Some strong competition has developed in pricing and menu products.

The reader is cautioned not to rely on any information provided in this example for making decisions about trading any security. Please refer to the **Caution—Limitations and Difficulties** section found at the end of the first chapter.

Assessment of Chipotle Using External Factors

These are factors that are out of the control of the company and the market, so they should not be considered under either fundamentals or technicals. Often, these factors can arise in an unpredicted fashion (the Barbero effect mentioned earlier). As an example, in 2010, if you had had a shipment of highly perishable lobsters from Maine that needed to reach France in 12 hours, you would have been blindsided by the unexpected eruption of the volcano Eyjafjallajökull in Iceland, which paralyzed air traffic over the northern Atlantic for six days due to volcanic ash. From April 14 to 20, 2010, about 20 countries closed their airspace, impacting approximately 10 million travelers and 200 lobsters.

24. **Favorable Legislation**
    The report from the CDC attributing the *E. coli* poisoning outbreak to Chipotle affected the bottom line.

25. **Change in Prime Rate**
   The prime rate has some effect on Chipotle because of the debt held by Chipotle. The company has debt, and paying down the debt with the decline in revenue became more difficult.

26. **Change in Oil Prices**
   Most shipping is done by truck or air, and the shippers will pass on increased fuel costs. So this will have a moderate effect on Chipotle, because of increases in food shipping costs.

27. **Change in Tariffs**
   Tariffs may have a limited impact on sales of Chipotle, but that remains to be seen.

28. **Negative Regulatory Change**
   The food chain supply has become more restrictive due to health concerns. The use of Romaine lettuce increased the risk of *E. coli* infection.

29. **Change in Stock Market in General**
   Chipotle does move with the market, so there is a moderate effect on the company.

30. **Force Majeure, Acts of God—Floods, Fires, Earthquakes**
   Like all force majeure events, none are anticipated. Any negative impact on farm product and food supply prices has a negative impact on Chipotle.

31. **Relative Strength Line**
   The slope of the line representing the stock price remains lower than the S&P 500 Industrial Average, with occasional dips into a parallel path. Being conservative, I would say that Chipotle is performing below the level of the S&P 500.

32. **Cup with Handle Breakout (after a 52-week high)**
   Look at the 50 dma and 200 dma in Figure 8.2. Normally, the handle being higher than the previous high indicates a buy situation. However, there really was never a cup with handle pattern, so this technical is not applicable.

33. **Common Sense and Discipline**
   Common sense says that Chipotle peaked at 785 in 2016, and was in a declining mode ever since, until February 2018, when the management changed. This category is my ultimate "fudge factor." My gut instincts tell me not to buy and hold Chipotle, since the recent rebound is not sustainable and the P/E ratio is still much higher than that of its peers.

34. Put-Call Ratio

The put-call ratio for Chipotle was above average compared to its peers'.

The reader is cautioned not to rely on any information provided in this example for making decisions about trading any security. Please refer to the **Caution—Limitations and Difficulties** section found at the end of the first chapter.

Interpretation of the Parnes Parameters

In 2016, the price of Chipotle ranged from roughly $450 to $758. This told me that if I had the opportunity to short more Chipotle, I probably would do so. I did short more. Chipotle fell to $245 for its lowest price, and as of February 2018 was selling for $290–$300, when I covered my short.

I offer this detailed evaluation of Chipotle to give an example of the thought processes I use in order to make a recommendation to short a stock, and more importantly, shorting for the long term.

I think it is important to note that trying to make money from short-term shorting is difficult and few people have mastered this. In my published recommendations in *Modern Trader*, the cover price listed is intended for sophisticated investors, but not for the average investor. Also, I do not follow the stop-loss price, either, because many of the stocks get stopped out in a one- to six-month period of time. This is not compatible with my investment philosophy, but traders and institutional investors want these recommendations, so I include them with my short recommendations. I am more risk tolerant and rely more on the fundamentals of a company to decide whether or not to cover my short. Sometimes I have paper losses of 25%–30%, but remember, it is not a real loss until I cover the short. So my byword is "slowly, slowly, slowly." If the fundamentals do not support a stock price, wait it out. The market will eventually recognize the flaws and the price will reflect this.

Moreover, remember that I typically hold only 10%–30% of investments in short positions, and I have already used the proceeds from the short to purchase more long positions. As long as the value of the long position keeps climbing, then I typically have more than enough of a margin to lessen my concerns about covering an out-of-the-money short position. When the market eventually responds to the fundamentals of a stock I have shorted, then I cover the short . . . in a year, a year and a half, even two years. Remember, I may have experienced 25%–30% paper losses, but I have never experienced a real loss (unless I covered a short out of the money).

Taking the basic premise of the evaluation process, I cannot report the selling price of each stock, since these varied for different accounts. The various clients may have covered a short at a less than optimal time for personal reasons. Some of the websites I used to obtain market information are:

https://www.marketwatch.com/investing/stock
http://www.stockcharts.com/freecharts/
http://www.buyupside.com/movingaveragechart/
    5yearmoveaveinput.php
http://www.ycharts.com

The reader is cautioned not to rely on any information provided in this example for making decisions about trading any security. Please refer to the **Caution—Limitations and Difficulties** section found at the end of the first chapter.

CHAPTER 9

Case Studies for Integrating Shorts for the Long Term with Longs

How can I make money shorting for the long term? Since business schools and law schools use case studies, I am going to use the same technique.

Principles of Shorting for the Long Term

As long as my long positions are increasing in their values at a higher rate than the paper losses in the short position, there is no need to sell off portions of the long positions. Do not forget that there is not a loss in a short until you actually cover it at a loss.

The only three times a short position will create problems for you is if (1) the company is being acquired, (2) the lenders call the stock back, or (3) a short squeeze occurs. Otherwise, I may continue to hold selected shorts for years by evaluating the chance of any of these three negative events occurring or not occurring. As long as the long positions I acquired with the proceeds from the short sale will pay for the cost of the lender's fee, dividends, and interest charges, if any, I hold both the long and short positions.

The most important distinction between buying a stock on margin and using proceeds from a short to purchase long positions is how the brokerage houses treat either transaction. Hypothetically, if I buy 100 shares of a stock at 50, and I want to increase my position, buying on margin, I pay the same interest cost as I do if I short a stock and use proceeds to buy a long position. The distinction between the two is simple. The short provides a hedge in a down market while my increased long position may drop to a level that can trigger a margin call.

When I have a profit on my long-term equities, I do not want to put the long stock at risk with a margin call. I would be at risk for a stock bought on margin in a down market. Then, when I want to cover a short, rather than take a loss on a long-term equity in a down market, I sell another short to cover the first short and I have hedged the long position.

The Use of Long-Term Shorts to Increase the Value of Long-Term Positions

How can I justify a number of short recommendations that lose money if a stop loss is used at the recommended price? I hold the short for the long term, as long as the long positions purchased with short proceeds continue to climb.

Traders typically are short-term-oriented and base their profit and loss on single-digit changes in money invested. These short-term traders may short a stock at the recommended short price with the hope of increasing their profit or limiting their losses. It is important to note that the trader determines the stop loss according to the movement of the stock. Additionally, the trader buys and sells options, such as puts, calls, straddles, and leaps. Do not forget that options have a time limit, usually 90 days. As I mentioned earlier, many are traded before the expiration date while many expire worthless.

Short positions are not designed to be an investment tool by themselves. Only a few traders make money trading shorts. William O'Neil, of William O'Neil and Company, and Gil Morales, managing director of MoKa Investors, LLC, and Virtue of Selfish Investing, LLC, are well noted for this. Most other traders lose money if they invest exclusively in shorts. Think of shorts as a hedge for the long positions. They are a vehicle to provide income to increase long position holdings, and they provide an opportunity to make a profit covering the short in a down market. Remember, shorts comprise only 10%–30% of my typical portfolios. If the shorts are used to increase the value of long positions in a down market, and if the shorts are held for the long-term, then they have a useful purpose.

It is important to remember that stocks with poor fundamentals often have an erratic and overextended technical pattern. However, eventually these stocks cannot support their technical pattern, and they will be faced with repeated plunges and eventually reach a death cross pattern. In a bear market, any corrections or retractions of major indices produce a valuable market hedge. The critical concept to understand is the discrepancy between the fundamentals and the technical aspect of a stock. The wider the gap between these two concepts, the more likely a stock price will fall, augmented by the high-frequency and institutional traders and major stock holders exiting en masse (the sheep mentality). Therefore, having short positions helps in a bear market or during corrections/retraction phases in the market due to conditions outside the market, such as geopolitical unrest, rising yields, and unforeseen commodity price increases.

It is difficult to assign a direct one-to-one use of proceeds from a short to be applied to long purchases. I try to pick high-growth areas for appreciation. It is safe to say I placed the proceeds from shorts in growth companies in different sectors, such as semiconductors, social media, Internet commerce, and medical supply companies.

Short sellers usually do not make money on short selling. Traders make money on the volatility of the stock and don't hold the shorts for the full term (full term = when the recommended cover price is reached). I occasionally make money on the shorts. Primarily, shorts are used as hedges and to generate proceeds to purchase longs and cover other shorts. I never take a long position and short the same stock, no matter how volatile it is. That is betting against yourself. If you think a stock has good fundamentals and good technicals, then buy it. If you think a stock has either poor fundamentals or poor technicals, or preferably both, then short it.

However, I have shorted a stock, watched it decline, and when something positive happened that led me to believe the stock would advance, I covered my short. At some later date, if the changes to the fundamentals were significantly positive enough, I might even take a long position.

If I want to cover a short, I have to buy it back. For meeting the cost of buying back the stock, there are several choices: (1) sell the exact amount from my long position, (2) keep the amount due in my margin account and pay interest on it, or (3) find another short position for the long term and reduce my margin account with the proceeds from the second short sale. This is the essence of shorting for the long-term.

Multiple Shorts

Very often, the fundamentals of a company warrant a continued decline in its price. Typically, this is the result of ongoing deficits in the fundamentals of a company.

Methods Used by Other Investors and Traders

The essence of this book is to explain how I use shorts for the long term, where the proceeds are applied to purchasing positions for the long term as an investment vehicle. It is only fair to explore how other investment advisors use longs, day trades, shorts, or long/short management as an investment tool, or, better said, as a trading tool. To understand this, you need an economic framework.

Brad Zigler offers a nice conceptual structure.[1] In the first place, he has a global perspective, comparing the 5% annualized domestic growth estimates in the United States to the decline in the Japanese, Chinese, and European economies. He said that economists are concerned by the longevity of the bull market and feels risk will be increasing, especially with increasing interest rates and inflation created by the impending trade wars. He describes the asset allocation in portfolios, spread between well-developed market equities, and investment-grade debt. He notes that smaller amounts of money can be placed in bonds and emerging markets to diversify a portfolio. He advances the strategy of a long/short equity typically found in hedge funds so that the net exposure to the equity market is less than 100%. He feels that this strategy gives fund managers "greater flexibility to search for alpha" and dampens the effects of market volatility. So he set about to test this theory by tracking five long/short equity funds with 60% exposure to global equities and 40% in global high-grade bonds. He found that only one fund outperformed a core portfolio of 60% share MSCI World ETF (URTH), 20% iShares Core International, and Bond ETF (IAGG) 20% iShares Core US Aggregate Bond ETF. The best fund was an "alpha engine" built on a 30-plus-factor framework that was designed to determine which factors were driving returns, and the relative strength of these factors, while keeping a beta of 0.5 against its MSCI World Index benchmark. The fund's net long exposure has been hovering around 70% at the time of his article. This differed from other funds, which sought a static beta exposure.

Todd Rosenbluth reports that, in recent years, advisors and investors have shifted to index-based equities (ETFs) and mutual funds.[2] He feels there is now a shift to indexing. The data supporting this statement comes from the fact that the large-cap core mutual fund in CFRAs (his company) did not perform as well as the S&P 500 Index. This was in part due to mutual fund management fees and less-than-optimal stock selection. Another factor cited was the volatility of the market, with 46% of the S&P companies moving at least 10% in either direction. Rosenbluth calls this a "stockpicker's market," but is quick to point out that stockpickers have generally made the wrong calls. He further notes that 16% of the large-cap core mutual funds lost money in the first half of 2018 while 29% were outperforming the iShares S&P 500 Index (IVV). He also draws the distinction between large-cap and small-cap funds, noting that the small caps outperformed the large caps for the first half of 2018, but active management lagged behind. The Russell 2000 Index, a benchmark for small-cap strategies, had nearly double the performance of the average small-cap core mutual fund. Overall, this led to a $48 billion shrinkage of capital in active equity funds. Classically, the performance records of active managers justified paying premiums for their management compared to indexes, but things seem to be shifting.

Megan Greene reports that a lot of current trading is no longer based on fundamentals.[3] She feels that there is a shift to a "rules-based, passive investment" approach and that there is less of a focus on the information from economists. According to Greene, JPMorgan Chase reports that only approximately 10% of US equities investments are executed by the traditional traders who evaluated stocks. The shift has been to artificial intelligence quant funds with huge memory and computing capacity to evaluate huge amounts of data to discover patterns and compare strategies in various markets in real time, without regard to why the markets move the way they do. They are using the analytic techniques I described earlier and are trying to develop trading strategies based on pattern recognition.

This system is a risk for a very simple reason. Like all artificial intelligence expert systems, the assumption is that

1. The data fed into the computer is accurate, and, more importantly,
2. All the factors that contribute to the outcome have been considered.

Inaccurate input of either the first or second cluster of information will result in GIGO—garbage in, garbage out. This phenomenon has been well described in medicine.

After years of work in the area of expert systems in medicine, a number of authors feel limited progress has been made.[4] One major hurdle to any developer of an expert system is the quality of knowledge used to create the system and the availability of accurate data.[5] Other authors emphasize the value of the longitudinal data collection and data mining to develop expert systems.[6] The accuracy of any expert system is a core issue. The expert systems that have the best results are those that focus on specialized areas of medicine. One questionnaire for rheumatologic disease evaluated 358 patients. It had 60 questions and evaluated 32 rheumatologic diseases.[7] The correlation rate was 74.4%, with an error rate of 25.6%. Forty-four percent of the errors were attributed to "information deficits of the computer using standardized questions."[8] However, in a prospective study of the expert system RHEUMA on 51 outpatients, there was a 90% correlation with clinical experts.[9] The diagnosis of jaundice has been addressed by other groups. The expert system ICTERUS produced a 70% accuracy rate[10] while jaundice also had a 70% overall accuracy rate.[11] An expert system for vertigo has an accuracy rate of 65%.[12] The expert system was named O to Neurological Expert (ONE), and it had same results reported in the earlier article.[13] Only in the narrow area of managing lipid levels was there an agreement of 93% between expert system management advice and a specialist, using the interpretation of laboratory and clinical data.[14] The best analytic models and expert systems come from a group of physicians at Johns Hopkins Hospital. The Pain Validity Test can determine which patient will have abnormalities on medical testing with 95% accuracy.[15-17] The doctors have also developed an Internet-based diagnostic system that gives diagnoses with a 94%–96% correlation with diagnoses of Johns Hopkins Hospital doctors.[18,19]

In general, the accuracy of expert systems in medicine is not particularly good, ranging from 65% to 93%. Only the Johns Hopkins Hospital group has developed expert systems approaching 95%

accuracy. This is of concern, since we would hope (especially if you were the patient) that levels of accuracy for medical care would approach at least 95%. The criteria seem to be less rigorous when stock trading is concerned. Further complicating the use of artificial intelligence expert systems is the sheep mentality, which manifests when traders run from one trading system to the other, based on performance, without regard to underlying fundamentals, as Greene reports.

Greene is quick to point out that "passive investments, such as exchange-traded funds (ETFs) and index funds, similarly ignore fundamentals." The structure of the ETFs mimics an index, so when equities increase in price, the ETFs must buy more of the equity, driving the price even higher. This is without regard to the fundamentals of the company. This creates a paradoxical effect, where ETFs buy high-price stocks, based on a self-fulfilling prophecy, while overlooking the better-value lower-price stocks. As Greene so astutely observes, this creates an investment bubble, without regard for fundamentals. This is a purely "technical" move—looking at graphs, charts, 50 dmas, and 200 dmas and not digging deeper into the real value of the company. Greene correctly mentions that when the ETF stock price falls below the asset value of the company, banks and other organizations assume the market-making role and buy the securities at a discount compared to the assets of a company.

To understand ETFs better, readers are referred to https://www.sec.gov/reportspubs/investor-publications/investorpubsinwsmfhtm.html, which is the website for the Securities and Exchange Commission. ETFs are SEC-registered investment companies that offer investors a method of pooling their money with other investors into a fund that makes investments in securities and receiving a prorated interest in that investment pool. Unlike mutual funds, however, ETFs do not sell individual shares directly. Instead, ETF shares are traded throughout the day on national stock exchanges and at market prices that may or may not be the same as the net asset value (NAV) of the shares.

ETF managers enter into contractual relationships with one or more authorized participants, which are typically financial institutions such as large broker-dealers. Only authorized participants purchase and redeem shares directly from the ETF and can only trade large blocks of shares (e.g. 50,000 ETF shares) commonly called "creation units." They typically "pay" for the creation units through an in-kind exchange with a cluster of securities that reflects the ETF's portfolio.

Once an authorized participant receives the block of ETF shares, the authorized participant may sell the ETF shares in the secondary market to investors. An ETF share is trading at a premium when its market price is higher than the value of its underlying holdings and is trading at a discount when its market price is lower than the value of its underlying holdings. A history of the end-of-day premiums and discounts that an ETF experiences—that is, its net asset value (NAV) per share compared to its closing market price per share—can usually be found on the website of the ETF or its sponsor. By law, an ETF must calculate its NAV at least once a day.

One of the most astounding facts reported by Greene is that the average holding period of a stock on the New York Stock Exchange has fallen from two months in 2008 to *20 seconds* in 2018.[20] This is related to a number of factors. The two major ones are day trading online and the electronically controlled automatic trading.

As the use of personal computers increased exponentially at the end of the twentieth century, so did online stock trading. In his book published in 1999, *Day Trade Online*, Christopher Farrell asks a most pertinent question in the introduction. He asks, "Does the little guy really have a chance?" He then goes on to explain the various hidden interests in Wall Street and even goes so far as to say that "Wall Street earns its money at the expense of the investing public." He makes a very important distinction between day traders and investors, and freely admits that day traders know virtually nothing about the companies whose stock they trade. He emphasizes focusing on the mechanics of the trade and 1/16-, 1/8-, and 1/4-point profits. He compares brokerage houses to a gambling casino, because the odds of winning are stacked in favor of "the house." He points out that, just like casinos, brokerage houses are content to make small but consistent profits on a daily basis. I mention day trading only because it is diametrically opposed to my investment philosophy. Day traders are exactly that—they trade multiple times within a day, often holding securities for as little as 10 seconds, assuming there's no "late fill," which is a situation where you buy a stock, and minutes or even hours later, the stock is not registered in your account. Even though you own the stock, you are unable to trade it until it is registered in your account. This is a disaster for a day trader and can quickly erode profits. The most common cause for this delay is technical problems with the online broker. However, this problem is nothing compared to a "system crash." In this situation, a day trader is denied access to his account or access to up-to-the-minute information until the system is repaired, which can take anywhere from a few minutes to a few hours—a lifetime for a day trader. Further complicating day trading are mistakes or discrepancies made by the online broker. Farrell points out that he "experienced overcharge for commissions, a failure to execute an order, or having shares in your account which you did not purchase." As Farrell says, "dealing with back-office problems is a nightmare." Of course, these situations require meticulous bookkeeping in order to correct any inadvertent errors. Most people do not have the time or personality to become involved in day trading. However, I mention day trading only because there are some valuable principles to be understood that are transferable to investing. First and foremost is the realization that you, as an investor, or even I, as a registered investment advisor, will never have all the resources needed to function as, or compete with, a large brokerage house. The transferable skill from day trading to investing is the ability to read the market. The specifics in reading the market for a day trader will differ from the specifics in reading the market for an investor, but the concept remains the same. In general, there is a herd mentality in many trades. Farrell describes this as momentum. This means that when a stock looks like it's trading up, there is a tendency for investors and traders to buy more and more of it, since they are fearful that they may miss out on a chance to make a profit as the stock increases in price. This momentum is often seen in "highflying" high-profile stocks, technology stocks, and stocks that are making headlines. An investing frenzy develops and people begin to buy a stock, based not on fundamentals, but rather on technicals, that is, the movement of the stock based on the graph for the day, the week, or the month. Typically, the individual stocks are trading in high volumes, on the order of 10 million to 20 million shares a day. That is not much, when you consider that "the New York Stock Exchange (NYSE) trading volume tops a billion shares a day. The newer NASDAQ's busiest days topped 5 billion shares, but its average is around 2 billion."[21]

Other examples of electronically controlled automatic trading are seen on the double, triple, and quadruple "witching days" on the stock market. On the third Friday of March, June, September, and December, the impact of program traders is apparent. On these dates, in the final hour of the stock market trading session, options contracts and futures contracts on market indexes expire. This overlapping expiration typically sets off high-volume trading in options, futures, and associated stocks, which can cause wide swings in stock prices, called "triple witching." "Double witching" is the same phenomenon, except it addresses only one-month options, not three-month options, while "quadruple witching" involves simultaneous expiration of stock index futures, stock index options, stock options, and single stock futures. The trades are dictated by the preset parameters, and when the options expire, the transaction is triggered.

These examples of electronic trading differentiate trading from investing. The electronic trades function as an automatic trigger when preset criteria are met. Investing infers that there is an evaluative process in the decision to buy or sell or short a stock, and the set point may change as conditions change.

There are other techniques of investing which differ from my long/short combination. Some investors focus on just the use of technicals. One of the best-known traders is William O'Neil. He founded the stock brokerage firm of William O'Neil and Company, Inc., in 1963, and the business newspaper *Investor's Business Daily* in 1983. O'Neil is the author of the books *How to Make Money in Stocks: 24 Essential Lessons for Investment Success* and *The Successful Investor*. He developed the investment strategy called CAN SLIM, which was evaluated by the American Association of Individual Investors. This group conducted an independent real-time study of 50 top investment strategies every month from January 1, 1998, to December 31, 2009. In this study, CAN SLIM produced a 2,763% result, which averaged 35.3% a year compared with 3.3% a year for the S&P 500 during the same time. O'Neil reported these findings in his book *How to Make Money in Stocks: A Winning System in Good Times or Bad*, which has sold over 2 million copies and was in its fourth edition in 2009.[22]

According to O'Neil, the CAN SLIM system consists of seven elements:

1. C = current big or accelerating quarterly earnings and sales per share
2. A = annual earnings increases: looking for big growth
3. N = newer companies, new products, new management, new highs off properly formed chart bases
4. S = supply and demand: big volume demand at key points

5. L = leader or laggard: which is your stock?
6. I = institutional sponsorship
7. M = market direction: how you can determine it

On pages 3 and 4 of his book, O'Neil shares some of his observations after years of investing. He advocates the following:

1. Buy stocks when they are on the way up but not on the way down. When you buy more, you do it only after the stock has risen above your purchase price, not after it is fallen below the purchase price.
2. Buy stocks when they are nearer to their highs for the year, not when they look cheap and are at their low. Buy higher-priced better-quality stocks rather than the lowest-price stocks.
3. You learn to always sell stocks quickly when you have a small 7% or 8% loss rather than waiting and hoping that they will come back. Many will not.
4. What was most striking to me was his recommendation that, historically, book value, dividends, and price-to-earnings ratio have little value, and the focus should be on historically proven factors, such as strong earnings and sales growth, price and volume action, and whether the company is the profit leader in its field with the superior new product.
5. He recommends against relying on market newsletters or advisory services and not being influenced by analysts, or, worse yet, friends.
6. He relies strongly on daily, weekly, and monthly price and volume charts, which he views as an invaluable tool.
7. He insists that you must use time-tested sell rules, which tell you when to sell a stock and take your worthwhile gains. He also indicates that you need buy-and-sell rules that help you determine when to enter the general market and lower your percent of capital invested.

The book provides 100 historical examples of stocks that have done well. However, where he differs from my selection process is his reliance on the technical aspects of the stock, by ignoring the 50 dma and 200 dma and focusing instead on just the price of the stock and its volume. He has noted 105 examples in the charts of a pattern that he calls "cups with handles." He reports that there are eight other distinctively different but repetitive chart patterns that appear cycle after cycle. One of these patterns is called the "high, tight flag pattern." He also reports that the use of charts plus earnings help you differentiate the best stocks in general markets from riskier stocks and markets. As described earlier, he uses pattern recognition and studies successful stocks. By studying the characteristics of successful stocks, you can determine whether the same characteristics are present in the stock you are considering for purchase.

O'Neil exhorts the reader to focus on stocks with big increases in sales, earnings, and returns on equity, plus a strong chart pattern. He feels that proper evaluation of chart patterns reveals institutional buying, which can significantly improve returns.[23] Interestingly, this is the same rationale offered by Farrell, that is, try to recognize what the institutional buyers are doing. By evaluating the 100 historical charts, beginning with Richmond and Danville in 1885, through the 2007 evaluation of Mosaic, he points out numerous cups with handles that appear in the charts. He illustrates these cup-with-handle chart patterns, which range in time from three weeks to nearly a year, as was the case with the evaluation of Taser in 2003. He also lists several stocks with multiple cup-with-handle patterns. The most consistent finding I saw when reviewing his charts was that the vast majority of the stock prices were above the 50 dma and were nearly always above the 200 dma. An example of a cup-with-handle stock chart pattern is shown in Figure 9.1.

The cup with handle is a bullish continuation pattern that marks a consolidation period followed by a breakout. It was developed by William O'Neil and introduced in his 1988 book, *How to Make Money in Stocks*. As its name implies, there are two parts to the pattern: the cup and the handle. The cup forms after an advance and looks like a bowl or rounding bottom. As the cup is completed, a trading range develops on the right-hand side and the handle is formed. A subsequent breakout from the handle's trading range signals a continuation of the prior advance.[24]

> The reader is cautioned not to rely on any information provided in this example for making decisions about trading any security. Please refer to the **Caution—Limitations and Difficulties** section found at the end of the first chapter.

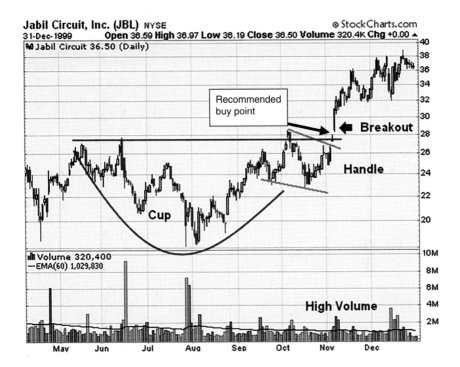

Figure 9.1   Example of cup with handle. Chart courtesy of StockCharts.com.

O'Neil also continues the use of a medical analogy, feeling that stock charts are equivalent to CAT scans, MRIs, and x-rays. He feels that thorough evaluation of chart patterns is essential before investing in the company and that the graphs of economic indicators assist with their interpretation. In order to determine whether a stock is healthy and under accumulation or if it is behaving in a weak fashion, he recommends looking at stock price and volume history on charts. He views chart patterns as a factual price performance of the stock. O'Neil feels the secret to investing is being able to decode the meaning of price movements on charts. He offers insight into the creation of chart patterns by saying that they are formed as a result of corrections in the general market the vast majority of the time. He advises against buying stock merely because it has good fundamental characteristics like strong earnings and sales. O'Neil feels that a stock chart can offer information on the proper position of the company, which allows an investor to determine the proper time to buy or sell the security. Like all good scientists, he recommends a retrospective analysis, looking for common patterns, the so-called pattern recognition that we discussed in earlier chapters. He feels that history repeats itself in the stock market and attributes this to understanding human nature and the law of supply and demand. This may in part explain the sheep mentality that was also discussed earlier.

O'Neill feels that the most common stock pattern, and also the most important one, is the cup with handle. He says that cup patterns last from 7 to 65 weeks, with most of them lasting three to six months. He says that the price variation from the absolute peak gains (top of the cup) on the left-hand side of the graph and the price of the stock may fall 12% to 15% but can fall as much as 33%. When the stock reaches its nadir (the very bottom of the curve) the shape of the cup should be U-shaped rather than a very narrow V. The depth of the cup should be 30% or less of the previous advance. However, with volatile markets and overreactions, this depth could be as great as 40%. The sustained time at the low price of the stock discourages unsure traders and diverts the attention of speculators away from the stock.

He cautions that the handle is a very important part of the decision-making process, and stocks that have a persistent climb in price are less likely to sustain this rise compared to stocks that emerge from the cup and then have a handle-like effect. The handle represents the final correction or sell-off before a major breakout and can have a fall in price up to one-third of the recent advance, but usually not more. The smaller the handle, the more bullish the formation and more significant the breakout. It is at the end of the handle phase that he recommends purchasing the stock (see Figure 9.1). He attributes this again to human nature, since there is a natural inclination to sell off a stock after a dramatic increase in price. This creates a handle-like effect, since stocks tend to fall 5–15% beyond their breakout prices. Most importantly, he feels that cups without a handle phase have a higher percentage of failures than stocks that have a cup-with-handle pattern. Despite that, he feels that stocks can advance without having a handle pattern.

One of O'Neil's most important concepts is that he follows the pattern of the stock price and volume, rather than the 50 dma and 200 dma. In fact, he doesn't mention daily moving averages at all, except to say that when a handle forms, it should be above the stock's 10-week moving average price line. Coupled with attention to the stock price is the attention to the volume of shares traded. O'Neil recommends that the daily volume should increase at least 40–50% above normal, although he indicates that during major breakouts it's not uncommon for new market leaders to show volume spikes of 200%, 500%, or even 1,000% greater than the average daily volume. He remarks that "in almost all cases it is professional institutional buying that causes the big above-average volume increases in the better priced, better quality growth-oriented stocks and pivot breakouts." Contrary to the commonly held belief of "buy low and sell high," O'Neil feels that 95% of the general public is afraid to buy stock at its very high price, although this is a strong indication that there is institutional buying power behind the stock that is driving the price even higher. Again, just like Farrell, he is recommending understanding the institutional buying mentality. If you can read the charts to find an indication of what the institutions are doing, you can duplicate or even outperform institutions. However, the most telling comment in all of O'Neil's book is where he says, "Your objective isn't to buy at the cheapest price or near the low, but to begin buying at exactly the right time, when your chances for success are greatest. This means that you have to learn to wait for stock to move up and trade at your buy point before you make an initial commitment. If you work and cannot watch the market constantly, small quote devices or quotes available on cell phones and websites will help you stay on top of potential breakout points."[25]

This statement is significant and powerful. It is the demarcation point between a trader and an investor. There are very few private investors who have the time or inclination to monitor the stock market on an hourly basis, as recommended by O'Neil. With the volume of shares currently traded on the New York Stock Exchange, and the speed with which transactions occur, no single individual investor can hope to compete with institutional investors. In fact, it was rumored that many brokerage houses move their operations closer to Wall Street, and the New York Stock Exchange, to take advantage of the speed at which they receive information on market activity, compared to having an office at a more remote location. The speed advantage they were hoping to achieve by being located closer to the New York Stock Exchange? It was less than 30 milliseconds.

Perhaps Nick Baumann tells the story of fast stock trades best.[26] He reports that stock exchanges can now execute trades in less than a half a millionth of a second. Financial firms employ sophisticated algorithms to make a profit of fractions of a cent more. Designed by the computer programmers who are known as quants, these programs capitalize on minute movements and long-term patterns in the markets. As an example, they buy a stock at $1.00 and sell it at $1.0001 a few thousands of a second later. If you do this trade 10,000 times a second, the proceeds add up. Constantly moving in and out of securities for those tiny profits, and ending the day owning nothing, is known as high-frequency trading.

There is a company called Spread Networks that specializes in high-frequency trades. Spread Networks is part of a growing industry dedicated to providing hyperspeed connections for financial firms. A faster trader can sell at a higher price and buy at a lower one because he gets there first. One estimate reports that a connection that is just one millisecond faster than the competition's could boost a high-speed firm's earnings by as much as $100 million per year. Because of this, trading firms are increasingly pushing the limits to establish the fastest connections between trading hubs like New York, Chicago, London, and other major exchanges globally. Every extra foot of fiber-optic cable adds about 1.5 nanoseconds of delay; each additional mile adds 8 microseconds. That is why companies like Spread Networks have linked financial centers to each other by the shortest routes possible.

This rapid turnover has reduced the average holding period of a stock. Half a century ago it was eight years, but today it is around five days. Most experts agree that high-speed trading algorithms are now responsible for more than half of US trading. Computer programs send and cancel orders tirelessly in a never-ending campaign to deceive and outrace each other, or sometimes just to slow each other down. They might also flood the market with bogus trade orders to throw off competitors, or stealthily liquidate a large stock position in a manner that doesn't provoke a price swing. It's a world where investing—if that's what you call buying and selling a company's stock within a matter of seconds—often comes down to how fast you can purchase or offload it, not how much the company is actually worth.

One of the first firms to use the high-frequency trading (HFT) technique was Renaissance Technologies, and it was quickly followed by KCG, IMC, Virtu Financial, Citadel LLC, Tower Research Capital, and Tradebot. Some research indicated that there are about 20,000 high-frequency trading firms operating today, which is only 2% of the market, but they account for 73% of all equity order volume.

The Bank of England suggests that European HFT activity accounts for about 40% of equity order volume. Even though the percentage of volume in the equity markets traded by HFT has fallen, it has remained a major force in the futures markets. In 2012, according to a study by the TABB Group, HFT accounted for more than 60% of all futures market volume in 2012 on US exchanges.[27]

No less an authority than Michael Spence, former dean of Stanford University's Graduate School of Business and a Nobel prize winner (2001) in Economic Science, has advocated outlawing high-frequency trading (25) at a conference sponsored by the International Monetary Fund (IMF) (Macro and Growth Policies in the Wake of the Crisis).[28] Dr. Spence feels that focusing on just inflation is not enough. Stability of financial systems requires much more oversight.

Spence laid out four post-conference points to consider, but the point most pertinent to this book is his opinion that high-frequency trading should be banned.[29] The algorithmic method of computer trading makes up as much as 70% of all equity volume in the United States. These type of trades result in "flash crashes," starting with the most notable on May 6, 2010, when the Dow Jones Industrial Average dropped nearly 1,000 points in less than 10 minutes. The SEC report showed that a single brokerage house tried to sell $4.5 billion of S&P 500 futures. The role of ETFs in this event created a needed for more controls over this practice. The Commodity Futures Trading Commission panel recommended that trading firms adhere to a set of standards, but then begrudgingly admitted that any rules would be impossible to enforce. Any controls are unpopular with financial institutions. Banks value their high-frequency source codes and aggressively protect them. The two most notable cases of attempted code theft have resulted in recent prison sentences. As I mentioned in my lecture before the Bank of England, a former Goldman Sachs computer programmer, Sergey Aleynikov, was sentenced to eight years in prison after he was arrested and accused of stealing Goldman Sachs' secret algorithmic trading code. In a similar case in France, a former Société Générale SA trader was sentenced to three years in prison for stealing the French bank's code. Therefore, since enforcement is virtually impossible, and with billions of dollars of profits to the banks and brokerage houses, self-regulation would not be supported. Spence feels that one way to protect the abuses created by high-frequency trading codes is to just ban them.

Michael Spence and Fred Hu offer the following insight:

With the entire global economy becoming inextricably linked to the Internet and digital technologies, stronger regulation is more important than ever. But if that regulation is fragmented, clumsy, heavy-handed, or inconsistent, the consequences for economic integration—and, in turn, prosperity—could be severe.[30]

Further complicating electronic trading are the securities issues with brokerage houses in general. In the book *Under Attack*, Robert Boles recommends brokerage houses protect themselves by the following methods.[31]

1. Have an attorney-approved written security and employee use policy
2. Follow the policies that are in place
3. Schedule regular DR testing
4. Schedule regular security audits
5. Limit user privileges
6. Filter spams and malicious emails in the cloud
7. Maintain best practices update cycles
8. Have an incident response plan
9. Ensure that archiving systems are functioning properly
10. Test backup systems monthly
11. Take inventory of each component of security systems
12. Stop believing it won't happen to you

High-frequency trading aside, if you really want a lesson in stock charts and their meaning, I highly recommend going to https://stockcharts.com/school/doku.php?id=chart_school: chart_analysis:chart_patterns. The StockCharts.com website has a wealth of useful information, presented in an easily understood fashion. They offer tutorials on various charts, called Chart Schools. They have a list of common chart patterns that can be useful in technical analysis. Following is a list of their patterns, offered with a disclaimer about their interpretation that reads, "Note that we have classified these chart patterns as to whether they are *typically* reversal or continuation patterns, but many can indicate either a reversal or a continuation, depending on the circumstances."

Reversal Patterns
- Double Top Reversal
- Double Bottom Reversal
- Head-and-Shoulders Top
- Head-and-Shoulders Bottom
- Falling Wedge
- Rising Wedge
- Rounding Bottom
- Triple Top Reversal
- Triple Bottom Reversal
- Bump-and-Run Reversal

Continuation Patterns
- Flag, Pennant
- Symmetrical Triangle
- Ascending Triangle
- Descending Triangle
- Rectangle
- Price Channel
- Measured Move—Bullish
- Measured Move—Bearish
- Cup with Handle

While a number of traders have different philosophies from investors, there are some similarities worth noting. Gil Morales and Dr. Chris Kacher, in their book *Trade Like an O'Neil Disciple: How We Made 18,000% in the Stock Market*, outline several techniques and rules that sound more like those of an investor than a trader.[32] Probably their most telling admonition is the quote from their mentor and teacher, Bill O'Neil: "Human nature being what it is, 90% of the people in the stock market—professionals and amateurs alike—simply haven't done enough homework."[33]

I think that is one statement with which we can all agree. Everyone is in a hurry today. Everyone wants short sound bites. Everyone wants instant gratification. Take Twitter as an example. Even if you are the president, you have only 140 characters to convey your message, and only 9% of all tweets reach that limit in English (the average length of a tweet in Japanese is 15 characters, and only 0.4% of tweets hit the 140-character limit).[34]

Tweeting aside, it seems that most people do not take the time to thoroughly research a stock before purchasing it—or shorting it. They want shortcuts. O'Neil, Morales, and Kacher all caution against this by once again using medical analogies. They observe that most investors "dabble in the market" but caution "they would rarely dabble in medical or legal practice. . . ." As William O'Neil said, "Outstanding stockbroker or advisory services are no more frequent than outstanding doctors."[35] Essentially, he says proficiency in any profession is the results of years of study, practice, hard work, and persistence. Morales and Kacher advance and reinforce some of the same principles advocated by O'Neil. They recommend buying expensive, not cheap, stocks. The psychology of the reverse of this behavior is the natural human inclination of a lazy investor to view a high-price stock that dropped in price as a bargain, rather than understanding the reason the stock dropped in price. This same rationale applies to another move by novices, which is "averaging down." People tend to fall in love with a stock, and when a stock they bought at one price drops, they average down and buy more. This is similar to dollar cost averaging, often applied to mutual funds by less skilled brokers, roundly disparaged by O'Neil.

Part of this behavior of sticking with a stock is explained by the natural psychological inclination to avoid changes and be stressed by new events. Interestingly, a change in a positive direction can be just as stressful as a negative change. This phenomenon has been well described by Hans Selye, MD, where he terms positive events that represent a change in a person's life as "eustress" while negative events that change a person's life are "distress."[36] When it comes to investing, if an investor has spent some time learning about a stock and investing emotional energy, as well as his money, into it, then he is going to be resistant to letting go of it. Often, brokers term this "getting married to a stock." Understanding this basic aspect of human psychology helps to explain the behavior described above.

This leads to another issue facing investors, which is "cutting losses quickly."[37] Various investment advisors recommend a stop loss ranging between 6% and 10% to limit the potential loss in the market, since all these advisors feel that losses are always difficult to make up. The flipside of this is taking profits too soon. All the advisors recommend following the market. Obviously, there is a great temptation to take a profit and run, but then what? The investor would have to find another winner. So, Morales, Kacher, and O'Neil recommend staying with a stock if the market is "acting right" and the stock is "acting right." They call this "letting the winners run."

Morales and Kacher offer another insight when they address market concentration. They advance the notion of handling a winning stock correctly by addressing position size. They feel that if you use small market positions, your portfolio will act like a market index and you will have average market returns. For this reason, they recommend avoiding a very diverse portfolio, with scores of stocks, which they term "pocket indexing." This is behaving just like a mutual fund manager, with only 1% to 2% of their portfolio in each individual stock but holding 100 or more stocks in their portfolio. This is analogous to going to a roulette table at a casino and betting every number with a single chip, because if that single number hits, you get back 35-to-1 odds. That's a fantastic return, until you realize that there are 38 numbers on a roulette table (36 numbers, 0, and 00). It doesn't take long to lose all your money that way. Morales and Kacher report that at times they have been fully invested in only two stocks and expand their portfolio by using full margin buying to wind up with 200% of invested capital in just two stocks (p. 8).[38] They feel that most investors overdiversify.

One way to do well in the market is to read the investment patterns of institutions. When the large institutions begin to accumulate a stock, the price just keeps climbing, based on their own in-house research, and it takes big purchases to push up stock prices. One of the ways of spotting these trends is the use of charts. Some investors look at stock volume and price, some look at 50 dmas and 200 dmas, and some use charts almost to the exclusion of other data, which earns them the title of a "chartist."

Morales and Kacher offer six basic principles of short selling, which they call "The Golden Rules of Short Selling," which comply with the O'Neil approach.[39] They advance the notion that when the bull market has topped and begins to "roll over," it is the result of changes in "big stock" leadership decisions and has far-reaching implications for the market in general.[40] In effect, this type of leadership led the market on the upside, so it stands to reason that this leadership will lead the market on the downside. They recommend focusing their short selling on the few big winning stocks, which had huge price moves in the bull market. In effect, what went up the fastest has the best chance of coming down the fastest. As I described in my earlier chapter on pattern recognition, Morales and Kacher focus on six patterns they have observed for stocks that should be good candidates for a short.

In Step 1, they recommend shorting only when there is a clear bear market and as early in the bear market as possible. Waiting several months may mean you miss the bear market all together, or you may be coming too late to the party.[41]

In Step 2, they recommend focusing on "big stock" leaders, which had large price increases in the preceding bull market and are showing "topping signs." This limits the choices of the best stocks to short. Again, the authors fall back on the technicals, looking for topping formations such as a head-and-shoulders top, which can take 8–12 weeks to develop. They again attribute this to the stubbornness of investors and the psychological make-up of humans. They watched the price of the stock soar, but had missed out on the skyrocket. When they see the price of this high-flying stock drop just a little, they feel that this is a good time to finally cash in on this missed opportunity. Even the brokerage houses recommend this type of stock as a strong buy when it dips, since it is now cheap. One example of this psychology was recounted by a friend of mine. He had bought some gold Krugerrands at $265 an ounce in 1999, but was soundly berated by his wife (now ex-) who claimed he didn't know anything about gold or business in general. His then-wife felt that only she and her advisors held the secret to successful investing. About seven years after he bought the gold, and about the time they separated, in 2006, he took with him the gold coins, which he sold for $650 an ounce in 2006. Of course, he couldn't resist telling that to his ex-wife. She then began to watch the gold prices, which steadily climbed to $1,000, and then $1,300, and then $1,600, and eventually reached a peak of $1,800 an ounce in 2011. She felt she had missed out on an opportunity. However, when the price dropped to $1,600 an ounce in 2012, she did exactly what Morales and Kacher predicted she would do, because of human nature. She did what most people do. She saw the drop in price of the high-flying commodity as an opportunity to get in gold, since she had missed the earlier meteoric rise. She bought the Krugerrands at $1,599 an ounce, which she felt was cheap, and mentioned to her ex-husband that she was now going to make money on gold as well. And when it went back to $1,800 an ounce in 2013, she reported that to him. When gold prices fell back to $1,600 an ounce, later in 2013, she held on, because gold had bounced back once before. At the time of this writing, gold is hovering around $1,200 an ounce, and my friend has wisely not said anything to his ex-wife. The graph in Figure 9.2 represents the price fluctuation. I mention this example of gold, even though it is not a stock, to demonstrate that the psychological factors that enter into stock market trades are also applicable to other aspects of life and should be taken into consideration. The similarity of the gold price chart and the stock price chart (Figure 9.3) demonstrating the head-and-shoulders pattern should be obvious.

> The reader is cautioned not to rely on any information provided in this example for making decisions about trading any security. Please refer to the **Caution—Limitations and Difficulties** section found at the end of the first chapter.

"A head-and-shoulders pattern contains three successive peaks with the middle peak (head) being the highest and the two outside peaks (shoulders) being low and roughly equal. The reaction lows of each peak can be connected to form support, or a neckline"

Figure 9.2   20-Year gold price in USD/oz.

Figure 9.3   Head-and-shoulders reversal.

Chart courtesy of StockCharts.com.

(https://stockcharts.com/school). Stockcharts.com offers a more comprehensive explanation and cautions that stock trading volume also influences interpretation of a head-and-shoulders pattern.

Morales and Kacher's Step 3 is timing the short sale 8–12 weeks after a stock's peak price following a major increase in price. They offer some insight into the anatomy of this type of trade. They report that most big stock traders are fairly liquid with trading volumes in excess of 1–2 million shares. They recommend that a short-sale candidate have more than 2 million shares traded daily, because anything less is too thinly traded and subject to rapid price run-ups. Again, this information is based on the knowledge of how the big traders on the stock market function.

This concept leads to Step 4, which is to stick with stocks trading more than 2 million shares a day, since risk correlates inversely with a stock's trading liquidity. The larger the trading, the lower the risk. For that reason, a stop loss on a short position should not be more than 3–5%. This is a personal preference that is dependent on the size of a position, personal psychology, and risk tolerance.

So based on the previous steps, Step 5 recommends using the 3% stop loss if a stock begins to rally against you. Again, the stop-loss spot is dependent on risk tolerance and personal psychology. Along these lines, they recommend setting 20–30% profit targets, or even lower, in fact as little as 15%, if you are worried that a rally might wipe out your profit. They suggest using the 20-day moving average for a trailing upside stop that is showing a decent profit.

Finally, in Step 6, they recommend using the 20 dma, but also the 50 dma and 200 dma, as a guide for readjusting the stop-loss price.

Morales and Kacher then explore several common failings of the small investor, which are falling back on emotions; relying on predictions; listening to opinions, news, and tips; and overtrading. The most important concept, however, is that of timing the market. They advocate following the trends in the market and having the patience to wait for a trend to develop and then jumping on it when it does. As in all things in life, timing is everything. However, in reviewing their writings, there seems to be a certain amount of anthropomorphism attributed to the market. There is some validity to this approach, since, after all, the market is controlled by human beings, fraught with the full range of human emotions, fears, greed, uncertainty, and herd mentality. As the electronic trading systems begin to intrude on the operation of the market, less and less of this behavior becomes obvious, until we step back to think . . . who programmed the electronic trading systems?

I have now explored three trading systems: my personal techniques, the day trading technique, and the highly touted O'Neil technique. Sorting out the similarities and differences can be most confusing, so I have created a table (see Table 9.1) comparing and contrasting the various approaches. I hope this will be of some help in understanding the various ways to approach the stock market.

The entire concept behind my investing philosophy is to take advantage of the potential profit from long positions. As I have mentioned before, I take proceeds from short sales and apply them to purchase long positions with good growth potential. Very often, I have paper losses in my short sales. But bear in mind, a real loss does not occur until I cover my short. However, I worry less about the prices of the short than I do about the growth in my long positions. As long as my long positions increase in value in excess of

Table 9.1   Investing for the Long Term versus Trading for the Short Term

	Investing	Trading	O'Neil Investing
1.	Holds the short as long as proceeds from short sales diverted to the long positions are profitable: weeks to years	Tries to make money on a short sale using stop losses to limit losses	Makes money on longs in a bull market and on shorts in a bear market
2.	Evaluates fundamentals of a company as well as technicals	Less regard for fundamentals and more reliance on technicals	Absolutely no use for book value, P/E ratio, and dividends
3.	Individual evaluations of equities	Relies on patterns analyzed by artificial intelligence programs	Relies heavily on technicals
4.	Holds longs and short positions for the long term: sometimes for years	Automatic trading: shorts and longs held for seconds	Tries to time the market to buy/sell
5.	Does not use ETFs	Uses ETFs	Sets stop losses at 5–10%
6.	Active management	Uses indexes to invest	Active management
7.	Evaluates many factors affecting the decision about shorting for the long term and diverting proceeds to long positions	Focuses on just sales, earnings, return on equity, and chart patterns	Trades longs and shorts independently Tries to profit on both independently
8.	Considers 50-day and 200-day moving averages in evaluation as well as other technical patterns	Relies on technical patterns to time the market	Focuses on just stock price and volume traded
9.	As an investor, you are less affected by daily and short-term market fluctuations.	Requires constantly monitoring the market as a trader, and becoming sensitive to hourly fluctuations	Requires constant monitoring
10.	Invests for the long term, so no need for day trades	Requires constant monitoring daily, if not hourly, to get the best trade	Times trades to market swings
11.	Makes money by increasing long positions using proceeds from shorts to buy longs: investing for the long term	Tries to make money on short sales or long sales or options: trading short-term	No relationship between long and short trading; stop losses of 3–5% on shorts and 5–10% on longs
12.	Understands what institutional investors are doing and tries to follow the trends	No interest in long-term trends of institutional investors	Understands what institutional investors are doing and tries to time sales or purchase

Consistency on short-term trading is difficult to achieve and cannot match the results of the long-term approach.

any expenses I might have in the short, I am ahead. I cover the short when the performance of the long position has slowed and the potential increase in performance is not sustainable. This strategy of enhancing long positions is optimized in a bull market, and in case there is a bear market, the shorts provide a hedge during that time.

Having said that, the next question is pretty obvious: How do I get money to purchase long positions and the stock that I think is going to appreciate? There are a variety of answers.

1. If an investor has cash on hand, the investor can simply use the cash to purchase a stock which the investor thinks is going to appreciate.
2. If an investor has cash on hand but doesn't want to take cash out of their account, the investor can do a "passbook loan."
3. An investor can sell a stock that they think is fully appreciated and use the proceeds to purchase the new stock that they think is going to appreciate even more.
4. If an investor does not have a ready supply of cash, they can buy the stock on margin if it is a qualified account (not an IRA or other restricted accounts).
5. If an investor thinks the stock is going to go up, they can buy a call on the stock.
6. If an investor thinks the stock is going to go up, they can sell a put on the stock.
7. An investor can sell a short on a stock that they think is going to decline and use the proceeds from the short to purchase a long position in the stock that they think is going to climb.

Each of these seven methods has certain advantages, certain expenses, and a certain degree of risk associated with it. Let us explore the pros and cons of each one of the methods. This will help you decide which method is best for you, based on your risk tolerance and investment needs.

Use Cash: This is the simplest mechanism of all. If you're lucky enough to have extra cash that is not being used, and you don't need a cash reserve, then the only cost of this type of transaction is the interest you will no longer receive if you take the cash out of your account.

Passbook Loan: This is a strange little mechanism that banks often recommend, in which you borrow money from yourself. You're being paid interest on your cash in the bank, but then you borrow from yourself and pay interest on the amount you borrow. Usually, the way banks make money on this type of transaction is with the transaction fees and the spread between the loan interest and interest on the cash in the account. This is a classic arbitrage situation.

Sell a Stock: This is a classic conflict. You may have made money on the stock and want to take your profit to invest in another stock. This raises a whole series of questions, as described by O'Neil and myself earlier in this chapter. Has the stock you plan to sell reached its maximum potential? Will the stock you plan to purchase grow as fast as the stock you are selling? If you hold the stock for less than six months, will your short-term capital gains tax on the profit reduce the value of this type of transaction? Associated with this transaction are brokers' fees for the sale of the original stock and for the purchase of the new stock. What guarantee is there that the newly purchased stock will not fall? Think of my physician friend who bought gold at $265, and sold it at a profit at $650 an ounce. When his ex-wife got in at $1,599 and watched it go to $1,800, then plunge to $1,200, in reality, he had not fared any better. When he sold at $650, he then had to find a comparable investment that would grow as fast and far as the gold. Had he held to $1,800 or $1,599 or even at $1,200, he would have made much more money than the $650 level at which he sold. He did invest the proceeds from the $650 sales price into a stock that went down so far that he has about as much money as he had when he initially invested in the gold. His net gain was nothing, which demonstrates that if you have faith in an investment, and a rationale for purchasing a stock is still valid, do not sell. When you have a good investment, hang on. There were reasons you bought the stock in the first place, and if those reasons are still in place, then there is room for growth in the stock. So, if you don't want to sell an appreciated stock, what other methods can you use for stock purchase?

Buy on Margin: Buying on margin is borrowing money from a brokerage house to purchase a stock. Margin trading allows you to buy stock in excess of the amount of cash in your account. A margin account is different from a regular cash account. The buying power of a margin account changes daily, depending on the price movement of the marginable securities in the account.

The brokerage house is required to obtain your signature and to get a minimum amount of money (usually $2,500) to open a margin account. The margin account may be part of your standard account opening agreement or may be a completely separate agreement. Once the account is operational, you can borrow up to 50% of the purchase price of a stock, if you have enough cash in your account. The portion of the purchase price that you deposit is known as the initial margin. You do not have to margin all your account at once.

You can keep your loan open as long as you want as long as you meet your obligations. First, when you sell the stock in a margin account, the proceeds go to your broker to repay the loan until it is fully paid. Second, there is a maintenance margin, which is the minimum balance you must have before your broker will force you to deposit more funds or sell stock to reduce your loan. If the value of your marginable account decreases, there will be a margin call from the broker. If you do not have enough cash in the account, the brokerage house will first ask for more money, but, if you fail to provide this cash, then the brokerage house expects you to sell positions to satisfy the margin call. If you fail to provide either, then the brokerage house can sell your positions as they wish.

You also must pay the interest on your loan. The interest charges are applied to your account unless you decide to make payments. Over time, your debt level increases as interest charges increase, because they are compounded. Therefore, buying on margin is best used for short-term investments. The longer you hold an investment, the more interest you are going to pay, so you need a greater return to offset compounding interest charges. If you hold an investment on margin for a long period of time, you reduce your chance for a profit. Individual brokerages may also decide not to margin certain risky stocks.

Buy a Call Option: When you buy a call option, you need to be able to calculate your breakeven point to see if you really want to make a trade. The components of buying a call option are the current price of the stock, the length of the call option, the strike price at which the call option can be exercised, which determines the price of the call option, and the volatility of the stock, which also determines the price of the call option. If the current price of a stock you want to buy is $50, and the price of a three-month call option is $2.50, then the stock you picked has to go to at least $54 before the call option expires in three months for you to break even. The costs associated with buying a call option are (1) the cost of the call option ($2.50), then (2) the brokerage fee to buy the call option ($.50), and if you are lucky enough to have the stock you picked go up above $53.75 in three months, (3) the commission for buying the stock ($1). Only the most popular stocks have call options.

Therefore, not many stocks are optionable. There is no set percentage of the current price of a stock to determine the sales price of the call option. The call option price is determined totally on a supply-and-demand basis. Typically, a three-month option of the New York Stock Exchange–traded stock carries a 5% strike price. If the price of a three-month call option is less than 5% of the current value of the stock, then not many people are expecting the stock to reach the strike price within three months. If the price of the three-month call option is more than 5% of the current price, then you know a lot of people are expecting that stock to rise in price and the call option costs increase accordingly. As you might expect, option prices are a function of the price of the stock, the "strike price," the length of the call (three months, six months, one year or a "leap," which is one, two, or three years), and the overall volatility of the stock. While the stock price, strike price, and length of option are obvious parameters, the number of call option contracts traded and all the other factors mentioned in this book determine the increase or decline and therefore the price of the stock and its associated call option. Most authorities report that the vast majority of all call options are either traded before expiration date or expired without being exercised, and therefore are worthless.

Sell a Put Option: This is one of the most interesting ways of purchasing a stock. This method works if you have extra cash and the discipline to wait for a stock to reach a certain price. Once you have determined that you wish to purchase a stock, you can sell a put option on the stock, which is essentially the reverse of buying a call. Instead of paying a broker a fee for the option of purchasing a stock at a certain price for a limited period of time, you are selling someone else the option of selling a stock to you at a prearranged price for a limited period of time. For the privilege of having a set selling price, some other investor buys a put option. This means the investor can sell the stock within a certain period for a prearranged price, regardless of the price of the stock at the time that he sells it. Most investors buy a put option to protect the downside of their investment. This put option allows an investor to limit any losses they may experience. So if another investor purchases a stock at $50 a share and wants to be certain that he can always sell the stock at $50 a share, regardless of the price of the stock within a certain period of time, he buys a put option. Just like a call, a put option has a fixed strike price and a certain period during which the put option can be exercised. Selling a put option allows an investor to establish the floor, or established price, for which he is selling the stock. Basically, this is like an insurance policy. The other investor is guaranteed that he can sell a stock at a given price, and is willing to pay for this option by buying a put option. Alternately, the other investor may be worried that the stock is going to drop in price, so by buying a put option he is guaranteed to always get at least a certain price for the stock. This can work to your advantage if you want to buy the stock. If a stock is selling at $50 a share and you think the price is going to go up or even stay the same, you sell a put option on that stock. Essentially, you get paid for guaranteeing that you will purchase the stock at $50 a share, within a given period of time (the term of the option). If the stock you picked is not volatile and remains around the $50 price without much fluctuation, you could expect to get 5% on the value of the stock every three months by selling puts on the stock. If the stock drops below $44 a share, then it is worthwhile for the other investor to put the stock to you at $50 a share, and you are obliged to purchase it at $50 a share, where you incur a loss. If the stock goes to $60 a share within the option period, then you have lost your opportunity to purchase the stock at $50 a share but have still made money by selling the put option.

Sell a Short Position: This is the method I use to purchase a long position in the stock that I think is going to appreciate. It is my method of generating extra cash to make a long purchase. I do not have to take money from my savings account; I do not have to borrow money from my savings account; I do not have the risk of a margin call; I do not have the time limitations imposed on me which I would otherwise have by using put or call options; and finally, I am using the proceeds from the short sales to purchase long positions that I think will appreciate. I am not focused on making money on shorts like other short sellers, who are trying to make money on only short sales. Finally, this method provides a hedge in a bear market.

The various approaches to buying a long position are summarized in Table 9.2.

Hypothetical Example of Shorting for the Long Term

(This is not a recommendation to buy, sell, short, or cover a short. This example is for demonstration purposes only.)

Table 9.2   Various Approaches to Buying a Long Position

	Cash	Passbook Loan	Stock Sale	Mar-gin	Buy a Call	Sell a Put	Sell a Short
Lost use of money	Yes	No	No	No	Yes	No	No
Bank transaction fees	No	Yes	No	No	No	No	No
Broker transaction fees	No	No	Yes	Yes	Yes	Yes	Yes
Pay loan interest	No	Yes	No	Yes	No	No	Yes
Pay short-term capital gain	No	No	Yes or no	No	No	Yes	Yes
Pay long-term capital gain	No	No	Yes or no	No	No	No	No
Pay dividend to owner	No	No	No	No	No	No	Yes
Transaction can expire	No	No	No	No	Yes	Yes	No
Transaction can be called*	No	No	No	Yes	No	No	Yes

* Short squeeze, being acquired, being called in

The reader is cautioned not to rely on any information provided in this example for making decisions about trading any security. Please refer to the **Caution—Limitations and Difficulties** section found at the end of the first chapter.

This following scenario is a totally hypothetical example, for illustration purposes only, of **shorting for the long term**. It gives you a model for the strategy I use. This scenario did not happen; it is a case study model.

Make no mistake about it . . . Amazon has a great fundamental picture and a good technical picture. I mention this stock individually for illustrative purposes, because the reader can see the performance of Amazon as a growth company. A number of investment advisors recommended purchasing Amazon in 2016. Based on this, an investor is motivated to increase his position in Amazon.com (AMZN). Where does he get the cash to increase the position?

1. September 28, 2016. Amazon.com/AMZN/"NSDAQ" Today's price: $827.58 52wk H. 828.97 52wk L. 474.00 Mkt Cap: $390.69B, P/E: 204.95, Beta: 1.64
2. November 30, 2016. Amazon.com/AMZN/"NSDAQ" Today's price: $752.26 52wk H. 847.21 52wk L. 474.00 Mkt Cap: $362.31B, EPS: 4.36 P/E: 174.68 Div/Yld: 0.50(0.65%) (see 1 and 2 on Figure 9.4).

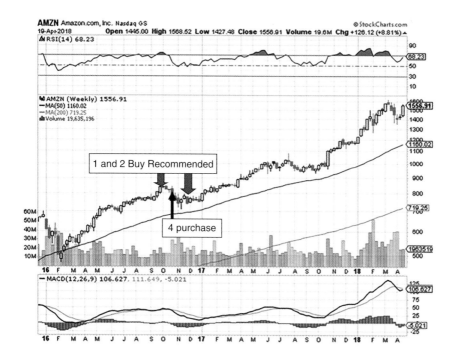

Figure 9.4   Chart courtesy of StockCharts.com.

(This is not a recommendation to buy, sell, short, or cover a short.)

The reader is cautioned not to rely on any information provided in this example for making decisions about trading any security. Please refer to the **Caution—Limitations and Difficulties** section found at the end of the first chapter.

Suppose I had already purchased Amazon on January 12, 2016, for $623.45. Even so, I would have thought that the fundamentals and technical aspects of this stock warranted increasing my position. Let us assume that I really want to increase my long position in Amazon, but I didn't have any ready. Let us also assume that I have been watching General Electric for a while and am concerned about its activity in various divisions of the company. This information is only for illustrative purposes. So, in this hypothetical example, at the end of September 2016, I might have shorted 3,000 shares of GE at $28 a share (see 3 in Figure 9.5). This provides $84,000 in proceeds, less fees, interest, and dividends, which might range to $4,000, leaving me, hypothetically, $80,000 to invest. Theoretically I could have invested approximately $80,000 in Amazon.com (AMZN) on October 15, 2016, when 100 shares of Amazon cost $800 a share, or $80,000 (4 in Figure 9.4). Alternatively, I could have selected some other growth company.

> The reader is cautioned not to rely on any information provided in this example for making decisions about trading any security. Please refer to the **Caution—Limitations and Difficulties** section found at the end of the first chapter.

From the end of September until mid-December, GE stock price increases to $30.75 (5 in Figure 9.5). I am now facing a paper loss of $30.75 – $28, or $2.75 on 3,000 shares, or $8,250—a 9.8% loss in two months, which annualizes to a 58.9% paper loss. Remember, this is not a real loss until I cover my short. I do not panic. I do not

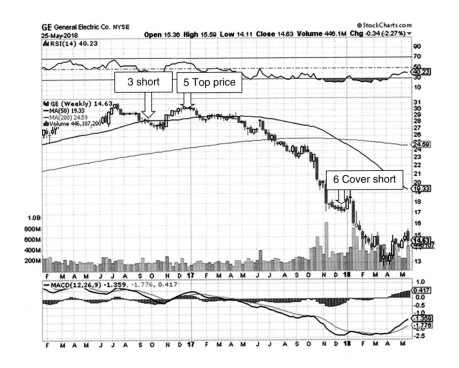

Figure 9.5   Chart courtesy of StockCharts.com.

use a stop loss. Typically, I would not cover my short. In the meantime, at the end of December 2016, Amazon.com has dropped in price to $750, so I am about even on my purchase price. Do I sell my Amazon stock to cover the paper loss in GE? **No.** Remember, I **short for the long-term**. I invest. I do not trade. I would maintain the short position, because the fundamentals of the company are not encouraging.

Let us see where this hypothetical transaction takes us. By the end of December 2017, GE has dropped in price to $17.25 a share, right after a death cross on December 1. I theoretically shorted 3,000 shares at $28, and now I theoretically cover my short at $17.25 (6 in Figure 9.5), making $10.75 a share on 3,000 shares, or a $32,250 profit on this hypothetical transaction.

In the meantime, by the end of 2017, Amazon has jumped to $1,200 a share. Theoretically, if I use the proceeds from the short on GE to buy 100 shares of Amazon at $800 a share, my paper profit is $400 a share, or $40,000. I realize this paper profit because I did not use a stop loss on the long position, just as I had not used a stop loss on the short. Taken in combination, this entire theoretical transaction would have increased a portfolio value by $40,000 + $32,250, or $72,250, over the course of a year.

Suppose an investor had selected ISRG to short, which did not produce a profit on the short, but rather produced a loss. Let us look at this hypothetical scenario (Figure 9.6).

> The reader is cautioned not to rely on any information provided in this example for making decisions about trading any security. Please refer to the **Caution—Limitations and Difficulties** section found at the end of the first chapter.

In this hypothetical scenario, an investor might have shorted ISRG on September 2016 at $225 a share (see 7 in Figure 9.6) to get $84,000, with a net of $80,000 to invest in Amazon.com. An investor would have needed to short approximately 375 shares of ISRG. So, just like the scenario with GE, an investor theoretically would have taken the $80,000 to invest in Amazon.com. However, ISRG increased in value, so that by the end of 2017, the price of ISRG was $375 a share (8 in Figure 9.6). Now, theoretically, the investor would have a paper loss of $150 a share. On 375 shares, this amounts to a paper loss of $56,250. However, during this same period of time,

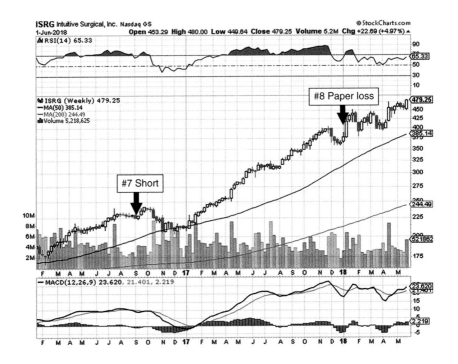

Figure 9.6   Chart courtesy of StockCharts.com.

the investor theoretically could have invested approximately $80,000 into Amazon.com (AMZN) on October 15, 2016, when 100 shares of Amazon cost $800 a share, or $80,000 (4 in Figure 9.4), and by December 2017, Amazon.com was selling at $1,200 a share. This resulted in a paper gain of $400 a share, on 100 shares, or $40,000. When the paper loss in ISRG is compared to the paper profit in Amazon.com (AMZN), the entire transaction has a paper loss of $16,250.

Notes

1. Zigler, B. (2018). Do Long/Short Equity Funds Work? *Wealth Management* (July/August), p. 19–22.
2. Rosenbluth, T. (2018). Active vs. Passive: Halftime Results. *Wealth Management* (July/August), p. 26.
3. Greene, M. (2018). *Financial News* (August 3), p. 9.
4. Metaxiotis, K.S. and Samouilidis, J.E. (2000). Expert Systems in Medicine: Academic Exercise or Practical Tool? *Journal of Medical Engineering and Technology* 24: 68–72.

5. Engelbrecht, R. (1997). Expert Systems for Medicine: Functions and Development. *Zentralblatt fur Gynakologie* 119: 428–434.
6. Babic, A. (1999). Knowledge Discovery for Advanced Clinical Data Management. *Studies in Health Technology and Informatics* 68: 409–413.
7. Schewe, S., Herzer, P., and Kruger, K. (1990). Prospective Application of an Expert System for the Medical History of Joint Pain. *Klinische Wochenschrift* 68: 466–471.
8. Ibid.
9. Schewe, S. and Schreiber, M.A. (1993). Stepwise Development of a Clinical Expert System in Rheumatology. *Clin Investigation* 71: 139–144.
10. Molino, G., Marzuoli, M., Molino, F. et al. (2000). Validation of ICTERUS, a Knowledge-Based Expert System for Jaundice Diagnosis. *Methods of Information in Medicine* 39: 311–318.
11. Camma, C., Garofalo, G., Almasio, P. et al. (1991). A Performance Evaluation of the Expert System Jaundice in Comparison with That of Three Hepatologists. *Journal of Hepatology* 13: 279–285.
12. Kentala, E., Auramo, Y., Juhola, M. et al. (1998). Comparison Between Diagnoses of Human Experts and a Neurotologic Expert System. *Annals of Otology, Rhinology, and Laryngology* 107: 135–140.
13. Kentala, E.L., Laurikkala, J.P., Viikki, K. et al. (2001). Experiences of Otoneurological Expert System for Vertigo. *Scandinavian Audiology, Supplement* 52: 90–91.
14. Sinnott, M.M., Carr, B., Markey, J. et al. (1993). Knowledge Based Lipid Management System for General Practitioners. *Clinica Chimica Acta* 222: 71–77.
15. Hendler, N., Gronblad, M., Cashen, A., LeRoy, P. et al. (2005). A Multi-Center Study for Validating the Complaint of Chronic Back, Neck and Limb Pain Using the Pain Validity Test. *Forensic Examiner* (Fall): 41–49.
16. Hendler, N., Davis, R.J. and Baker, A. (2008). An Internet Questionnaire to Determine the Presence or Absence of Organic Pathology in Chronic Back, Neck and Limb Pain Patients. *Pan Arab Journal of Neurosurgery* 12:15–24.
17. Hendler, N. (2017). An Internet Based Questionnaire to Identify Drug Seeking Behavior in a Patient in the ED and Office. *Journal of Anesthesia & Critical Care Open Access* 8: 00306.
18. Landi, A., Speed, W., Hendler, N. and Davis, R.J. (2018). Comparison of Clinical Diagnoses versus Computerized Test (Expert System) Diagnoses from the Headache Diagnostic Paradigm (Expert System). *SciFed Journal of Headache and Pain* 1:1. 1000004.
19. Hendler, N., Davis, R.J. and Berzoksky, C. (2007). Comparison of Clinical Diagnoses Versus Computerized Test Diagnoses Using the Diagnostic Paradigm (Expert System) for Diagnosing Chronic Pain in the Neck, Back and Limbs. *Pan Arab Journal of Neurosurgery* 8–17.
20. Greene, Financial News.
21. Haring, B. Define Volume in the Stock Market. Zacks. https://finance.zacks.com/define-volume-stock-market-6839.html.
22. O'Neil, W. (2009). *How to Make Money in Stocks: A Winning System in Good Times or Bad.* New York: McGraw-Hill.
23. Ibid.

24. https://stockcharts.com/school/doku.php?id=chart_school:chart_analysis: chart_patterns:cup_with_handle_continuation.

25. O'Neil, *How to Make Money in Stocks.*

26. Baumann, N. (2013). Too Fast to Fail: How Hi-Speed Trading Fuels Wall Street Disasters. *Mother Jones* (January/February). https://www.motherjones.com/politics/2013/02/high-frequency-trading-danger-risk-wall-street.

27. Grant, J. (2010). High-Frequency Trading: Up Against a Bandsaw *Financial Times* (September 2).

28. Philips, M. (2011). Should High-Frequency Trading Be Banned? One Nobel Winner Thinks So. *Freakonomics* (March 28). http://freakonomics.com/2011/03/28/should-high-frequency-trading-be-banned-one-nobel-winner-thinks-so/.

29. Ibid.

30. Spence, M. and Hu, F. (2018). Preventing the Balkanization of the Internet. Project Syndicate (March 28). https://www.project-syndicate.org/commentary/internet-regulation-must-preserve-economic-openness-by-michael-spence-and-fred-hu-2018-03.

31. Boles, R. (2015). Security Consideration for Financial Professionals. In *Under Attack*, Chapter 26, pp. 243–249. Winter Park, FL: Celebrity Press.

32. Morales, G., and Kacher, C. (2010). *Trade Like an O'Neil Disciple: How We Made 18,000% in the Stock Market.* Hoboken, NJ: Wiley.

33. Ibid., p. 3.

34. Newton, C. (2017). Twitter Just Doubled the Character Limit for Tweets to 280. *The Verge* (September 26). https://www.theverge.com/2017/9/26/16363912/twitter-character-limit-increase-280-test.

35. O'Neil, *How to Make Money in Stocks*, p. 256.

36. Selye, H. (1974). *Stress Without Distress.* Philadelphia: JP Lippincott.

37. Morales and Kacher, *Trade Like an O'Neil Disciple*, p. 3.

38. Ibid., p. 8.

39. Morales and Kacher, *Trade Like an O'Neil Disciple.*

40. Ibid., p. 187.

41. Ibid., p. 188.

CHAPTER 10

Modern Trader Charts

(**The following reprinted *Modern Trader* articles are simply an analysis of a particular securities price and volume movements, and do not represent any current recommendation for purchase or sale or short or covering short of any security. Any recommendations to buy or sell or short or cover a short that appeared in any reproduced article are not current recommendations, and should not be construed as such.)**

The reader is cautioned not to rely on any information provided in this example for making decisions about trading any security. Please refer to the **Caution—Limitations and Difficulties** section found at the end of the first chapter.

For two years I regularly wrote articles for *Modern Trader* magazine. All the articles I wrote for *Modern Trader* over those two years are reproduced here. This represents everything in print, reproduced with permission from *Modern Trader*. I have made some minor changes to the wording of these articles, to try to make them less cryptic and more grammatical than the originally published articles, but neither the content nor technical information was changed. Additionally, I included one article that was submitted but absent in print due to human error.

I did not cherry-pick these articles; every article I wrote is included. Some of the stocks made money while others lost money. Some were recommendations for long positions and others were recommendations for short positions. These articles are offered as a way of providing an insight to the thoughts behind picking a stock in real time, either to short or to purchase.

One thought to bear in mind is that shorting a stock cannot be done on technical information alone. This is best exemplified by the path of ISRG. In a report in *Modern Trader*, I focused on the technical aspects of ISRG, as you can see in the following report. This assessment, taken in isolation, worked against me. Also, the evaluation of the fundamentals led to the assumption that competition would slow earnings growth, but this did not materialize.

As you read through these articles, try to apply the parameters I described in Chapter 5, which discusses the Parnes Parameters. It will be interesting for you to determine whether your evaluation of a stock corresponded with my own. You may find that you would assign a different weight to the various factors in both the fundamentals and technical sections, or you might choose to focus more on the technical aspects of a stock than I did. As they say, "That's what makes horse races."

You could further test your application of the Parnes Parameters by reviewing one of the companies below from a historical perspective, and then try to predict what it might be doing today. Write it down . . . don't cheat. Then look at the stock performance for the past 12 months. Even if you expected something other than what actually happened, at least you will have a way of assessing your selection process.

Remember, this is not a book designed to tell you what to think. Rather, I am sharing with you how I think so that you can develop and enhance your options, becoming an informed independent investor.

ISRG (An Intuitive Surgical Short, *Modern Trader*, #529, February 2017, p. 12)

Technicals Scream Sell. ISRG took out its 50 dma and 200 dma after setting a double top in October, which coincided with breaking a trend line from the February 2016 low (upper trend line in Figure 10.1) and occurred with the record volume. The lower trend line, which was recently broken, connects the 2015 and 2016 close and corresponds with the breach in the 200 dma.

Fundamental Picture

It appears that there is a "short" circuit within the well-known surgical robotic system manufacturer Intuitive Surgical Inc. (ISRG). The Sunnyvale, California–based company is responsible for the design, manufacturing, and marketing of the da Vinci Surgical System and associated accessories. ISRG is also recognized for its EndoWrist instruments, which include surgical tools that build off the company's "hand-like" movement systems enabling surgeons to operate in complicated procedural environments through singular incisions.

ISRG has also diversified its offerings to include endoscopes and other surgical items to work with its robotic assisted systems. ISRG's main product line retails for about $1.5 million per unit, and is intended to create briefer hospitalization stays, less surgical intrusion, and less pain. The company is a primary marketer and distributor of its products but works with secondary resellers in the United States, Europe, and Asia.

The company's seemingly perfect free cash flow and its record double-digit earnings per share increase of more than 35 times this past year suggest robotic force primed for 2017. Its market cap of $24 billion and the current price/earnings ratio of 34 is signaling it may be primed to short.

In light of any overtly perceived question of its sustainability, its third-quarter earnings report shocked the Street in its revelation that there were considerable slowdowns within the urology unit. This timing is particularly ominous when viewed together with the election of Donald Trump and his commitment to repeal and replace the Affordable Care Act (Obamacare), in addition to losing competition within this niche market.

Not every hospital can afford ISRG's price point on its main product line. And there remains uncertainty over whether the price savings it produces in terms of shorter hospital stays and fewer complications is truly balanced, as well as claims its machines offset the need for superior trained surgeons.

While ISRG's products are unique, there is mounting competition from large players who are ready to take stabs at the automated industry in the healthcare sector.

Specifically, the competition from Google (GOOG) and Johnson & Johnson's (JNJ) new venture VERB aim to continue to reduce the human factor and the reliance on human skill and increase the robotic efficiency of surgeries at a lower price point.

Technical Picture

ISRG gained more than 40% in 2016 from February through September and is now in correction mode. After setting a double top at $727 in the fall, ISRG broke through both its 50-day and 200-day moving averages and is threatening a death cross as the 50-day moving average appears close to crossing below the 200-day moving average (see Figure 10.1). The failure at the double top also drove the trend line from the 2016 low.

The stop gapped lower following the US election, ending an upward correction that was threatening to move back above the 50-day moving average. Since topping in October, it has taken out support at $675 and $625, levels representing brief correction lows before the 50-day moving average (see Figure 10.1).

The breach of the 200-day moving average also corresponded closely with the break of a long-term trend line connecting the 2015 and 2016 lows. ISRG's technical weakness now warrants lower P/E multiples. In a market that may place more constraints on the healthcare sector based on a new president's aim, its technical pattern and its P/E sustainability, combined with new methods of cheaper technology and ISRG basic challenges, perhaps we'll see a test of its 2016 low near at $502.

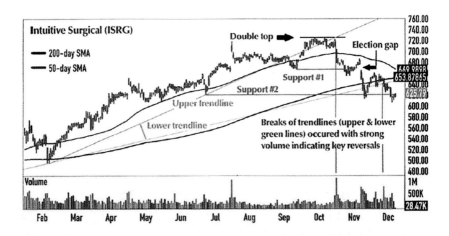

Figure 10.1   Technicals scream sell.

The reader is cautioned not to rely on any information provided in this example for making decisions about trading any security. Please refer to the **Caution—Limitations and Difficulties** section found at the end of the first chapter.

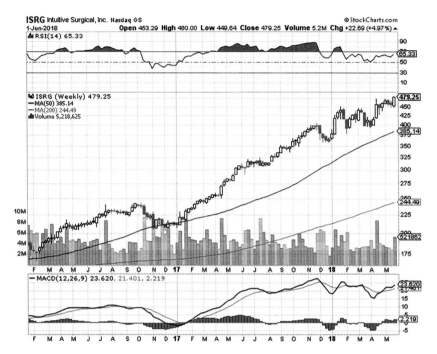

Chart courtesy of StockCharts.com

The reader is cautioned not to rely on any information provided in this example for making decisions about trading any security. Please refer to the **Caution—Limitations and Difficulties** section found at the end of the first chapter.

BHP Billiton (The BHP Bottom Isn't Near, *Modern Trader*, June 2016, #521, p. 13).

This stock was also reviewed in the December 2017 issue (Iron Ore Bust, *Modern Trader*, December 2017, #538, p. 15); however, the June 2016 issue best illustrates the rationale for a short on a purely fundamental basis, which is why this publication was used. The December 2017 article follows this one from June 2016.

Chart courtesy of StockCharts.com.

The reader is cautioned not to rely on any information provided in this example for making decisions about trading any security. Please refer to the **Caution—Limitations and Difficulties** section found at the end of the first chapter.

Fundamental Picture

After a two-year bear market in commodities, some analysts may be looking to the sector to find value. While there are certainly long opportunities out there amid the volatility in commodities, BHP Billiton Limited (formerly BHB Limited) stands out as a strong short opportunity, with more downward momentum left.

Billiton LTD (BHP) discovers, acquires, develops, and markets natural resources worldwide. Its primary commodity interests are in petroleum, coal, potash (as agricultural fertilizer), copper, and iron ore. Formed in 1851, headquartered in Melbourne, Australia, BHP's global business model has continued to expand with iron-ore extraction as one of the world's leading producers.

Although BHP's diversified commodity interests allow for a certain degree of financial hedging from individual commodity fluctuations, the recent drop in iron-ore prices is taking its toll on the company's earnings, with put options on the short side and higher risk calls. Recent spikes on March 17 and March 30 generated hope that a continued rally is in the offing. However, any specific global economic correction must be examined in tandem with the macro geopolitical and economic realities. The six-month stockpile of iron ore in China will continue to push global inventory to its highest supply levels. And while some analysts predict that increased demand for iron ore will help the HP regain momentum, the 2016 consensus predicts a 2.85% decline in demand. There are also other mitigating factors in pairing a potential iron ore rebound, making the March rebound in BHP a shorting opportunity.

China is not the only global factor driving iron ore demands down, resulting in increasing inventory and lowering expectations for BHP. The recent mud and iron-ore dam breach in Brazil, now flowing down the Rio Doce River toward the Atlantic Ocean as a result of BHP Billiton and Vale's co-venture has led to an unprecedented environmental and media branding disaster. BHP's attempt to mitigate the situation with a $262 million payout has not assuaged public anger surrounding the mining operations and future litigation could rise to upwards of $7.2 billion.

Even if you attempt to ignore these aspects—China's production of iron ore and the fallout in Brazil—worldwide iron ore production is forecast to increase. Producers' efforts to limit production may be insufficient, with iron-ore prices sinking to $30 per metric ton from a high of $60 in March 2016. As a result, BHP's earnings risk level will play a critical role in its subsequent dividend yields. Any possible reduction or elimination will force BHP to lower its dividends for the first time in 25 years (currently at 1.56 trailing 12 months or 6.08%), possibly resulting in its prices falling into lower teens.

Technical Picture

BHP's chart has been in a stair-step decline since the second half of 2014 (see Figure 10.2). A reversal from its January low under $20 recently failed as it hit resistance at $29. This downtrend step has been reestablished and a test of its previous low of $18.46 set on January 19, 2016, is likely.

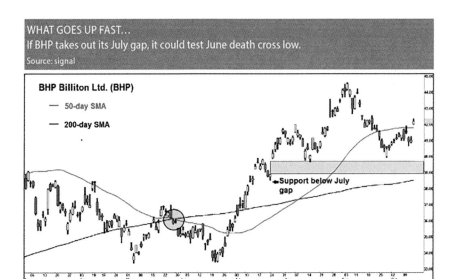

WHAT GOES UP FAST…
If BHP takes out its July gap, it could test June death cross low.
Source: signal

Figure 10.2

FAILED REBOUND

BHP failed after bouncing 50% from its fourth quarter drawdown.

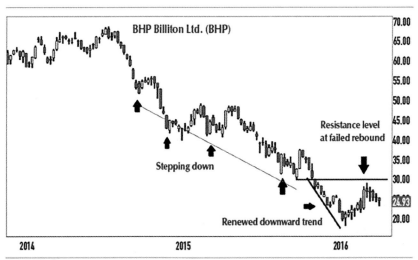

Figure 10.3   Failed rebound.

BHP Billiton (Iron Ore Bust, *Modern Trader*, December 2017, #538, p. 15)

HP Billiton Limited (BHP) discovers, acquires, develops, and markets natural resources worldwide. It was founded in 1851 and is based in Melbourne, Australia. BHP operates through four segments: petroleum, copper, iron ore, and coal. Iron ore constitutes 38% of its revenue. BHP has enjoyed an overly positive growth rate due to the worldwide demand for iron ore for the production of steel. However, due to the sluggish price of iron ore, BHP's recent positive run could be coming to an end and it looks like it is ready to short.

BHP had reported significant and robust growth for the six months ending June 30, 2017, which was responsible for an increase of 13.4% in BHP shares. Contributing to this upbeat trend were productivity gains of $12 billion and a significant reduction of capital exploration expenses in its onshore plans. In its fiscal year 2017, BHP reduced capital exploration expenses by $5.2 billion, resulting in a 32% plunge in total expenses.

Such momentum is simply unsustainable, due to its massive iron ore interests, the prices of which have fallen sharply. Mining companies continue to produce more supply while inventory has significantly increased as a direct result of China's demand for iron ore. Specifically, BHP anticipates iron-ore productivity to be within 239–243 million tons in fiscal year 2018, representing year-over-year upside of 3% to 5%. Improved productivity will come on the back of an increased yield of the Western Australia iron ore mine. Quite simply, iron-ore prices are in a bear market, with volatility paving the way, with prices reaching a high of $95 per ton in February 2017, then falling to $53 per ton in June 2017.

Additionally, metal commodities' price fallout will adversely affect BHP's dividend policy. BHP's dividend policy differs from other companies where payouts are based on 50% of its cash flow rather than a flat dividend payment in each quarter. Its recent dividend payment is 43¢ per share (including a 33¢ per share minimum payment plus an additional 10¢). This phenomenon cannot be repeated in upcoming quarters.

Technical Picture

BHP rebounded sharply from a death cross pattern in June, thanks to its positive growth report, productivity gains, and China's Belt and Road initiative (See figure 10.3). This resulted in up to 150 million tons of additional steel demand, which drove up demand for raw materials. This all led to its sharp upward reversal from $33. However, increased production has led to a drop in iron ore prices and the formation of a double top in BHP around $44. A correction should test support at $40 from the September low and a gap around $38.50. If that support is taken out, BHP could test its June lows. BHP is a shining candidate for a short position.

[Please note that in these examples of recommended short positions, I actually went against my normal procedures. In the case of ISRG, I relied heavily on the evaluation of the technical aspect of the stock while for BHP I relied equally on the fundament evaluation of the stock. The fact that both of these shorts lost money unmistakably illustrates the need to incorporate a balanced evaluation of both fundamentals and technical aspects.]

Six Examples Where the Evaluation of Both Fundamentals *and* Technicals Warranted Shorts

> The reader is cautioned not to rely on any information provided in this example for making decisions about trading any security. Please refer to the **Caution—Limitations and Difficulties** section found at the end of the first chapter.

General Electric (GE) (submitted as Short Burn?, Modern Trader, *#539, January 2018)*

Fundamental Picture (submitted to *Modern Trader*, January 19, 2018)

The General Electric Company (GE) is a world-known industrial giant that may be burning shortly. GE operates as an infrastructure and technology company worldwide. It has multiple segments, including power, renewable energy, oil and gas, aviation, healthcare, transportation, energy and lighting, and capital financing. GE was founded in 1892, and is based in Boston, Massachusetts. GE shocked the market by its formal announcement of a Q4-2017 after-tax charge of $6.2 billion and a $3 billion cash capital contribution to its legacy reinsurance portfolio—specifically, its capital financing segment inclusive of its insurance portfolio of North America Life & Health Insurance, which was retained. The reinsurer buys the right to receive premiums from the primary insurers.

GE's reason for its retention was based on the assumption that its current insurance-related business contains approximately 60% of long-term care insurance and that the transfer of such claims would be more profitable than the outright sale of its segment. The announcement can be seen as a major setback for its turnaround campaign, led by John Flannery, the new chief executive of GE. Flannery was installed only in August 2017 and has been busy selling assets and slashing dividends. This activity and the requirement of having to set aside $15 billion over seven years to bolster its insurance portfolios within its capital segment may not sit well with investors, stockholders, and analysts. Within these massive cracks there are clear indicators of potential breakups or complete spinoffs in order to attempt to manage its precarious status. This is in direct comparison to GE's prior initiatives in expansion under the reins of its former CEO, Jack Welch, who ran GE from 1981 to 2001. It was during the late 1980s that GE acquired RCA and retained NBC, leading to further expansion in the 1990s, launching media initiatives including NBC/CNBC television programs and its financial services segment. GE's turnaround may be faced with two critical obstacles: the first being that many analysts believe that any such revival may take at least two years and the second being its notable and consistent lower market value of $270 billion since November 1999. Regrettably for GE its red tag sell-off by slashing costs, halving GE's dividends, and potential corporate restructuring may not be enough to bring solidification to its financial dilemma.

Technical Picture for GE

GE has been trading below an established death cross pattern since mid-June 2017. It has formed prominent stepper-plungers: first plunge (28–26), second plunge (26.30–25/10), third plunge (25–23.80), fourth plunge (23.50–22.15), fifth plunge (20.10–18.90), and sixth plunge (19–17.90). Evidence of short selling was apparent, as it stabilized in a trading range of 17.40–17.90 during mid-November and the end of December 2017. Then GE rocketed through primary resistance (18.50–19.10), hit its seventh plunge (19.10–17.79) and challenged primary support (17.60–17.15) with an eighth plunge (18.12–17.01). There was an acceleration of exiting seen by institutions and high-frequency traders (HFTs) and smart position holders. The expectation of further dividend slashing is a prime indicator of poor performance, and forces share prices to continue falling.

Chart courtesy of StockCharts.com.

> The reader is cautioned not to rely on any information provided in this example for making decisions about trading any security. Please refer to the **Caution—Limitations and Difficulties** section found at the end of the first chapter.

IBM (Buffett Bailed on IBM: Is Watson Next? Modern Trader, *June 2018,* #544, p. 14)

Fundamental Picture for IBM
In the 1968 movie *2001: A Space Odyssey*, the spaceship's advanced cognitive computer, HAL—"foolproof and incapable of error"— suffers a malfunction that leads to the derailment of the mission.

International Business Machines Corporation (IBM) has been commonly associated with the naming of HAL (attributable to movie myth), but in reality, IBM's enhanced computer solutions may not be enough to save its mission to drive revenues from its downward trend as a short position.

IBM, the Armonk, New York–based company founded in 1924, has been faced with a drastic and lengthy transition from its prior business segments due to its declining sales of its legacy server hardware. This led to IBM's "strategic imperative" mission to reinvest and focus within emerging markets, including cloud computing, data analytics, mobile technologies, and social and security services. This shift in conjunction with its seemingly flat year-over-year reported margins have led to investor hesitancy and apprehension.

IBM's cognitive solution segment is the only one of its five major divisions functioning with improved margins. Its other business segments have been shrinking faster than the growth of its new business initiatives. IBM's reported Q1 2018 earnings of $2.45 per share and revenue of $19.1 billion vs. the consensus estimate of $2.40 per share and revenue of $18.7 billion led to immediate investor unhappiness with both its margin and its strategic restructuring plans. While it announced better-than-expected earnings and revenue, IBM reaffirmed guidance for 2018 earnings of $13.80 per share. This was IBM's first revenue growth after 20 straight quarters of decline, and it was projected that this would continue for 2018, but this did not impress investors, leading to a significant 6% fall.

Although there was some success reported by its cloud and autonomous database products in relation to its competitors, a growth of 15%, the market was still skeptical. Viewed in the most favorable light, this can be seen as a mixed success, as Warren Buffett's Berkshire Hathaway (8RK-8) liquidated its entire stake of IBM in Q4 2017. IBM's overall lack of growth has been evidenced through its Q3 2017 numbers, down 2% for the year, and its Q1 2018 unsatisfactory reassurances by IBM's finance chief, James Kavanaugh, that its Q1-2018 numbers were lower due to its storage segment. IBM's statement that it has "all the confidence in the world" it can improve the storage segment by the second half of 2018 seems eerily reminiscent of HAL's "enthusiasm and confidence" in 2001's fated mission.

Technical Picture

The lack of enthusiasm for an IBM recovery by the markets is matched by a challenging technical picture (see Figure 10.4). The February sell-off pushed IBM below both its 50- and 200-day simple moving average (SMA). This followed a golden cross—inspired rally in January. Although IBM rallied above both its 50- and 200-day simple moving average in March, it failed to take out its January high. On April 17, IBM failed to take out the March high and set a double-top resistance level at $162 as it awaited its post-close Q1 2018 earnings announcement.

The disappointing announcement coupled with technical weakness led to further losses. With its stock trading below both its 50- and 200-day DMA. IBM entered a death cross on May 11 as the 50-day DMA crossed below the 200-day SMA. The next support area is the 2017 low of $139.13, but strong downward momentum should be able to take that out.

Recommendation

Short Range: 139–149 Cover Short: 119
Stop Loss: 154
*Price as of intraday May 9, 2018
**Joseph Parnes has short position holdings in IBM.
IBM INC/IBM/"NYSE" 142.11*
52-week high: 171.53; 52-week low: 138.13; market cap: $130.45 billion; EPS: 6.13; P/E: 23.16; beta: 1.05; DIV/YLD: 6.28 (4.32%)

The global computer services company has been in a lengthy turnaround toward becoming a cognitive solutions and cloud platform operator. Unfortunately its other business segments are shrinking faster than its growth within its new segments. IBM's current growth rate is in the single digits and warrants lower P/Es. Rebounding through golden cross formation (148–150) (see "golden cross" in January) to upped-gap (152–156) to (158–162). Meeting resistance at (164–167), plunging (164–158) to (154–150) to (150–146). Trading with erratic pattern. Reversal challenged 50-dma (152–154) with a brief ascend to (158–160). Pressured with a new plunge (160–152) through 50 and 200 dma (154–148) to death cross pattern: (148–146) to (144–141) (see "death cross" at far right of graph).

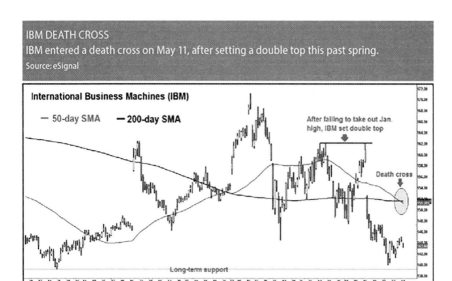

Figure 10.4   IBM death cross.

Chart courtesy of StockCharts.com.

The reader is cautioned not to rely on any information provided in this example for making decisions about trading any security. Please refer to the **Caution—Limitations and Difficulties** section found at the end of the first chapter.

Advance Auto Parts (Advance Auto: Downshifting, Modern Trader, #537, November 2017, p. 15)

Advance Auto Parts: Symbol: AAP; market cap: $7.24 billion; 52-week high/low: $177.83/$82.21; EPS: $5.52; PE: 17.77; short range: $95–$104; cover short: $69; stop loss: $116

Advance Auto Parts, Inc. (AAP), the provider of automotive parts, accessories, and maintenance items for domestic/imported vehicles and industrial vehicles, has been given a "ticket to short," due to a 20% plunge in a single trading day. The Roanoke, Virginia–based company founded in 1929 sells its products online through AdvanceAutoParts.com and Worldpac.com. It serves do-it-for-me and do-it-yourself customers, as well as 5,062 independently owned stores, 127 WORLDPAC branches, and approximately 1,250 independently owned Carquest-branded stores in the United States, Puerto Rico, and the US Virgin Islands. Internationally, it serves Canada, Mexico, the Bahamas, Turks and Caicos, the British Virgin Islands, and the Pacific Islands.

AAP's 20% single-day plunge was primarily due to its reported lower than expected sales outlook for its Q2 2017. The company's profit fell 30% to $8.7 million. It suggests that AAP is experiencing broad industry sector headwinds where sales for Q2 were flat instead of beating by an expected 0.2%. To make matters worse, this guidance was lowered by 1% to 3% in same-store sales for the year. AAP's adjusted earnings fell to $1.58 per share from $1.90, leaving flat revenue of $2.26 billion.

AAP's principal audience is comprised of do-it-for-me and do-it-yourself customers. Acceleration of new car sales in and around 2010 has reduced AAP's customer base in 2017 and in its 2018 projections. Or another way of saying this is that AAP's inventory and maintenance services are increasingly unfavorable to its customer base as they are partially comprised of batteries and battery accessories, belts and hoses, brakes, clutches, engine parts, exhaust parts, ignition components, radiators, starters, alternators, tire repair, fuel and oil fluids for engine maintenance, which has little demand in an environment of cars that are self-regulating, computer-centric, and less prone to repair issues.

Technical Picture

AAP's stock price has plummeted to its current low of $82.21, which marks its lowest level since September 2013, skidding consistently lower since its 2016 high above $175 (see Figure 10.5). AAP traded below its 50- and 200-day moving averages and continued its retreat through mid-May 2017. This led to a failed rebound above its 50-day moving average, followed by continued weakness reaching its new low of $82.21. AAP's recent rebound challenging the $100 level is being carried out with little conviction. There is a difficult task ahead on AAP's horizon to fill the prior plunges, as well as its capacity to meet its primary resistance at $110, and its secondary resistance at $115. AAP is on a seemingly long ride in the short lane.

> The reader is cautioned not to rely on any information provided in this example for making decisions about trading any security. Please refer to the **Caution—Limitations and Difficulties** section found at the end of the first chapter.

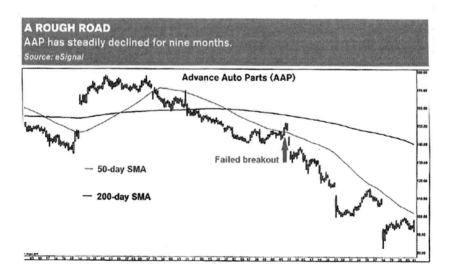

Figure 10.5   A rough road.
Courtesy of eSignal.

Chart courtesy of eSignal.

The reader is cautioned not to rely on any information provided in this example for making decisions about trading any security. Please refer to the **Caution—Limitations and Difficulties** section found at the end of the first chapter.

Core Labs (Core Fundamentals & Technicals Point Lower, Modern Trader, #519, April 2016, p. 12)

Energy stocks have taken a beating, and continue to provide sufficient short trading opportunities. One such company is Core Laboratories N.V. (CLB), which was recommended initially in November 2015. CLB provides oil reservoir, production, enhancement, and managerial services within the oil and gas industry domestically and abroad. CLB was founded in 1936, and is headquartered in the Netherlands, though it maintains a sizable share of the US market. The company, once a golden child during the hot energy sector boom, differentiated itself among other competitors through its focus on evaluating and developing comprehensive solutions to optimize oil extraction and recovery. Its prior economic growth was justified by obvious factors including the geopolitical demand for oil and the race to optimize oil recovery.

Core Laboratories N.V.: Symbol: CLB; market cap: $4.01 billion; 52-week high/low: $134.87/$84.50; sector: energy; short range: $92–$97; cover short: $67; stop loss: $105

Core Laboratories' fourth-quarter 2015 results were rather disappointing and provide sufficient signals of continued contraction. Its reported $178 million revenue had a sequential 7% decrease while its fourth-quarter earnings of 65¢ per share (excluding severance and miscellaneous charges of 29¢ per share) is a significant consideration to factor. Core's 2015 total-year revenue was down a staggering 27%. Its rig count, used to monitor the number of rig drillings for oil in the United States, also plummeted 16%, and led to a 60% decrease from its year-over-year basis.

Here the market's disdain for uncertainty has clouded investor confidence, continuing to push the price lower. As hedge funds continue to add shorts, a clear manifestation of a death cross on January 11, 2016, signals further technical weakness for CLB. A significant rebound is not in the immediate offing.

Any expectation of a meaningful recovery in the broader energy sector is far from certain. While many analysts have concluded that the price drop within oil is simply reflective of the dollar's value versus the demand for oil itself and has run its course, the potential lifting of Iran's oil sanctions furthers the expectation of higher supplies of oil. This, taken together with the slowing global economy, is sufficient evidence that a recovery is not likely to be seen in the coming quarters.

Focusing on the chart's patterns, CLB has broken its 50-day moving average, now down 8.55% for the past 12 months, signaling a clear downward pattern leading to a base building around $125 to $120, then $120 to $110 and failing again at $113 to $104. While there was an attempt of a reversal in December at $105 to $120, the downtrend has resumed under the death cross (see Figure 10.6), falling below $90 before rebounding to $100.

CROSSING OVER

CLB entered a death cross early in 2016.

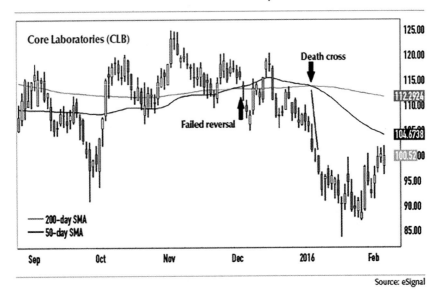

Figure 10.6   Crossing over.

Core Labs (Core Labs Is Out of Gas, Modern Trader, #533, June 2017, pp. 11–12)

Fundamental Picture

Core Laboratories N.V. (CLB), founded in 1936 and based in Amsterdam, is a provider of reservoir descriptions, production improvements, and reservoir management services within the petroleum sector in the United States, Canada, and internationally.

CLB operates via three segments: reservoir description, production enhancement, and reservoir management. All three segments are expressly targeted to crude oil, gas, and petroleum refinement; subsequently conforming to one specific commodity, independent of CLB's internal investments. Such conformity is illustrated via its reservoir description segment analyzing petroleum reservoir rock, fluid and gas samples. Their production enhancement segment includes services and products relating to reservoir well completions, perforations, stimulations and production; and their reservoir management segment integrating the reservoir and production enhancement services to increase the production and improve recovery of oil and gas from its client's reservoirs. CLB markets and provides its services via its sales representatives, technical seminars, trade shows, media advertising, and third-party distributors.

CLB's specific business operation is intrinsically and extrinsically dependent on one sector, putting the company in a precarious position. The reduction of US drilling and related activities has had a direct effect on CLB. This is evidenced by CLB's last earnings report where shares have declined 5% from its prior valuation within a substantial 30- to 40-day period. Additionally, CLB's Q4 2016 adjusted diluted earnings of 41¢ per share was substantially below its year-prior quarter of 65¢ per share totaling CLB's revenue of $150 million. This accounted for a 20.8% decline from its prior-year quarter of $180 million. Its reservoir segment reported an operating income of $17.3 million, its production enhancement operating income was $2.9 million, and its reservoir management suffered a $1.3 million loss.

CLB's future guidance for Q1 2017 is equally indicative of potential decline, based on expected earnings of 42¢ per share on revenue of $150 million. This subpar growth rate and value places CLB in the 20% lower quartile for investment strategies. While some believe this is an opportunity to either hold or buy, the signals point toward a prime short candidate.

CLB will also be affected by external factors that will remain volatile. These include the overall global economic outlook, potential OPEC taxation, and the continued technological advances in alternative energy production. As a result, any immediate or near-term bounce in CLB's stock performance and perceived growth in earnings should be questioned in light of these precarious factors and seen as a shorting opportunity.

Technical Picture

CLB has been in a declining mode since setting a high of $214 in April 2014. Continued declines with plunges brought the price to a low of $92.75 in January 2015. The election bounce reversed the share price above its 50- and 200-day moving average. The rebound continued to $125, but failed to take out the 2016 high.

A downtrend established of the high has not been broken by early April rebound to $117 (see Figure 10.7). The prospects of energy and soil services sectors may invite more short-sellers in light of such variance. The retesting of its previous low of $96.30 may be expected.

Figure 10.7   CLB short energy.

Chart courtesy of StockCharts.com.

The reader is cautioned not to rely on any information provided in this example for making decisions about trading any security. Please refer to the **Caution—Limitations and Difficulties** section found at the end of the first chapter.

Ralph Lauren (*Ralph Lauren: More Style Than Substance,* Modern Trader, #523, August 2016, p. 14)

Ralph Lauren Corp. (RL), the global apparel and lifestyle retailer focusing on three segments—wholesale, retail, and licensing—is suffering from severe performance declines from 2015, making it a ripe candidate for shorting.

The company, which was founded in 1967 and operates 493 retail locations and an additional 583 sub-retail facilities, ranks as one of the most iconic brands in the world. However, while RL's cachet may be still intact, its overall operating margin continues to contract.

Ralph Lauren Corp: Symbol: RL; market cap: $7.89 billion; 52-week high/low: $141.03/$82.15; sector: retail; short range: $88–$99: cover short: $71; stop loss: $110; price as of intraday June 1, 2016

New York City–based Ralph Lauren's fiscal performance rose 1% to $7.4 billion in 2016, which is a 26% decline from 2015. Its wholesale revenue dropped 3% to $3.3 billion from North American sales alone. This, in tandem with its operating margin, currently at 25.15% compared to 27% in 2015, and its 4% increase in retail via the Internet and new store expansion, has led to a 1% decline to $3.9 billion with comparable store sales decreasing by 3%. As a result, RL's operating margin stands at 10.7% (a 260-basis point decline). A downward revision of the EPS projection for 2017 from $6.73–$6.90 to $6.34–$6.46 is a sign that RL's chance of rebounding in the near term is slim.

RL's operating profit and revenues are being squeezed by insufficient sourcing and extreme costs. Their dependence on department stores and discounting was created by bloated costs which continue to linger. Management has been slow to react, and as a result they are now overwhelmed with expenses in excess of 45.8%, putting them at a disadvantage with their competitors. There are also internal management structuring issues which have become less streamlined and consequently inefficient as a result of their high numbers of entry-level employees and upper-level management. For the June 2016 quarter, RL is expecting to earn 98¢ per share year-over-year on revenue of $1.56 billion, down 3.7% year-over-year. For the fiscal year ending March 2017, projected earnings will decline 0.47% to $6.33 per share on expected revenue of $7.10 billion, which is a 4.1% decline year-over-year.

RL has been in a consistent declining mode since November 2015. Its reversal in early January 2016 from $97.64 met resistance at $115, followed by its one-day plunge below $90 that gapped lower from $110 to $103, and that continued on to set a new low of $81.72. This reversal continued to have difficulty during a breakout attempt through its primary resistance at $96.99. Now, trading below its 50- and 200-dma has positioned RL in a critical divergence mode. This is a result of continuous negative accumulation and distribution evident through its March-to-May trading range of $89 to $99. A retesting of its previous low of $81.72 set on February 8 was also not an optimistic sign and the subsequent reversals from $83.66 to its early June 2016 level are simply the hallmarks of short-covering boosts (see Figure 10.8). During the past 12 months, RL shares have declined 30% while the S&P 500 Index has risen 0.23%. Facing the difficult task of penetrating its primary resistance and secondary resistance of $103, an additional plunge is in the offing. Ralph Lauren's elevated volatility may appeal to some as an opportunity

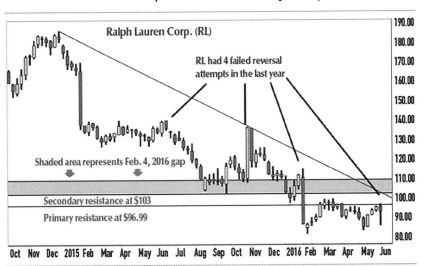

NO RELIEF IN SIGHT
Despite severe losses, no relief in sight for Ralph Lauren.

Figure 10.8   No relief in sight.

to trade on its attempted rebounds, but the short-selling potential far outweighs any such variance. While Ralph Lauren's clothing and lifestyle line imbue a life of luxury, currently, in the words of Hans Christian Andersen, "The Emperor has no clothes."

Ralph Lauren (This Retailer Is Out of Fashion, Modern Trader, #531, April 2017, p. 13)

Fundamental Picture

Ralph Lauren (RL), previously shorted in *Modern Trader*'s July 19, 2016, issue (published #523, August 2016) is still unraveling at the seams (then, we recommended to short at $96.91 and to cover short at $71.00). One of the world's most visibly known apparel and lifestyle retailers focuses on three segments—wholesale, retail, and licensing—and is still suffering from its continuous performance declines from 2015, making this a long-term short position.

The company, which was founded in 1967 and operates 493 retail locations plus 583 sub-retail facilities, ranks as one of the most iconic brands in the world. While RL's brand cachet may still remain intact, its overall operating margin continues to contract further from July.

Overall, retail stocks continue diving as companies mark down their higher-end inventory. The recent news marking the sudden and abrupt departure of Ralph Lauren's CEO Stefan Larsson has made investors concerned over the company's managerial decisions. Larsson, who was hired by RL only one year ago, reportedly stepped down from his role due to disagreements with founder Ralph Lauren, who serves as executive chairman and chief creative officer, over the direction of the brand. This "changing of the guard" is not exclusive to RL, as the purge of executives within the retail sector has heightened anxiety, as evidenced by Frederic Cumenal's departure from Tiffany & Co. (TIF) due to disappointing earnings results only 22 months after moving from LVMH Moet Hennessy Louis Vuitton (MC).

Ralph Lauren's reported results for its fiscal Q3 pertain to the period ending Dec. 31, 2016. Surprisingly, it delivered better-than-expected earnings and in-line revenues. Its earnings-per-share (EPS) fell 18% while its year-over-year revenue reported at $1.86. On average, analysts were expecting a 28% year-over-year fall to $1.64 per share. RL's total revenues fell 12% year-over-year to $1.7 billion, signaling its seventh straight quarterly decline. Fiscal Q3 wholesale revenues were 26% lower year-over-year primarily due to the strategic reduction in North American shipments.

RL's stock price touched a six-year low on February 2, closing at $76.61, or 12.3% below the previous day's closing price. Currently RL is trading 48% below its 52-week high price and has fallen 15% year-to-date (YTD). By comparison, apparel and accessory competition including Coach (COH) and Hanesbrands (HBI) have gained 5.6% and 5.3%, YTD respectively while PVH Corporation (PVH) and VF Corporation (VFC) have stayed in the red. Notably, the S&P 500 Apparel and Accessories Index, a seven-company index based on Ralph Lauren, Hanesbrands, VF Corporation, Coach, PVH Corporation, Michael Kors, and Under Armour, have all fallen 6% YTD.

Technical Picture

In decline since late 2014, RL rebounded beyond the 38.2% Fibonacci level in late 2015 before once again retreating, and traded

Chart courtesy of StockCharts.com.

Figure 10.9   Marked down.

The reader is cautioned not to rely on any information provided in this example for making decisions about trading any security. Please refer to the **Caution—Limitations and Difficulties** section found at the end of the first chapter.

between $90 and $114 during the second half of 2016. After a post-election rally that saw RL rocket through the 50 dma and 200 dma, RL topped at $114 and began a step pattern decline. A tepid rebound failed at $92 in late January leading to a further decline that pushed the 50 dma below the 200 dma (see Figure 10.9). That technical weakness most likely exacerbated the recent plunge on Larsson's departure, which was accompanied by heavy volume and could carry the price in a stairstep decline into the $50 area. An attempt to fill the February 2 gap between $81 and $86 is possible, but not likely, so shorts can place a stop just above the high of the gap.

These six cases of short positions mentioned above reinforce the scenario in which the proceeds obtained from each short were placed into long positions. If, during the time the short positions were held, the long positions went up, there was no need to cover the short. These shorts were maintained independent of any stop loss, because the fundamentals of the company suggested a long-term decline, and the technical pattern is in a deterioration mode. The chances of acquisition are limited, and the growth rate is a declining mode. Using a stop loss for these positions creates a trading scenario, rather than an investment scenario that is shorting for the long term. Very often, there are wide fluctuations in stock prices, and these spikes may be caused by short sellers covering their positions or by traders taking advantage of short-term gains, or a bullish announcement by a brokerage firm or an institution. These spikes are short lived. However, the short positions above were designed for the investor, to increase asset value of the portfolio by selecting an issue for the long term and using the proceeds from the short positions to increase positions in selected long positions. The short positions are not sold to make money on the shorts. They are sold to use the proceeds to increase positions in selected long stocks where there is an increase in value anticipated, and the **short position maintained for the long term**, until changes in the fundamentals of the company warrant covering the short.

There are other stocks mentioned in *Modern Trader*, and their write-ups are reproduced next.

Polaris Industries (Recalling Polaris Stock, *Modern Trader*, #527, December 2016, p. 14)

Polaris Industries: Symbol: PII; market cap: $4.85 billion; 52-week high/low: $124.39/$67.80; short range: $73–$79: cover short: $52; stop loss: $85

Polaris Industries Inc. (PH), with its segments of off-road vehicles including snowmobiles and motorcycles, and global adjacent markets, is skidding down the short track. The company, founded in 1954, has faced significant downgrades since the recall of its off-road vehicle RZR ROV due to fire hazard considerations. Polaris, a fixture in off-road industry designs, engineers, manufactures, and markets these products in the United States, Canada, Western Europe, Australia, and Mexico. However, the recent recall has exceeded costs and turned Polaris into a fading star.

Medina, Minnesota–based Polaris is known to market its products via dealers, secondary distributors, and directly through its website Polaris.com under the following brand names: Ranger, RCR, Ranger Crew, Polaris Rush, Victory Vision, Victory Crossroads, Cross-Country, Indian Chief Classic, Indian Chief Vintage, Indian Chieftain, Roadmaster, Scout, Scout Sixty, Victory Magnum, and Hammerhead Off-Road.

The recall of its off-road vehicles lowered earnings guidance for 2016 to $3.30–$3.80 per share from $5.80–$6.80 per share. This was lessened additionally to a flat to down 2%. The recall costs of roughly 284,000 vehicles have exacerbated internal cost overruns. Polaris's attempt to repair its previously recalled off-road vehicles was also met with an underestimation of its assumed expenses and is now poised for the delay of its 2017 models, signaling weakness and pessimism.

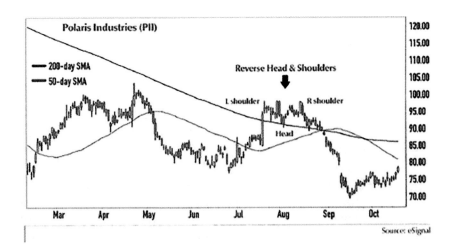

Source: eSignal

Chart courtesy of StockCharts.com.

The reader is cautioned not to rely on any information provided in this example for making decisions about trading any security. Please refer to the **Caution—Limitations and Difficulties** section found at the end of the first chapter.

However, there is more than just a recall that is behind Polaris's failing, which started well before when the company stock was trading above $110 a share. That was well within the high-digit multiples based on $7 per-share earnings on year- to two-year extended patterns. Note that the multiple recalls were causative of its plunge through its 50-day moving average in early May 2016 when it was still trading near $100. This developed into a reversal head-and-shoulder pattern with a left shoulder at $98.34, right shoulder at $98.13, and a head at $90.44 set in mid-August 2016.

Prior to that Polaris attempted a reversal, rallying through its 50- and 200-day moving average in July, but the severity of the recall caused PH to fail and plunge into a step pattern that took out support at the 50- and 200-day moving averages, and finally skidded to a bottoming at $70.14. Any reversal attempt since September 19 has failed to refill this downed gap of $82–$77. Its recent reversal attempt from an established low of $70.14 met a resistance at $79, before sliding back to the $73 area. It second reversal attempt was simply too shallow to complete any filling of its downward gap of $82 to $77.

Polaris is challenging its primary support of $65 with a secondary support of $51 in the offing.

> The reader is cautioned not to rely on any information provided in this example for making decisions about trading any security. Please refer to the **Caution—Limitations and Difficulties** section found at the end of the first chapter.

SINA (Shorting SINA: China's Twitter, *Modern Trader*, #525, October 2016, p. 13)

SINA Corporation. Symbol: SINA; market cap: $4.89 billion; 52-week high/low: $70.50/$32.61; sector: social media; short range: $65–$70; cover short: $52; stop loss: $75

Social media companies have been all the rage due to their growth prospects and the likelihood of merger and acquisition activity in the space, but one firm stands out. SINA Corporation (SINA), via its subsidiaries, operates as a significant social media content provider within the People's Republic of China. SINA .com provides a wide variety of online commerce and content, and through Weibo.com offers seemingly analogous content of US social media giants Facebook (FB) and Twitter (TWTR), but with a specific region-based formatting. Significant and sufficient losses of $25.2 million versus year-to-date and its non-generally accepted accounting principles (GAAP) income is poised to single SINA out on the short list in comparison to its social media competitors. The SINA Corporation was founded in 1997 and is headquartered in Shanghai.

SINA's first quarter 2016 operational losses of $25.2 million versus $8.5 million from the same quarter in 2015 have started to illustrate the erosion of SINA's growth capacity. Additionally, SINA's continued non-GAAP adjusted earnings have still declined in its income generation of 2016's reported $5.6 million versus previous year-to-date income of $13.6 million.

Weibo.com (WB) is SINA's singular powerhouse (listed separately in the United States) and its social media subsidiary. It can create and post a feed of up to 140 Chinese characters and attach multimedia or long-form content.

SINA has been waiting for its positive second-quarter projections to alleviate the Chinese Facebook/Twitter regional superpower uncertainty and speculation, based on SINA's 2016 substantial decline, which has been carrying the weight of most of SINA's positive growth.

Weibo hit an all-time high of $43.56 per share, after a positive earnings result in mid-August. The positive report may not be able to save the downward trend in staggering momentum SINA has incurred since the beginning of this year. Weibo's second-quarter results released on August 8 were met with enthusiasm with high trading volume and active traders, but in relation to SINA, this is simply indicative of an unstable bump and only further emphasizes SINA's retracted and overall decline. In fact it could prove a selling opportunity.

A short covering rally rocketed the stock to just past $70, taking out its primary resistance levels. Such violent moves often lead to equally fast retracements. Expect SINA to return to its primary support level between $57 and $60 and secondary support level between $52 and $55.

While many analysts and investors are now similarly content with SINA's adjusted 2016 revenue of just under $1 billion versus its previous guidance of $852 to $950 million, simply because of a stronger second quarter, it does not inherently cure the underlying devaluation of SINA. SINA's dependency on Weibo as its lead player in revenue growth cannot simply mitigate the bright-line issues that are dragging SINA downward. SINA's operational costs and diversified Internet offerings are laggards that cannot simply be ignored and will continue to erode its value moving forward.

SINA's overall technical picture has been broken up with the upward spike following the second-quarter earnings surprise from Weibo. The spike pushed SINA to test the 62% Fibonacci retracement level from the sell-off from its October 2013 high to its March 2015 low. See Figure 10.10.

TIME TO SELL

SINA has extended a move higher thanks to a surprisingly strong earnings report from Weibo, which is providing an opportunity to short.

Figure 10.10   Time to sell.

Chart courtesy of StockCharts.com.

Stamps.com Inc. (Stamps Stock: Return to Sender, *Modern Trader*, #540, February 2018 p. 15)

Symbol: STMP; market cap $2.98 billion; EPS: 6.18; P/E ratio 29.70; short range $171 to $190; cover short $138; stop loss $108

Stamps.com, Inc., the Internet-based mailing and shipping solution provider, is sending short signals this holiday season. STMP offers mailing and shipping solutions through the US Postal Service under the Stamps.com and Endicia brands. STMP, formally known as StampMaster, Inc., was founded in 1996 and serves individuals, large businesses, and warehouses. The El Segundo, California–based company operates multi-carrier shipping solutions and offers customized postage solutions to its customers.

STMP's street approval, demonstrated by its substantive earnings increase, is poised for a slowdown, leading to short selling opportunities. STMP reported a $2.68 per share earnings increase for Q3 2017 on revenue of $115.1 million. This beat the consensus expectation of $1.91 per share in earnings on revenue of $109.4 million, of 142% and 24% respectively. Also, STMP's yearly earnings guidance of $9 to $10 per share versus the consensus of $8.05 will significantly project a reduction in its P/E ratio. STMP's reported earnings and revenues did not impress investors, which adds to the negative outlook.

Competition has slowly eroded STMP's hold on the shipping industry with Amazon's (AMZN) entry into similar shipping and mailing business models. These noticeable signs of a slowdown warranting a lower P/E ratio are a sign of holders and momentum traders exiting positions, and makes the STMP a short selling candidate.

STMP has been in an ascending mode since mid-June 2017, with two major gaps following its last two earnings announcements (see Figure 10.11). Its overly impressive Q2 2017 earnings report resulted in a gap opening on August 3 from the previous day's close of $151.20 to $180.40. This is indicative of a short squeeze with high volume and an increase in the Relative Strength Index to 78.9% in conjunction with the STMP stock price breaching $200 on the day of the gap open.

Signs of overextended patterns made STMP prime for a correction. The reversal threatened to be extreme given the gap higher and the severity of the move. STMP was vulnerable when met with the news of the AMZN's entry into its business model. This literally spooked investors and traders when STMP gapped lower on November 3. STMP closed November 2 at $221.25 and opened November 3 more than $25 lower at $195.15. The stock continued to bleed, settling at $171.25 with heavy volume and penetrating the 50-day moving average.

STMP's bearish pattern has pushed the price close to oversold territory, but it has not yet completely filled the August opening gap. Exiting now is rampant with an average bearish trend, which could find STMP's closing price attempting to refill the August gap from $151. This could be followed by challenging its secondary support at the 200-day MA, a breach of which would leave STMP in a vulnerable position.

> The reader is cautioned not to rely on any information provided in this example for making decisions about trading any security. Please refer to the **Caution—Limitations and Difficulties** section found at the end of the first chapter.

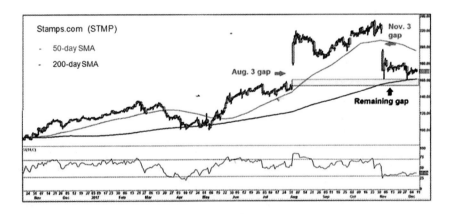

Figure 10.11   Pick your gap.

The reader is cautioned not to rely on any information provided in this example for making decisions about trading any security. Please refer to the **Caution—Limitations and Difficulties** section found at the end of the first chapter.

Goldman Sachs (Goldman Will Rebound, *Modern Trader*, #520, May 2016, p. 10)

Finding applicable shorts in a volatile market presents its own dangers; however, the prospects for long-term growth potential equities in the banking/financial sector have been fraught with uncertainty. One such company, Goldman Sachs, is poised for a maintainable rebound, and should be differentiated from its competitors.

New York–based Goldman Sachs global investment banking firm provides investment banking services, trading, and asset management.

Goldman Sachs: Symbol: GS; market cap: $61.79 billion; 52-week high/low: $218.77/$139.05; sector: banking; buy range: $149–$157; stop loss $141.

Goldman's investment banking division handles mergers and acquisitions and underwriting (including its role as a primary dealer in the US Treasury security market), distressed debt, and commercial real estate lending. With the current market volatility, mergers and acquisitions and IPO business are down. However, Goldman's diversified business provides sustainable growth in the upcoming quarters.

In comparison to other lenders, Goldman is not as attached to lending to energy-based entities, which are under considerable stress because of the long bear market in crude oil and natural gas.

Such energy exposure leaves other lenders primarily saddled with investment-grade-rated debt compounded by European banks using contingent convertible bonds with hefty coupon payments. Of course, Goldman can't escape some of this debt but is distinguishable as its creditworthiness is likely a nonissue and it's ripe with appreciable dividends as a substantive benefit from credit spreads contracting the yield curve (between the short and long-term Treasuries).

Goldman's 2015 Q4 earnings fell 71.8% to $574 million or $1.27 per share versus $2.03 billion or 4.38 per share. The earnings decline was largely because of its long-overdue civil settlement of $5.1 billion, from the 2007 banking crisis. Its net revenue fell 5.4% to $7.27 billion, topping the consensus of $7.07 billion (see Figure 10.12).

Goldman's primary income, almost 70%, is derived from its trading and investments divisions focusing on fixed income, commodities, and merchant banking while its asset management divisions provide investment advisement and securities services offering financing and securities lending to its large intuitional clients. This is where Goldman's ability to extend shorts and significant money to hedge funds, large institutions, and high-frequency traders will be enhanced by such increased market volatility generating significant asset potential in the current market.

LONG WAY BACK

Shares plunged approximately 25% last summer from a high of $218.40 set on June 23, 2015. After rebounding back to $200, it fell more sharply in January's correction, crossing the neckline of a bearish head-and-shoulders pattern on Jan. 6. Now it has crossed back above its 50-day moving average and is poised to go higher.

*price as of intraday March 9, 2016   Source: eSignal

Figure 10.12   Long way back.

Goldman Sachs (GS: Anticipating the Swamp Bump, *Modern Trader*, #534, August 2017, p. 14)

Goldman Sachs: Symbol: GS; market cap: $87.66 billion; 52-week high/low: $255.15/ $138.20; EPS: 18.79; PE: 11.40; buying range: $210–$218; near-term objective $238; intermediate objective: $259; stop loss: $199; price as of June 2, 2017

The Goldman Sachs Group Inc., founded in 1869, continues to offer long-term growth in upside potential, despite recent political interference and intermittent plunges. Goldman's recent volatility should be construed as a golden fleece, without a tragic ending, providing strategic timing for investors/traders seeking long-term growth on equities within the banking sector.

New York–based Goldman offers its worldwide investment banking, securities, and investment management company through four segments: investment banking, institutional client services, investing and lending, and investment management. Goldman's primary year-to-date income—more than 70%—stems from trading investments, specifically lending to institutional clients such as hedge funds and high-frequency traders.

Unlike its competitors, it has limited its exposure to investment financing within energy-based entities and sectors. This intrinsic insulation, which has been a hallmark of Goldman's growth power and previously recommended as a long holding, has continued to keep it in a position worthy of accumulation.

Goldman had been in a strong ascending pattern since President Donald Trump's election, passing through resistance levels at $219 and $232 before settling on a continued base building area between $237 and $242 during March 2017.

Following a correction and retraction with a plunge to $235 and then to $227, Goldman stock reversed higher through its 50-day moving average around $232 and rallied to a new high of $255.15. Shares have since plunged 20% from that high set in early March, as promised tax cuts and regulatory relief have stalled. The stock began crossing its neckline set in early May at $226, which was reflective of a bearish "head-and-shoulders" signal, subsequently followed by a plunge to an intraday low of $214.08.

Goldman's recent weakness stemmed from international bond purchases positioning Goldman in the middle of a political storm when it was revealed that its asset-management division acquired $2.8 billion of 2022 October bonds issued by Venezuela's oil company PDVSA on the secondary market, rather than directly from the Venezuelan government. Goldman's activity, which has been similarly enacted with other discounted sovereign bonds, including those from Greece, was met with opposition from the Venezuelan US Congress members, accusing Goldman of aiding and abetting the country's dictatorial regime.

This was the primary culprit for Goldman's stock sinking to $212. Keeping in mind that Goldman is not alone in this practice, operating with sound business judgment abiding by "ex fida bona," as other discounted deals have been derived by similar global asset management firms, most notably Nomura Securities purchasing $100 million of Venezuelan government bonds.

With exposure to Venezuela no longer a serious threat, investors have an opportunity to take advantage of these momentary dips in Goldman stock as its price-to-earnings ratio has fallen way below its peers. Goldman's May low of $211.26 could serve as a long-term bottom (see Figure 10.13). The stock faces primary resistance at $224 and secondary resistance at $232. Base building and short covering could challenge its upper head resistance at $239. Though technicals still appear weak, it is not a good idea to bet against Goldman as it has friends in high places.

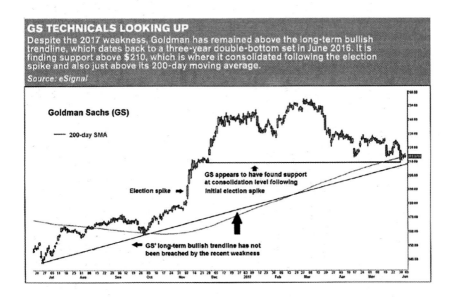

GS TECHNICALS LOOKING UP
Despite the 2017 weakness, Goldman has remained above the long-term bullish trendline, which dates back to a three-year double-bottom set in June 2016. It is finding support above $210, which is where it consolidated following the election spike and also just above its 200-day moving average.
Source: eSignal

Goldman Sachs (GS)

—— 200-day SMA

GS appears to have found support
at consolidation level following
initial election spike

Election spike ➡

GS' long-term bullish trendline has not
been breached by the recent weakness

Figure 10.13   GS technicals looking up.

The reader is cautioned not to rely on any information provided in this example for making decisions about trading any security. Please refer to the **Caution—Limitations and Difficulties** section found at the end of the first chapter.

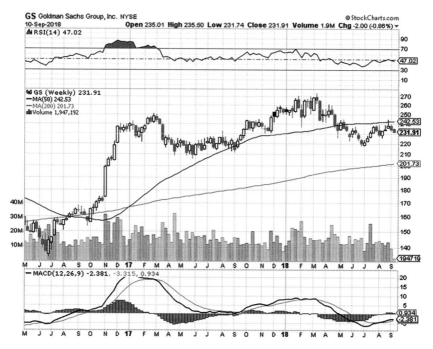

Chart courtesy of StockCharts.com.

The reader is cautioned not to rely on any information provided in this example for making decisions about trading any security. Please refer to the **Caution—Limitations and Difficulties** section found at the end of the first chapter.

Fiat (Fiat Chrysler in Low Drive, *Modern Trader*, #524, September 2016, p. 13)

Fiat Chrysler Automobile: Symbol: FCAU; market cap: $7.87 billion; 52-week high/low: $10.93/$5.45; sector: automotive; short range: $5.00 to $7.00; cover short: $2.25; stop loss: $7.93; current price $6.12 as of July 8

While oil prices may be down, not all consumers are taking advantage of automobiles this summer. Fiat Chrysler automobiles N.V. (FCAU), a designer, manufacturer, and distributor of automobiles, componentry, and production systems, is driving its way to a short position. The company operates via six segments: NAFTA, LATAM, APAC, EMEA, Maserati, and Components, producing passenger cars, light trucks, and light commercial vehicles under the brands of Abarth, Alfa Romeo, Chrysler, Dodge, Fiat, Fiat Professional, Jeep, Lancia, and Ram.

Its component segment produces lighting, body, suspension, molding, electronic, exhaust, powertrain, and various parts under its Magneti Marelli brand, iron systems for its Teksid brand, and industrial automation systems under its Comau brand.

Founded in 1899, the company has sizable interests in media and publishing. Based in London, this global company is currently operating in more than 150 countries and has three recent factors, combined with a preexisting technical downward trend, placing it on the short list. These factors include Brexit, debt exposure of Fiat Chrysler Automotive, and the current media bias and customer uncertainty due to the untimely death of the mega movie franchise *Star Trek* actor Anton Yelchin. Brexit's inherent volatility has caused an increase in the company's own stock risk, which simply places the equity in a cautionary state for investors in tandem with an already slow demand in the European market for automotive purchases. Such apparent weakness in its operating cash flow, which currently is contrasted with its increase in earnings per share, some believe suggests growth is outweighed by the lengthy macro picture of the company. While Jeep and Ram sales have posted a 17% increase in sales in June—the highest for the company in more than 10 years—there is heavy technical and fundamental data, which does not translate to a rebound.

The unexpected death of Anton Yelchin in late June, whose *Star Trek* film's July release will continue to highlight a 2015 unofficial recall of 1.1 million Jeeps, will potentially negate the optimism for Jeep sales in June, and will undoubtedly hang over the company's star product line, casting insecurity regarding safety amongst Jeep's largest market. Contrary to June analysts' consensus of optimism for FCAU, this third factor will only lead to a decline in its net income and projected revenue growth.

While these are recent occurrences, what makes FCAU, which has an earnings-per-share of 0.53 and a P/E ratio of 11.50, particularly vulnerable are the technicals (see Figure 10.14). Its position has already been in a progressive decline since December 2015, when it was trading at 7.2% below its 20-day moving average and its respective 50 dma and 200 dma.

It rallied 33% from a February low below $6, but failed on a double-top in March and April. Since then, it has made a series of lower highs and lower lows, eventually taking out its February low this July.

FCAU broke below its 50-day in May, which served as resistance, and it subsequently failed to take out resistance at the 50 dma SMA several times. This most recent downward gap from $7.10 to $6.10 presents an extremely difficult position for FCAU to fill, with only a reversal at a primary resistance of $6.50 to $6.90 and a secondary resistance at $7.20 able to change its technical outlook.

The reader is cautioned not to rely on any information provided in this example for making decisions about trading any security. Please refer to the **Caution—Limitations and Difficulties** section found at the end of the first chapter.

OUT OF GAS
Fiat Chrysler has made a series of lower highs and lower lows after its rebound attempt failed this spring.

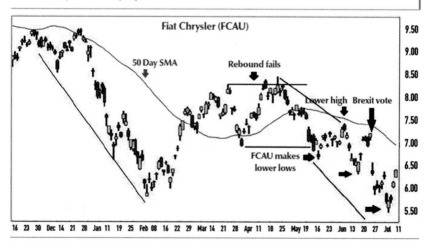

Figure 10.14   Out of gas.

Chart courtesy of StockCharts.com.

The reader is cautioned not to rely on any information provided in this example for making decisions about trading any security. Please refer to the **Caution—Limitations and Difficulties** section found at the end of the first chapter.

Chipotle (Short Sell: Tainted Grub, *Modern Trader*, #518, March 2016, p. 12)

Selecting shorts is a difficult art; however, particular companies stand out as potential shorts when critical technical patterns emerge. One has to make sure that the issue will not be called by the lender and that the stock will not split, all while analyzing stocks where the growth rate has slowed.

One stock that has been in the news is Chipotle, most notably after the media coverage surrounding its food tainted by *E. coli*.

While this has sent the stock moving lower, ripe for shorting, there were signs that made this a long-term short for us since April 2015.

Chipotle Mexican Grill: Symbol: CMG; market cap $12.97 billion; 52-week high/low: $758.61/$411.61; sector: food; short range: $448–$462; cover short: $387; stop loss: $475

Chipotle Mexican Grill, Inc. (CMG) is a fast, casual Mexican restaurant chain with approximately 1,900 locations. We first shorted CMG on February 4, 2015, after it violated its 50 dma at $670. We increased our short position in May at $630 despite the temptation to take profits and after it reversed to $750 in August.

We felt this reversal was an exaggeration, not an example of a true recovery but a response to the April 22 plunge. The chart pattern showed that it boosted the price excessively above its 50 dma and a reverse death cross appeared where the 200 dma crosses the 50 dma, signaling the potential of further declines. This continued before the *E.coli* outbreak scandal was fully reported in October and the subsequent report from the Centers for Disease Control on November 12.

It was easy to recognize CMG as a short after the *E. coli* news, but CMG signaled further short possibilities as no visible V-shaped rebound materialized. Also, any rebound was unlikely while not penetrating its 200 dma. Its third plunge, from $614 to $539, indicated a death cross, where the 50 dma fell below its 200 dma, was forming (see Figure 10.15). This convergence gives one the belief that the short trend will continue and has not hit its final low.

An actual death cross appeared on November 27, leading us to conclude that the subsequent rebounds since CMG's third plunge were not strong enough to become a true reversal. Continued losses on low volume led to a fourth plunge around December 7. Another short rebound at $577 gave a false indication of accumulation but had particularly shallow volume. The fifth plunge showed negative accumulation below the "flat line," with continued selling taking CMG to its sixth plunge. This has continued to manifest into a seventh plunge on January 4 and an eighth plunge on January 7.

Many think Chipotle has reached its bottom. However, we continue to maintain our short because it's trading below its 50 and 200 dma, below its death cross suggestive of continued losses. A rebound will be very difficult and typically requires it to meet a primary resistance at

TAKING A DIVE
Chipotle dropped in waves in the fourth quarter and into 2016.

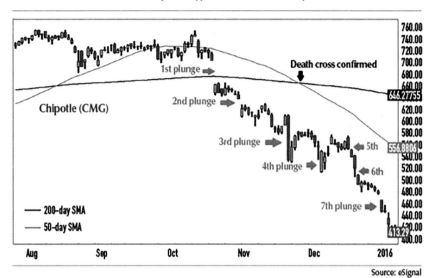

Source: eSignal

Figure 10.15 Taking a dive.

$459 and a secondary resistance at $489. Normally as this is happening a company's market value will fall and they subsequently slash their growth rate. In the case of CMG, this is decelerating significantly and these falling prices are suggestive of further short potential.

Aside from the chart pattern, CMG lowered its guidance for Q4 to $2.45–$2.85 per share, substantially below its previous year of $3.84 for Q4. December sales were down 30% and same-store sales fell to 14.6% during Q4 while CMG previously predicted an 11% decline. In addition, there has been another investigation instituted in California from August regarding Chipotle in Simi Valley, California. The declining double-digit growth maturity rate of 30–40%, the rising completion and lofty P/E ratio in contrast to its competitors, cutting its Q4 guidance, and slashing its sales and earnings forecast are all evidence of a cloudy outlook. Markets don't favor uncertainty, which discourages reversal.

CMG announced that it would close all stores on February 8 to discuss food safety.

Chipotle (Chipotle: New Health Outbreak, New Short, *Modern Trader*, #536, October 2017, pp. 14–15)

Chipotle: Symbol: CMG; market cap $9.82 billion; 52-week high/low: $499/$336.51; EPS: 3.23, P/E ratio: 103.81; short range: $330–$349; cover short: $199; stop loss: $361; price as of August 19: $334.61

    Chipotle Mexican Grill, Inc. (CMG), the trendy Mexican-style restaurant chain founded in 1993, develops and operates more than 198 Chipotle Mexican Grill restaurants in the United States, 29 international restaurants, and 23 non-Chipotle style restaurants. Denver-based CMG has become famous for its unique food services while also becoming infamous for its candidacy as a long-term short position.

    Since 2015, CMG has signaled its short-selling potential and has been continuously recommended as a short. CMG relished its notoriety and its growth rate in 2015, sending the equity to an all-time high of $758.61 with a market cap of $15.19 billion, an earnings per share of $16.76, and a P/E ratio of 29.07.

    In the fall of 2015, the *E. coli* outbreak at various stores in multiple locations across the United States and the subsequent media coverage generated by the Centers for Disease Control's 2016 formal declaration of its direct association, led CMG to slash its sales and earnings forecast. This sent the stock's price plunging from its then 52-week high of $521.52, a market cap of $12.82 billion, earnings per share of .77, and a P/E ratio of 525.84, as of March 8, 2017. During the same period, CMG was faced with a secondary offering of 2.9 million shares by a prominent shareholder activist, which further reduced the market's trust in CMG.

    In July 2017 it was reported and confirmed that 130 customers in Sterling, Virginia, were contaminated by food from a Chipotle restaurant and infected by the norovirus. CMG has been unable to distance itself from its food poisoning reputation, and solidified its June 2017 guidance warning that CMG's operating costs would be higher and that its promotional mitigation costs would rise significantly. Despite CMG's multifaceted attempts to recover from its damaging and hurtful press coverage as well as hindered goodwill, CMG's stock has continued to decline. Its continuous disappointing earnings have reinforced it as a volatile short position, with more declines in the offing.

Technical Picture

CMG warrants lower P/E multiples to reflect today's slower growth rate versus its competitors. It has plunged with a down gap since mid-October 2015 with multiple plunge milestones.

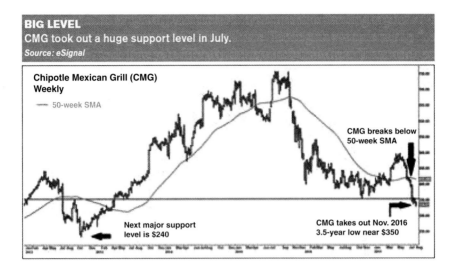

Figure 10.16   Big level.

Courtesy of eSignal.

CMG soared above its 50 dma and 200 dma in late March 2017 after straddling those averages for most of the first quarter, establishing a clear reverse head-and-shoulders pattern before topping at $499 on May 16. CMG then began a stark decline, breaking below its 50 dma and 200 dma in June as well as its 50-week moving average.

The sell-off accelerated in July following the norovirus outbreak. CMG took out its 3½ year October 2016 low, making the next clear technical support level the 2012 low of $240 (see Figure 10.16). This accelerated weakness pushed CMG into a death cross on August 2, with the 50 dma crossing below the 200 dma, while the market traded below both. CMG last entered a death cross (Figure 10.17) in late November 2016 and subsequently dropped $576 a share to just below $400 in six weeks. It entered a golden cross (the bullish opposite of a death cross) this past March before rebounding 25%.

CMG's troubles are clearly not over, and the recent fundamental weakness following the norovirus outbreak has created extreme technical damage.

> The reader is cautioned not to rely on any information provided in this example for making decisions about trading any security. Please refer to the **Caution—Limitations and Difficulties** section found at the end of the first chapter.

Figure 10.17   Death cross.

Courtesy of eSignal.

Chart courtesy of StockCharts.com.

The reader is cautioned not to rely on any information provided in this example for making decisions about trading any security. Please refer to the **Caution—Limitations and Difficulties** section found at the end of the first chapter.

American Express (AXP: Don't Leave Home Short, *Modern Trader*, #532, May 2017, p. 12)

American Express: Symbol: AXP; market cap $272.93 billion; 52-week high/low: $82.00/$55.57; buying range: $77–$82; objective: $93–$104; stop loss: $73

New York-based American Express Company (AXP), founded in 1850, has suffered competitor encroachment and significant decline, leading AXP to reveal a remarkable offense in 2017, making AXP a solid buy opportunity.

AXP, including its subsidiaries, provides charge and credit payment card products to consumers and businesses worldwide, operating through four segments: US consumer services, international consumer and network services, global commercial services, and global merchant services. Its products and services comprise financial lending services, merchant acquisition and processing, servicing and settlement, merchant financing, and point-of-sale marketing. AXP sells its products and services to consumers, small businesses, mid-sized companies, and large corporations via online, direct mail, in-house, third-party vendors, and direct response advertising.

AXP is in the process of increasing its benefits to its platinum charge card holders. Subsequently, it will increase the annual fee by 22% to $560 from $450 (its first increase since 2007). AXP's fee increase is to offset the cost of the rewards that they provide to their special customers as an incentive to retain the card. AXP is taking this bold step in the face of its competitors who have attempted to erode AXP's prolific rewards program. This competitive intrusion put AXP on the defensive, leading to its current restricting campaign, incurring marketing expenses of $1.4 billion, adding to its total expenditures. This necessary expense is expected to help AXP retain its customer base, and put AXP on the offensive within the credit market share.

AXP suffered a severe decline in its share price in 2016 as a result of its termination agreement with Costco (COST). AXP, through its established and exclusive reward and travel agreements, has put an unprecedented carrot in front of its customer segment, leading to customer retention and increasing customer acquisition, as most of the consumers within this segment are encouraged to increase the reward points as well as using the card that offers the most value.

AXP reported in Q4 2016 an earnings-per-share (EPS) of $.91 on revenue of $8.02 billion versus the consensus of $.98 EPS on revenue of $7.94 billion. Its net income of $825 million or $.88 EPS is down from $899 million or $.89 EPS. These lower-than-expected results are attributable to higher marketing and promotional expenses. Specifically, the loss of its exclusive partnership with Costco Wholesale Corporation: however, AXP experienced an increase in its adjusted revenue. AXP expects its EPS for 2017 to be within the range of $5.60 to $5.80 per share versus its previous guidance of $5.60 per share on revenue of $32.04 billion. The card the made famous the slogan, "Don't leave home without it," may now be referring to its stock purchase price.

Technical Picture

AXP's upward correction from its February 2016 lows ran out of gas in the fall of 2016 as it retraced back below its 50 dma and 200 dma. Signaling a resumption of its upswing, AXP rocketed back above its 50 dma and 200 dma on October 20 and continued to rally. See Figure 10.18.

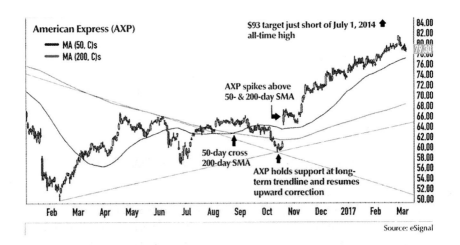

Source: eSignal

Figure 10.18   American Express.

Courtesy of eSignal.

Prior to the move, the 50 dma cost crossed above the 200 dma (a "golden cross"), signaling bullish momentum. Since then, AXP has rallied, taking out various resistance levels, including a long-term trend line, and is poised to make an 18-month high.

Chart courtesy of StockCharts.com.

The reader is cautioned not to rely on any information provided in this example for making decisions about trading any security. Please refer to the **Caution—Limitations and Difficulties** section found at the end of the first chapter.

Amazon (Yes: Amazon Is Different, *Modern Trader*, #536, October 2017, p. 16)

Retail online giant Amazon Inc. has been the focus of intense investor speculation due to its pending acquisition of Whole Foods (WFM). However, those who have marked Amazon (AMZN) for a short position are being shortsighted and undoubtedly fail to see the opportunity to accumulate a position for solid long-term growth.

Amazon's downward momentum is not fundamentally sustainable, and its upward movements will be generated by high volatility within bid-ask prices, resulting in a short squeeze.

AMZN, currently boasting a stock capitalization of nearly $500 billion, was founded in 1994 and is headquartered in Seattle. The company engages in the retail sale of consumer products and service subscriptions in North America and internationally. From its humble inception focusing expressly on books, AMZN has expanded into unanticipated retail segments such as artificial intelligence, food, music, media content, publishing, manufacturing electronic devices, and consumer products.

AMZN's June 2017 quarterly report indicated a 25% increase in its revenue to $38 billion while its operating income slid 51% to $626 million (adjusting for periods of earning expansion with increased investing). AMZN's recorded capital investment comprised of its yearly capital expenditure of $2.5 billion (up 46%) and its capital leases such as property and equipment—up 50% to $2.7 billion—has astonished the street. These numbers are indicative of AMZN's demonstrative efforts to reinvest and refine its shipping capacity, digital video segment, Echo device, and affordable cloud services solutions.

Those who hold onto traditional methodologies and try applying them to AMZN fail to understand that AMZN has never followed a traditional business model. They are expecting corrections and retractions similar to other stocks, rather than embracing AMZN's 20-year proven model as sufficient evidence that AMZN is different and has a unique growth metric. AMZN's surprising acquisition of Whole Foods only serves to provide further support that the company has not topped off, and will continue with its forward momentum.

This all has implications that will boost AMZN's bottom line. Even in the face of potential failure to acquire Whole Foods and expand its physical offerings, Amazon has proven itself capable of handling defeat, as it has with other failed expansion attempts (i.e. Amazon's Fire phone). AMZN's window for investors to purchase will eventually shut as AMZN continues to evolve and reshape the future for both its shareholders and the world. Hence, keeping AMZN in your portfolio as a long-term growth solution is a smart and lucrative future investment.

AMZN has broken the traditional valuation model since 1995 from its sporadic profitable quarters versus the belief in sacrificing profitability for growth. Its technical outlook indicates a status of reinforcement rather than divestment due to its P/E ratio dropping to low triple digits from a commanding high triple digits and has been on a clear pattern of ascension since 2016.

Continually trading above its 50 dma and 200 dma, AMZN has been a picture of consistency leading to its rise through early June when its price temporarily breached $1,000. A sell-off has held above its July low near $950.

Sporadic correction and retraction operating above the 50 dma may challenge support below this level, perhaps testing $910. Shorts, in general, are difficult to master because of the scarcity of float/liquidity, requiring a contrarian sense of objectivity and Amazon's business model is equally contrarian by its nature. In the context of the market, AMZN is most solidly a long position and provides a unique opportunity for any portfolio accumulation. AMZN may not have reached the low of this correction, but there is more room on the upside.

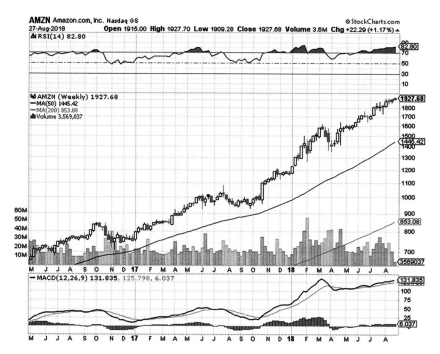

Chart courtesy of StockCharts.com.

The reader is cautioned not to rely on any information provided in this example for making decisions about trading any security. Please refer to the **Caution—Limitations and Difficulties** section found at the end of the first chapter.

Long Fangs, Short Fangs (Long Fangs, *Modern Trader*, #522, July 2016, p. 12)

No book on investing would be complete without mention of FANG. Many traders and investors, looking at the extreme volatility from "FANG" stocks (Facebook (FB), Amazon (AMZN), Netflix (NFLX), and Google (GOOGL)), are tempted to find what appears to be visually appealing shorting opportunities. However, as is often the case, looks can be deceiving.

Large institutions are heavily invested in FANGs with an expectation of long-term growth holdings, based on the FANG's collective projected earnings and cash flow. For this reason, shorting FANGs is not recommended. While the volatility might suggest that of a typical short, this is misleading. The sheer lack of liquidity available, low float, and short interest will inherently squeeze and force covering of shorts, making FANG stocks candidates for growth accumulation or new lows.

In taking short positions we typically put on a 10% to 15% decline from a current value as a stop loss, depending on volatility. The FANG stocks appear to be overheating from both a technical and fundamental perspective. Support and resistance levels have been challenged, gaps have formed, and volume is higher. The long bull move in these issues may be getting old but doesn't appear to be over. In fact, these tailwinds make FANG stocks a reliable buy going forward.

While some factors may qualify FANG for short selling, the compulsion to cover the short by the lender at any time there is an unexpected extreme uptick in stock minimizes the return. As a potential short, their volatility is so dramatic that the typical investor will face the "greatest fear" of subsequently erasing any gains normally expected, or worse.

The reasons for avoiding FANGs as shorts stem from their immense reversal power and the implied wider bid-ask spread that is manifested in these positions from large institutions to ETFs, who appear to be holding them as long-term collateral with little intention to liquidate. Thus, with less liquidity and the potential for purchase becoming higher, the bid-ask will quickly dominate and overwhelm the short investor. In contrast to the larger players, even in a situation where they may be forced to cover, their disproportionate liquidity in the market affords them a protection not guaranteed to mid- to small-sized investors. This inherently prevents a smaller investor from capturing the full value of a typical short position and places a pressure, literally like a gun to the head, to cover, which is too great to disregard. If one would even consider naked shorting, the risk is exponentially more damaging. Additionally, regulatory agencies—often fearful of shorting in general—can make lending availability harder, as they fear the companies' devaluation could impact the market more broadly.

The FANGs' one-year chart properly analyzed puts this risk into perspective, and as such, makes the FANGs' squeeze potential, analogous to a closing vice, more obvious. FANG is better thought of as a holding for a long-term growth consideration. Using a variation of our strategy, often coined as a "constrained long-short portfolio," shorts should be included as a hedge, using their proceeds to capture the momentum in conjunction with long positions. As explained earlier in this book, we look at using a 130/30 model for selecting long positions that equal up to 130% of the nominal capital invested and short positions that equal up to 30% of the nominal capital, for a net market exposure of 100%. Under this technique, short proceeds are then applied to the FANG specifically for their long-term growth rate, since these companies have enjoyed triple-digit growth earnings and less overhead expenditures. For all of these reasons—the extreme volatility, deviation, and capacity in terms of float and liquidity—the FANG is simply not worth the risk of being squeezed in a short position. It's not hard to find lower-hanging fruit than FANG, since there are bountiful and ripe shorts in today's market that are better suited for investing for the long term.

These are examples of my application of the Parnes Parameters for evaluating the fundamental, technical, or external factors that influence the price of a stock. Clearly, the assignment of values is subjective and experiential. My judgments about the ranking of the variable will mostly likely differ from yours. However, you now have the basic framework for creating a more objective way of assessing stocks and their values. I hope that this will prove productive for you.

Glossary

Accumulation mode   A positive direction, indicative of more buyers than sellers.

Alpha   A measure of the difference between the actual returns of a stock and its expected performance, given its level of risk as measured by beta. A positive alpha figure indicates that a stock has performed better than its beta would predict. In contrast, a negative alpha indicates that the stock underperformed, given the expectations established by beta.

Ascending pattern of a stock   When the current price of a stock is above both the 50-day and 200-day moving averages and has maintained this pattern, it forms an "upward channel."

Asymptotic   In statistics, describes an inflection point of graphing a number of items compared to the significance of the research. Typically, this type of graph becomes asymptotic at 33 items, meaning that increasing the sample size beyond 33 stocks under study does little to increase the significance of the data. Therefore, statistics on 33 items are almost as accurate as statistics on 100 items.

At the market, or at market   Usually refers to a buy or sell order at whatever market price the stock is trading at the time, without specifying a particular price.

Assets   Cash, land, buildings, investments, vehicles, accounts receivable, inventory, supplies, equipment, and anything else of value.

Assigning a weight   Determining how likely the occurrence of a single factor will be in influencing an event outcome. An underinflated football has less of a weight in determining the outcome of a football game than the star quarterback breaking his leg just before the game. The genius comes in determining how much of a weight should be assigned to each factor. This comes only from experience and historical data.

Backtesting The process of testing a trading strategy on historical data to ensure its viability. It is the reverse of pattern recognition, and retrospective analysis, which looks at patterns and then formulates a strategy.

Barbero effect When a totally unexpected event occurs. This references the great racehorse Barbero, who won the Kentucky Derby and was favored to win the Preakness, the middle race of the Triple Crown. Only 50 yards out of the starting gate, Barbero's leg audibly snapped, thus ending his racing career and eventually, after tens of thousands of dollars in veterinary treatments failed to heal the leg, his life. In all the years of the Triple Crown (Kentucky Derby, Preakness, Belmont Stakes), no horse, before or since, ever broke its leg at the beginning of the race. The odds of this event occurring were astronomical, and no one had considered it as a possibility. Millions of dollars were lost on betting. It would be analogous to insuring a ship and not considering its sinking due to a meteor hitting the boat, or buying a stock in a restaurant chain and having 10 people die because of botulism in a can of vichyssoise that was used to make soup in one of the restaurants.

Basis point One-hundredth of one percentage point. Obviously, 100 basis points equals 1% of a price, or return, or a deal.

Bayesian logic A logical technique that is based on experience. Experience allows you to determine how likely it is for an event to occur, and be able to assign a weight to it.

Bear market When most of the issues in the general stock market are retreating or falling back.

Beta The beta coefficient is a measure of the volatility of the price of a stock compared to a market benchmark. A higher beta indicates greater volatility than the market as a whole, and a lower beta means less volatility.

Black cross Also called the "death cross"; when the 50-day moving average falls below the 200-day moving average; it is an indicator to sell or short the stock.

Bottom line Typically, it means the earnings before income tax, depreciation, and amortization (EBITDA), or how much money the company actually earns. This has less significance with accrual accounting practices, since earnings are subject to manipulations, but in the old days, when "cash was king," you really knew how much cash the company earned if you looked at the bottom line.

Boolean logic   The logic commonly used to program computers. It is binary thinking, in which the chances of an event occurring are determined by a branching diagram. So clearly, the choice is either on or off, "yes or no" or 0 or 1.

Book value   The net worth of a company after subtracting the value of preferred stock, bonds and/or debt.

Branching diagram   A visual representation of the logic behind a computer program. It allows a programmer to determine which road to take, just like coming to a fork in a road. The question is "Do I go left or do I go right?" The flaw with this system is that the choice is always limited to one item or another without any consideration for the likelihood of the event occurring.

Bull market   When most of the issues in the general stock market, are advancing or increasing.

Buy a put   An option trade in which the investor pays money for the guarantee (for 90 days or some fixed period of time) to sell stock at a certain strike price. The investor is betting that the stock price will go down.

Call options   A contract that gives the investor the right to buy a stock or other asset at a "strike price" within a set time period, usually three months. The invest is betting the stock will go up within that period of time.

Churning   An unscrupulous practice in which a stockbroker buys and sells more frequently than need be, with the purpose of generating more commissions.

Circuit breaker   A mechanism to shut down trading when the major indices of the market fall below a certain amount. The percentage deviation is set by regulatory agencies.

Climax top   A climax top occurs at the top end of a bull market and has the highest prices with increased trading volume.

Closely held   A closely held company is one with very few stockholders owning all the shares of the stock.

Covering a short   When an investor purchases back the stock he borrowed, (effectively sold) when he shorted it in the first place.

Cup with handle   A visual pattern seen on the 50-day and 200-day moving average graph, where the price of the stock falls below both the 50-day and 200-day moving averages in concert with a death cross and then the price of the stock and the 50-day moving average rebounds above the 200-day moving average.

Current debt The amount of money owed and payable over the next 12 months.

Cyclical industries Companies that deal in commodities, such as iron, copper, housing, car manufacturing and oil.

Dark pools An undetected stock transaction that occurs between brokers. These are broker-run markets outside the public stock exchanges that allow investors to trade large batches of stocks.

Death cross When the 50-day moving average falls below the 200-day moving average on the charts, indicating a time to consider shorting or selling a stock. Also called the "black cross."

Delisting A process in which a security listed on one of the stock exchanges loses sales so it no longer meets the requirements to be listed on the exchange.

Deregistration See *Delisting.*

Distribution mode A pattern of more sellers than buyers.

dma Daily moving average; usually expressed as a 50-day or 200-day.

Downtick The most recent price of a stock, where the stock moved down in price.

Earnings The gross earnings EBITDA, which really is the difference between income and expenses.

Earnings multiple Price-to-earnings ratio of stocks or indices.

EBITDA Earnings before interest, tax, depreciation, and amortization.

ETF Exchange-traded funds.

Ex clearing Unreported trade hidden from regulatory agencies.

Ex dividend When a stock has recently paid a dividend to a previous investor. For several days thereafter, it is traded "ex-dividend," meaning that no dividend will be forthcoming on the shares recently traded to the new investor, since the dividend has already been paid.

F test A statistical test used to determine if correlation of data (cause-effect) is statistically significant.

Failure to deliver When a brokerage house cannot locate shares of stock to collateralize a short sale but executes the short sale anyway. This is called a failure to deliver and is in violation of FINRA Regulation. T. Essentially, this creates a naked short sale. There are regulatory penalties from FINRA for this violation.

FAANMG The acronym for Facebook, Amazon, Apple, Netflix, Microsoft, and Google (Alphabet).

FASB Financial Accounting Standards Board.

Federal Reserve A Federal agency established by an act of Congress in 1913, which sets the rate at which money can be borrowed or lent to banks.

Fee-based advisor An investment advisor who is paid a set fee, based on total assets managed, not commissions or transactions, which is the way a broker is paid. A fee-based advisor is motivated to increase the wealth of the client, not buy and sell securities.

50-day moving average Often abbreviated as 50 dma. This represents the average price of a stock in the previous 50 days.

Financial Transaction Tax (FTT) A tax added to all financial transactions in European Union (EU) countries.

FINRA Financial Industry Regulatory Authority. This is the successor regulatory agency to NASD.

FINRA 4320 This rule requires a brokerage house to buy securities to cover a delivery failure of short positions within a 13-day period of time.

FINRA 2010-043 This rule requires that any "short sale–exempt" trade be reported to FINRA. This situation would arise if a brokerage house does not locate a stock before executing a short sale, thereby creating a naked short sale, which is against FINRA regulations.

FINRA Regulation T This regulation requires a brokerage house to locate shares of stock to collateralize a short before allowing a short to be executed.

Flash crash A computer algorithm–driven sell-off.

Force majeure A force of nature, such as "acts of God," like hurricanes, floods, fire, electrical storms, and so on. This is usually included in a contract to release both parties from any obligations if something untoward happens and prevents the completion of contractual obligations.

GAAP Generally accepted accounting practices, which is an accounting methodology used by all public companies.

Goat Used to describe an individual who thinks for himself and doesn't "follow the herd" the way sheep do. In fact, sheepherders in Texas always put a goat in the herd to keep the sheep from doing stupid things like walking over a cliff, or being unable to find water.

Golden cross   When the 50-day moving average crosses the 200-day moving average on the charts, signifying an opportunity to buy. This is a reversal of the death cross pattern.

Gross earnings   A company's income after the deduction for expenses, but before allowances for income tax and the depreciation allowance on equipment, buildings, and other assets.

Head-and-shoulder top   The shape of a 50-day moving average resembles three peaks, with a left shoulder, head, and right shoulder. Typically the right shoulder (later rally) is lower than the left shoulder (earlier rally) and the head can be about the height of either shoulder or above either shoulder. If this pattern is seen over a course of two to three months, some experts recommend shorting.

High-frequency traders (HFTs)   A group of individuals who invest in stocks or bonds for the short term and take whatever profits they can.

Holding period   The time an investor owns a security.

Index   The average of a group of stocks picked by market managers, such as the Dow Jones Industrial Average, or the Standard & Poor Stock Index, or the NASDAQ Composite.

Industry groups   A group of companies all functioning in the same market sector or industry, such as automotive, which would include Ford, Chrysler, General Motors, Toyota, and so on.

Inflection point   A point in the 50-day or 200-day moving average graph, where the graph goes up, bends 90 degrees, and comes down. This is also called a "knee."

Jumping in and out   Trading for short-term gain, usually done by day traders.

Knee   An inflection point in the 50-day or 200-day graph, where the graph goes up, bends 90 degrees, and comes down. This is also called an "inflection point."

Latency   How long it takes to execute a financial transaction over a network connection. Recently, two tech companies proposed the lowest-latency link yet between Illinois and New Jersey. This will be a 733-mile chain of microwave towers to hurtle data in an 8.5 milliseconds round trip.

Leap A put or call option written for one year or more, rather than the typical 90 days.

Letter ruling A legal opinion issued by a regulatory agency.

Limit Also called a stop limit. A designated price for a buy or sell.

Liquidity A liquid asset can be easily bought or sold without changing in value—cash, for example, is more liquid than real estate.

Long-term debt The amount of money owed by a company, including the current debt.

Marked to market In real estate evaluation, the appraisal based on what the appraiser thinks the property is worth, regardless of the applied depreciation or fully depreciated value.

Margin call When an investor has borrowed money to execute a transaction, if the value of the transaction declines below an acceptable level for the lender, the lender then demands a margin call, or payment of the projected losses. If the investor still believes in his position, he will meet the margin call by paying the lender the requested sum and retaining his position. If he cannot meet the margin call, then the position will be taken from him by the lender, and the investor will have to produce cash to make up for any losses.

Market penetration The percentage of sales for all companies in a market segment, compared to the overall potential sales available for their product.

Market share The percentage of sales for a particular company compared to all other companies selling the same product.

Matrix A mathematical array of data.

Multiples Shorthand for "price-to-earnings ratio." This is the earnings of a company divided by the number of shares outstanding.

Naked short sales An illegal operation, not allowed by FINRA or the SEC, where an investor shorts a stock but does not have the securities to cover the transaction.

NASD National Association of Security Dealers, which was a regulatory agency overlooking the securities business. This organization was succeeded by FINRA.

One-trick pony A company that has only one product and no other prospects for diversity.

Options Puts, calls, spreads, leaps, or any contract with a time limit.

OTC   Over the counter. Stocks that are sold OTC are securities in companies that are too small to be listed on the NASDAQ or New York Stock Exchange. This means that their sales, the number of stockholders, and the number of shares do not meet the minimum requirement of the other exchanges.

OTC Bulletin Board   A listing of OTC stocks.

Outcome studies   Documented results of a process.

Out of the money   A situation where the price of a stock is outside of the option range that would be profitable, so covering an option would result in a loss of money. This is term adopted from horseracing, when a horse doesn't finish "in the money," that is, first, second, or third (win, place, or show), and therefore bettors make no money from betting on the horse.

Overhead resistance   A price barrier to the movement of a stock price in ascension mode.

P value   The level of statistical significance.

Pattern recognition   A cluster of events.

Pink sheets   Listings of public stocks (printed on pink paper, hence "pink sheets") that are OTC shares in companies that do not have large enough sales to be listed on other exchanges. These are usually start-up or developmental-stage companies.

Predictive analytics   A method of analyzing patterns to predict what will happen.

Precious metals   Gold, silver, platinum.

Price-to-earnings ratio   Earnings divided by the number of shares outstanding.

Proprietary trading   When financial institutions trade for the benefit of their companies rather than for their customers. The Dodd-Frank financial reforms put some restrictions on proprietary trading at big banks, but loopholes abound.

Quant   In investment management and stock trading, a slang term for a person who is an expert in the use of mathematics and statistics for trading purposes.

Quick ratio   Represents the short-term liquidity of a company. It compares the current debt (less than a year) with its most liquid assets, such as cash and current accounts receivable. Quick ratio = (cash and equivalents +

marketable securities + current accounts receivable) / current liabilities. This can be manipulated by accrual accounting methods, such as booking long-term accounts receivable as current or current bad debts as current account receivables.

Quote stuffing: Placing and quickly rescinding a large number of buy or sell orders to confuse or slow down rival traders.

R test   A statistical test to compare one set of events against another to see if there is a correlation.

Railroad tracks   A graph pattern where the price of the stock sharply increases in one week and then the next week follows the same pattern of price increases, on a high volume of trades. The price both weeks increases to the peak level, and the graph of the stock price looks like parallel railroad tracks.

Resistance line   A temporary plateau, which is limited by sell-off such as profit taking. When the resistance line is penetrated and held, then it is a time to buy.

Retrospective analysis   Reviewing historic data. Starting with results, the analysis looks backward to see what features can be identified that led to the results under analysis.

RS line   Relative strength line, a comparison of the performance of a stock against the performance of the S&P 500. If both lines have an upward slope, but the slope of the stock has a steeper gradient, then the stock is outperforming the S&P 500.

SEC   The Securities and Exchange Commission, which is the federal regulatory agency that governs stock exchange transactions.

SEO   Search engine optimization, a process where the website of a company is forwarded to a number of search engines, and by various manipulations of the search parameters, moves the website to the first or second item to show up when a customer does a search of a topic.

Sheep   A term used to describe a herd mentality, when a group of people act in a certain fashion only because other people are acting the same way without thinking for themselves.

Short interest   The percentage of total shares of a company that are held in a short position.

Short squeeze   When short sellers cannot cover their short positions because there are not enough shares available.

Single earnings-consensus miss   When a stock fails to meet projected earnings, it "misses" the target that institutions and traders have set for the stock. Then, due to sheep mentality, they all rush to sell the stock in response to the failure to meet projected earnings and therefore growth. They then put the proceeds into other stocks they feel will climb faster and higher.

Split   When a company splits the number of shares to give investors a larger number of shares. Usually, stock splits are 2 to 1, meaning that for every share of stock an investor owns, the investor receives two shares at half the original price. So a $10 share of stock that splits 2 to 1 gives an investor two shares of stock worth $5 each. Rarely, there will be a 3-to-1 stock split or some other ratio.

Spread   In trading, commonly the difference between the highest price a buyer will pay and the lowest price a seller will take.

Stalling   A description of the price of the stock that stalls or remains stagnant while a stock is rallying. If a stock closes below the mid-point of the weekly price range for one to three weeks, it has stalled. This often is a warning sign that a rally is being met with systematic selling, which means the stock is likely to be dropping again. There is also positive stalling, where a base is being established, a probable rally into the resistance line.

Statistics   A mathematical way of evaluating a situation.

Stock borrowing fee   A fee that an investor pays to a brokerage firm for borrowing their stock to collaterize shorts.

Stock splits   See *Split.*

Stop loss   A designated price that limits the loss when the stock is falling.

Strike price   A negotiated price at which a transaction will occur, whether it be a sale of a put or call, or a purchase of a put or call, or any other transaction.

Support line   A temporary floor in the stock price, resulting in buys, because the stock is attractive at this price.

***t*-test**   A statistical test to determine if the difference between groups is significant.

Thin float   A company that has a small number of shares available to the public compared to its peer group.

Triple E   Earnings, earnings, and earnings. A way of establishing the value of a company.

200-day moving average   Abbreviated as 200 dma, which is the average price of a stock over the previous 200-day period.

Uptick   The most recent trade of a stock in which the price of a stock moved upward.

Uptick rule   A law banning investors from shorting shares when the most recent previous trade had been a downtick, or drop in the price of the stock. SEC release No. 34-55970 removed this restriction, leading to the market collapse of 2008.

Upward channel   When the current price of a stock is above both the 50 dma and 200 dma, and has maintained this pattern for several weeks, it is said to form an upward channel.

Value of stock   Determined by different variables for evaluating the value of a stock, for example, the P/E ratio of a stock compared to its peers.

Wedging   A description of a rally in price, which is based on light trading volume, and as the stock price climbs, the trading volume drops. Typically, this is seen after multiple rallies, above the 50 dma. Again, it is likely that the stock price will begin to fall.

Xeroxing   Duplicating or copying a technique.

Year-end earnings   Set by the company to be either year-end or fiscal.

Zero plus tick   A rule for shorting.

Index